FROM
BIRMINGHAM
TO THE BOARD
A RAILWAYMAN'S ODYSSEY
CONTINUES

FROM
BIRMINGHAM
— TO THE BOARD —
A RAILWAYMAN'S ODYSSEY
CONTINUES

STANLEY HALL
MBE

Ian Allan
PUBLISHING

A Railwayman's Odyssey Continues

Stanley Hall MBE

First published 2015

ISBN 978 0 7110 3821 9

Published by the author and distributed by Ian Allan Publishing, Riverdene Business Park, Molesey Road, Hersham, Surrey KT12 4RG

Packaged by Unique Publishing Services Ltd — www.uniquepublishingservices.com
Designed by Mark Nelson
Printed in China

Contents

Foreword

Stanley Hall MBE

IN *A Railwayman's Odyssey*, my father Stan Hall recounted his career working in the railway industry from starting work in the booking office at Keighley station in 1943, when it was still part of the London Midland & Scottish Railway, to 1970 when he was appointed to the position of Divisional Operating Superintendent (DOS) in Birmingham. This was a prestigious job, responsible for all railway operational matters in the West Midlands. Along the way he worked in many railway operational roles, while he gained seniority, working in locations as diverse as Luton and Barrow-in Furness. *From Birmingham to the Board* continues the story, and covers the period from his appointment as the DOS at Birmingham up until he retired from the position of Signalling and Safety Officer at the British Railways Board in 1982. This was just before the end of the traditional railway with the soon to be created business sectors paving the way for the ultimate privatisation of the railway and the structure of the railway that we have today.

The period working in Birmingham was one of relative optimism following the Beeching retrenchments of the 1960s, many of which had affected the West Midlands such as the downgrading of the former Great Western main line to London Paddington, which ultimately led to the complete closure of Birmingham Snow Hill station and the former main line from there to Wolverhampton Low Level. Staff whose loyalties were still, as recounted by my father, with the former Great Western Railway and its successor the Western Region of British Railways must have keenly felt these cutbacks. The many positive developments of the period are covered such as the continuing development of electrically hauled services to and from the West Midlands, including the opening of the new station at Birmingham International to serve the National Exhibition Centre; the opening of the new power signalbox at Saltley covering many miles of track and resulting in the closure of many small signalboxes. The West Midlands Passenger Transport Authority was also established spearheading the development of many local services such as the creation of the Cross City line by extending the route from Lichfield City across Birmingham to the new station opened at Longbridge, and its eventual connection to the upgraded Redditch branch. The North Warwickshire route from Birmingham to Stratford-on-Avon, which had been slated for closure, was reprieved. On the other hand there was the final closure of the by then freight-only route from Stratford-on-Avon to Cheltenham Spa (the Honeybourne Line), the occurrence of frequent derailments — mainly of freight trains — to deal with, and often difficult industrial relations to address. Although my father was a senior manager by this time, he was still very much 'hands on' in his approach to these matters and was also not averse to taking the controls in the driving cabs of trains on occasions. One of the facets that shines through the book is his belief that you could only be an effective manager by knowing how those at the sharp end of the business felt and his regular contact with footplate staff was but a part of his attempts to keep his 'finger on the pulse' during this difficult period.

The move to the Board led to a very different workload and method of working. There were numerous trips to Europe to attend meetings of the Union Internationale des Chemins de Fer (UIC). My father was also at the forefront of developments affecting level crossings; the development of a novel system of radio signalling (Radio Electronic Token Block), which was probably the saviour of the rural railway routes in Suffolk, mid-Wales and Scotland that were equipped with it; and the adoption of battery electric tail lamps, consigning the old oil-lit tail lamps to history. All these and more are described in the text. The reader will also be struck by the often fractious industrial relations of the period with numerous strikes occurring on the railways.

The reader will also find that the working culture of the period was very different from today's privatised railway and was very much a case of taking the 'rough' with the 'smooth'. This was a time before strict limits on alcohol consumption were introduced for railway staff and the impression gained of a somewhat lavish lifestyle concerning meals and trips in the inspection saloon has to be balanced, for the period in Birmingham at least, against the often unsocial hours required, responding to mishaps and dealing with other matters that came up at short notice such as threatened industrial action. The railway was not (and is still not) a nine to five operation. For the period working at the Board, conducting business while eating a decent meal in a restaurant was seen to be an effective way of getting things done. It should, perhaps, also be stressed that much of the time was involved in routine matters — meetings, paperwork, discussions with colleagues — that were essential to the job but which don't necessarily make for a fascinating read more than 30 years on. A book of this type can, by its nature, only be episodic and so the reader should not regard the various highpoints mentioned as being typical of daily life.

Unfortunately, just following the completion of the basic text for this book, my father had a serious stroke and it has been left to me, one of his sons to complete the book, along with Peter Waller, whose help I gratefully acknowledge. I have had a lifelong interest in railways, both as an enthusiast and in various jobs working in and with the railway industry. This books charts a bygone period of railway history and the developments since, in the West Midlands and elsewhere with new services and many more passengers, would have astonished those at the time had they known what was to follow. This book makes an excellent companion — and successor — to *A Railwayman's Odyssey*.

Chris Hall,
Derby,
December 2014

6

1970

PART 1: ANOTHER DOOR OPENS

Still at Nottingham

THE major upheavals of the last few years were by now almost behind us. Line closures, power signalling, elimination of steam, rationalisation of marshalling yards and track layouts, all less-than-trainload traffic channelled through Toton, expansion of merry-go-round (MGR) working and many minor changes had all been achieved. Now the emphasis was on seeking economies and maintaining high standards of operational performance.

We had been introduced to the terrors of 'The Budget'. We had thought, in our innocence, that this was the province of the Chancellor and only heard of once a year, but now we were required to forecast our total expenditure in staff costs for the following year in great detail, and to achieve a saving of X% over the previous year. A new Finance Section had been created to assist with this, but they only did the number-crunching and it was up to the operators to seek economies, better known as staff cuts.

The enormous savings in staff costs over the previous five years had been achieved mainly through changes in freight traffic

patterns and the application of technology. Now we were going to have to look elsewhere, and a great deal of time and effort was expended on this. The fact was that BR had to meet its target imposed by the Government, and as HQ's expenditure was relatively small, the Regions were given their targets. The Regions didn't spend much, so the Divisions (which was where staff costs mainly occurred) were given their share, and that meant putting pressure on the poor unfortunate Area Managers. Just like the Army, promotion depended on achieving that share. Cutting costs became top priority.

Cab-riding was much more fun. This was the real railway and was far better than being closeted in some smoke-filled room trying to squeeze another job out of the system. I was doing my share of this in order to maintain standards when some interesting news emerged about a vacancy for the post of Divisional Operating Superintendent (DOS) at Birmingham. Bobby Gardiner, my Divisional Manager, told me that I was being considered for the post. Great excitement – even my wife Val was moderately excited. This was 22 January 1970.

Two contrasting diesels stand almost side-by side at Nottingham Midland station on 29 May 1969. A memory to take to Birmingham with me! A Brush Type 4, Class 47, No.D1516 departs gently with train 1E19, the 14.50 St Pancras to Sheffield, whilst one of the many named Class 45s, No.64 *Coldstream Guardsman*, waits to take over the 'Thames Clyde' express, 1M86. *D. L. Percival*

In March 1966, a DMU awaits departure from Bilston Central with a service from Wolverhampton Low Level to Leamington Spa via Birmingham Snow Hill.
Andrew Muckley

The chain of events

On 26 January I was called for interview at Regional HQ, Euston, to be seen by Dougal Fenton, Assistant General Manager, LM Region; John Pollard, Divisional Manager, Birmingham; and some staff folks. I had known Dougal F. when he was on the Eastern Region and I was one of the Yardmasters. Although I had not previously met John Pollard, he seemed very friendly and was a pal of Bobby Gardiner's. It was a genial interview and I went home feeling that things had gone well. I recognised, of course, that a genial interview can mean one of two things – either they want you and there's no point in wasting time, or they don't want you and ditto. But which one was it?

A few days later news came that Bobby Lawrence, General Manager of the LM Region, wanted to see me. He was another member of the ex-Army clan, like Bobby Gardiner and John Pollard. So, on 10 February, I travelled to St Pancras in the driving cab with Inspector Cyril Jones, my footplate mentor, because I had found from experience that it put me in the right mood for a critical interview. I cannot remember much about the interview, except that the GM had been at pains to stress that Birmingham was the most important Division on the LM Region, and that the job was the most demanding. I do not know what happened in the next ten days, but on 20 February Bobby Gardiner called me into his office and told me unofficially that I had got the job. Three days later it was official. To say I was overjoyed would be a massive understatement. DOS posts were probably the most coveted in the Operations Department. You were still sufficiently near the ground to be able to keep in touch with what was going on; you could walk into a signalbox; you could climb into the driving cab; you were amongst the rough and tumble; but you were also part of senior management with all the status that that implied.

I had had two ambitions in my railway career. I had not been long in the service when I decided that I wanted to be a Stationmaster (SM), and I had achieved that in 1951 when I was

appointed at Battyeford. It was only a small station, but it was a start. Then it was a question of climbing the ladder to more important SM posts. Ambitions of being a DOS were too far in the distance at that stage, but it came within the bounds of possibility when I was selected for the Management Training Scheme and it was then that I set my sights on becoming a DOS. Finally, fortune had favoured me, as, I suspect, had Bobby Gardiner, who I am quite sure backed me all the way with his pals. He was a martinet but a first-rate manager who let you get on with the job.

My first day

On Monday 2 March, I met John Pollard again (or JP as I called him) and he introduced me to his other officers (yes, it sounds a bit military and old-fashioned, but we were officers, not managers – that came later), then to the locum, who had been keeping the job warm and stayed on for three days to show me round and introduce me to my 'team'. I had several assistants (what luxury!) covering Operations, Train Planning, Freight Depots, Parcels Depots, and Train Crews, and the Central Services, covering Works and Accidents, Staff, Productivity, Finance and Public Relations. Under them were the respective Heads of Section and their staff, and the all-important Control Office. I also had about thirty inspectors (yes, thirty!) covering Train Crews, Freight Traffic, Passenger Train Working and Signalling. They were my eyes and ears and had direct access to me, although they would normally work to my assistants or Heads of Section.

So I had a pretty strong team composed of men (no women, except my secretary – this was 1970) some of whom came from the LMS part of the Division and some from the Great Western part. I was well used to LMS men, but the GWR men were a new breed. They were very good at the job, reliable, knowledgeable, dependable and, above all, loyal. Very traditional too, and proud of their GWR heritage.

Continued on page 14

The exterior of the new power signalbox at Coventry. *British Rail*

At the start of 1970 the Birmingham Division still included the branch lines from Bewdley to Hartlebury and to Kidderminster; these were, however, not to last long as both closed on 5 January that year. On 9 June 1969 a single railcar forms the 08.38 service from Bewdley to Hartlebury at Stourport-on-Severn. The section from Bewdley to Stourport closed completely on 5 January; the section east of Stourport remained open to serve the power station at Stourport. *John Glover*

Photographed in the summer of 1969, this is a scene which really tells a story. Toton's 'Peak' Sulzer Type 4, Class 44, No.D8 *Penyghent* coasts gently past an adverse distant signal as it approaches Leicester on its way south with quite a modest load of coal in 16-tonners, probably one of the many Toton-Northampton trains. The major goods depot seen top-left had recently been transferred from BR to a new company, National Carriers Ltd, by the 1968 Transport Act. A major change.
J. H. Cooper-Smith

Shrewsbury represented the western boundary of the
Birmingham Division; on 19 June 1969, Class 47 No.1696 hauls
a northbound freight through Shrewsbury station, passing
the 14.00 local service from Shrewsbury to Crewe standing
in platform No.4. *A Wyn Hobson*

Class 86 electric No.86234 runs into platform 4 at Nuneaton with the 12.20 service from Blackpool to Euston on 14 August 1975. *Philip D. Hawkins*

The front of St Pancras station on 17 April 1971. Built originally as a hotel, the building was converted to serve as offices in 1935. *J. H. Cooper-Smith*

On 10 September 1974, Class 47 No.47106 arrives at Banbury station with the 07.02 service from Newcastle upon Tyne to Poole. *Philip D. Hawkins*

Below: The power signalbox at Birmingham New Street. *British Rail*

LNWR route from Euston had been electrified, reaching Birmingham and the West Midlands in 1967. New stations had been built at Coventry, Birmingham New Street and Wolverhampton, and at each of those stations there was a new, modern, push-button signalbox covering the surrounding area. A PTA (Passenger Transport Authority) had been created following the Transport Act of 1968 and was soon flexing its muscles. Local railways figured large in its vision of the future.

The Divisional boundaries were Rugby, Nuneaton, Stafford, Shrewsbury, Worcester and Oxford (all exclusive), so it was a compact Division with the exception of the former GWR route to Paddington, which stretched for some distance beyond Banbury. The latter was a good place to find refuge to escape from the cares of the office. It also had a fairly new station and a genial former GWR Stationmaster who was now Area Manager. He was a very reliable man, as were all the ex-GWR men I came into contact with. My Chief Inspector, Bill Gillett, another ex-GWR man, was a treasure – utterly reliable and loyal. He was one of the founders of the Severn Valley Railway, but he left in disgust when Gerald Nabarro came along and wanted to run it on more commercial lines.

One of the side-effects of electrification of the LNWR route was the rundown of the ex-GWR. The two had been in competition since before the First World War and the LNWR had finally won. I got the impression that the GWR was top of the popularity poll in Birmingham and that Snow Hill station was greatly preferred to New Street, but tremendous savings had accrued from the rundown of the GWR route and the withdrawal of through services on the Paddington to Birkenhead route. The Snow Hill–Wolverhampton line now had only a meagre DMU service, and that survived only until 1972, when Snow Hill became a car park – what an indignity. But former GWR men were loyal not only to the Great Western but also to the greater concept of the railway system, and they transferred their loyalties to the new regime. They were a pleasure to work with, and I never had any problems with them at all.

Learning the road

The first essential was to get to know the 'parish'. On my second day the locum had arranged a saloon tour covering Coventry, Leamington, Stratford and the North Warwick line, and then in the evening JP took the two of us out for a meal in Solihull.

The geography of the Division

The Birmingham Division was quite unlike the Nottingham Division. Nottingham was widely dispersed with no natural centre and coal was its business. Birmingham proudly boasted that it was England's second city and was the centre of a huge conurbation. Its trade was metal-bashing, ie taking steel and making it into all manner of things from cars to trinkets, and it had a very intricate and extensively modernised layout of railway routes, which happily provided flexibility in case of trouble. In the 1960s, the former

'What a wonderful welcome,' I thought, but it was back down to earth the next day when up to a foot of snow fell overnight and everything on wheels was at a stand. Fortunately, it thawed rapidly and I was able to begin house-hunting.

The following week road learning began in earnest. On Monday it was the Banbury area; on Tuesday the steel terminals with my Freight Terminals Assistant. We had about a dozen of these spread around the West Midlands and they received trainloads of steel plate etc, which was then delivered by railway-owned lorries to the local factories and works. It was big business, and I had a graph on my office wall showing the upward trend, which continued almost throughout my stay in Birmingham. It collapsed soon afterwards in the late 1970s with the massive change in industry (and was completely unconnected with my departure).

The following day I went out with my Parcels Assistant to visit the Parcels Concentration Depots (PCDs) at Coventry and Wolverhampton. The latter was located in the now-closed former GWR Low Level station. Parcels traffic was still big business, and we had a huge depot at Birmingham Curzon Street, where the old London & Birmingham Railway offices of 1838 were still standing, unused. The Assistant Area Manager at Wolverhampton was Dick Holmes, whom I had previously met at Shipley 20 years earlier when he was the station master. He was an ex-RAF type and still had the moustache to prove it.

On Thursday that week I spent several hours in New Street power signalbox, which had been opened as part of the mainline electrification. It was very busy, with trains going to and coming from all directions. Instead of having an Area Controller, as we had at Derby and Trent, it had a Regulator who had come from the signalling grades. Finally, on Friday, for a change, we had a visit from a couple of VIPs. The Parliamentary Under Secretary at the Department of the Environment (DOE) wanted to see how the railway worked and the Regional General Manager thought it would be a good idea for him to see a Control Office in operation. Fortunately, I had made it a habit to call in at the Control Office first thing each day, so at least I knew a bit about it, and everything went off OK. So ended a busy week, and I returned home to Nottingham for the weekend.

PART 2: IN AT THE DEEP END

The essentials

The first essential was to find somewhere to lay my head. The arrangements provided for paid hotel accommodation for two weeks, after which a lodging allowance was paid and you had to find your own. In practice I never had any difficulty – the Staff Office usually kept a list of suitable digs and I tried some at Olton, two or three stations along the Solihull line. They were excellent. It was almost a private hotel, and about half a dozen other people were staying there. Breakfast next morning was an eye-opener – starting with two fried eggs and four rashers, freshly cooked. I was clearly going to be spoilt, as the evening meal was just as good. The second essential was to find somewhere permanent to live. My wife and I spent a couple of Sundays armed with a pile of estate agents' leaflets, plus two days during the week which I took off, and we finally concentrated on Solihull and Sutton Coldfield. However, Solihull was too expensive, so after another weekend of house-viewing we settled on one at Sutton Coldfield, 15 minutes' walk from the station. Financial details were quickly concluded and, on 20 April, we agreed on a price of £6,925. The Birmingham area was 50% more expensive than the Nottingham area.

A slight difficulty then arose. I was friendly with the headmaster at my elder son's school, as I had been secretary of the PTA, and he recommended that I should not move until the summer holidays, almost three months ahead. Not wanting the house at Sutton Coldfield to slip through our fingers, we went ahead with the purchase, based on a completion date of 30 June. Euston were happy to give me a bridging loan for the intervening period until I had sold my house at Nottingham, which was very helpful.

Meetings with the staff reps

I was pitched immediately into a series of meetings about changes due to take place in the Division. New carriage sidings had been constructed at Oxley on the site of the old marshalling yard and the staffing arrangements had to be agreed with the staff representatives (always referred to as staff reps), and as well as the conversion of the old GWR Low Level station at Wolverhampton into a PCD to deal with parcels traffic for the whole area there was a third scheme in the offing, which concerned the rundown

At the south end of the marshalling yards at Bescot on 16 January 1975, Sulzer Type 2, Class 25, No.25206 backs a freight into the west sidings in order to attach more wagons. *Philip D. Hawkins*

of Banbury yard following the closure of the GCR route. The detailed staffing proposals had already been notified to the staff reps through the consultation procedure.

The consultation arrangements, introduced when the railways were nationalised in 1948, required management to discuss the proposals with the staff reps. 'Discussion' was the operative word, but management had the last say. The aim of the staff reps was to secure as many jobs as possible and at as high a grading as possible, whereas the aim of management was the implementation of the proposals. The result was almost always a compromise. One or two hostages to fortune were always conceded, which kept the staff reps happy.

The reps consisted of the Local Departmental Committees (LDCs) from all the stations affected, each station electing four representatives annually. At consultation meetings where several LDCs were present the next tier up in the consultation procedures, known as Sectional Councils, took the chair on the staff side. They were also elected from the staff, but the volume of work meant that such posts were almost full time. They were paid their normal rate of pay and were experts on the consultation procedures. There were separate Sectional Councils for salaried staff, train crews, wages grade staff, and some others for the Engineering Departments. Separate consultation meetings were held for each Sectional Council.

On major schemes such as those just mentioned, the DOS was expected to take the chair (and the flak). The detailed proposals had been issued before my arrival in the Division, which perhaps was not a bad idea, as I was able to be a little detached in the discussions and could concede reasonable counter-proposals from the staff side. This went down well with them, but politically you had to make some concessions. The Sectional Councils had to be seen to be extracting some concessions from management otherwise there would be

The view south from Redditch station on 2 March 1968 on the occasions of an enthusiasts' special. The derelict ex-Midland Railway signalbox and the abandoned trackbed towards Evesham are visible. Passenger services south of Redditch to Evesham ceased on 1 October 1962 as a result of the poor condition of the track between Evesham and Redditch, although a replacement bus service operated until the date of formal closure (17 June 1963). *Andrew Muckley*

Below: On 1 June 1967 Class 47 No.D1517 heads through Droitwich Spa with a northbound freight of condemned wagons heading for the line towards Stourbridge and Dudley. *Anthony A. Vickers*

considerable unrest in the ranks. Looking back, the whole thing was always a bit of a charade. The Sectional Councils knew they had to make a fuss about the meanness of the proposals and achieve some concessions for the sake of appearances; equally, management knew they had to make some concessions as face-savers. Those at HQ, neatly insulated from the hurly-burly of life on the line, did not always appreciate this, and considered any concessions a sign of weakness. My reply was blunt and to the point: 'You had better take the chair next time, then.' That quietened them. These meetings were attended by large numbers of staff reps and could quickly dissolve in uproar if not carefully controlled. In practice, the schemes could not go forward until agreement had been reached, and I soon found that staff in the West Midlands were several degrees more bolshie than those in the Nottingham area, who had generally been as good as gold.

There's trouble at t'mill

I had my first taste of such bolshieness within a few weeks of my arrival. The shunters at Bescot marshalling yard, one of our main yards, downed tools and threatened to go on strike. I went out there with the Chief Staff Clerk to see what it was all about, and after two and a half hours of 'talks' a formula was devised which allowed a return to work. Unfortunately, I cannot recall what the issue was.

On 1 May, the signalmen at Crewe decided to have a one-day strike, which upset some of the train service, but fortunately the signalmen in the Birmingham area did not join in. However, I spent a long day in the office and the Control Office, just in case they did.

Train crew affairs

I always got on well with the train crew LDCs, who were generally reasonable chaps with whom you could have a sensible discussion. I took their complaints seriously, and I think they appreciated the fact that I spent quite a lot of my time in driving cabs. After the closure of motive power depots and the loss of Shedmasters, train crews felt a little out on a limb. Their boss was now an Area Manager, who was unlikely to have such an intimate knowledge of drivers' jobs and responsibilities as their former Shedmaster. He may even have come from a commercial background and be reliant on an assistant on train crew matters. It took a while before it all settled down, and that was where the Traction Inspectors were so valuable. I could well appreciate the problem, so I arranged to transfer some of my Traction Inspectors to the Area Managers, one to each, so that they would have some expertise on the spot. It pleased the Area Managers, but the Traction Inspectors who were transferred were rather unhappy about it and felt that they had been demoted, although their rates of pay and their gradings were unchanged.

There was a particular problem with Tyseley train crew depot. The closure of the GWR route north of Birmingham meant that it had lost all its long-distance freight and passenger work on that route. Moreover, Saltley men worked all the freight south of Birmingham over the GWR route because the diesel locos were domiciled at Saltley. So the GWR men were left with DMU work and felt the loss of their former long-distance work very acutely. The answer appeared to be the transfer of all the Tyseley men to Saltley and the closure of the Tyseley depot. The two depots were only two or three miles apart, so that was not a major problem. Soundings at Tyseley indicated that the men there would jump at the idea, because it would give them a much wider range of routes and work, although the Saltley men might not be so overjoyed at being invaded by GWR men. However, I discussed the issue with them and they could see the problem. Indeed, they sympathised with the Tyseley men's predicament. They were very reasonable, so a joint meeting of the two LDCs was arranged, with me in the chair, and it was left that they would jointly review the links at Saltley and see how best the Tyseley

A view taken looking towards the north from Stechford station on 27 October 1984 shows a Metro-Cammell DMU, forming a Motor Show special to Birmingham International, crossing the junction. The lines to the left head towards Birmingham New Street; those to the right are the freight-only lines towards Bescot. *Michael J. Collins*

work and the men could be integrated. The Saltley LDC was formed of reasonable and professional men, and they worked it out well. The Tyseley men were delighted, and so was I, as closure of the train crew depot helped my budget considerably.

Saloon tours

On 21 April, John Pollard took me on a saloon tour with several other officers from the Division along a number of routes that were new to me, including Redditch, Droitwich, Stourbridge, Dudley, Walsall and finishing up at Rugeley. Then it was nonstop back to base. A couple of days later we went to Banbury to visit the station and the yards. The station had been rebuilt some years earlier in a novel style, with all the platforms being accessed from a wide overbridge. The latter was the site of a commodious refreshment room/waiting room from which there was a good view of the line in both directions. Facilities on the platforms were rudimentary, the plan presumably being that passengers would wait on the bridge until they saw their train approaching, then dash down the staircase on to the platform. That was OK for the fleet of foot, but not for older people with luggage. We had lunch in a pub at Adderbury, which was the first station on the long, winding cross-country line that turned off the Oxford line at Kings Sutton and wended its laborious way through Kingham to Cheltenham. I believe that in previous years it had been used for iron-ore traffic from the Banbury area to South Wales, but that traffic had ceased.

Before April was out I went on another saloon tour, organised by the Divisional Freight Manager, which took us to Wolverhampton and Wellington, and along the branches to Donnington, for the MoD Depot, and to Buildwas, for the power station, which had been converted to MGR working.

Back to Crewe, and to cab-riding

It was becoming obvious that I was going to spend a lot of time going backwards and forwards to Crewe. I set off the same evening to Crewe and spent the night at the Webb Orphanage Training School, the next morning being spent with an Operating course discussing their syndicate reports. The DOS's job was proving to be very diverse.

Tyseley Open Days attracted large crowds, indicating that interest in the steam locomotive was far from dead, especially when it is such a famous engine as LNER Class A4 Pacific No.4498 *Sir Nigel Gresley* on a shuttle working at the depot. The date is 3 June 1973. *Chris Hall*

Another new field of interest was opening. The former LNWR main line from Rugby to Stafford via Birmingham and Wolverhampton had recently been electrified at 25kV on the overhead wire principle, and it was time to learn all about it. As well as the main line, the old Grand Junction line from Stechford to Wolverhampton via Bescot, which avoided Birmingham and was a valuable asset, was electrified, together with some short connecting lines, including Bescot to Walsall. Accordingly, I spent a whole day with my Chief Traction Inspector, Eddie Allcock, riding around on Class 86 locomotives and electric multiple-units, learning the intricacies of the job. It was the prelude to many happy miles of riding on electric locos, and eventually sitting in the driver's seat.

PART 3: I BEGIN TO SETTLE DOWN

More route learning to do

On Monday 4 May I went to New Street station to see the departure of a new express train from Birmingham to Glasgow – the 'Midland Scot'. This train had happy memories for me because I recall seeing it as a schoolboy train-spotter at Carnforth or Hest Bank during wartime school holidays. It always preceded the Down 'Royal Scot', which in turn was always followed by the 10.05 Euston to Perth. For some reason, which I have never been able to fathom, Birmingham always had a poor service to Glasgow.

However, after I had seen off the 'Midland Scot', Bill Gillett took me on a tour that embraced Selly Oak (Cadbury's chocolate factory, Bournville), Longbridge (British Leyland Motor Corporation factory), Stourbridge Junction and Wolverhampton. Going south-west from Birmingham, you were very soon in some rather pleasant countryside, and we had ham and eggs in a pub in the Clent hills. The following day I went with Bill Evison, my Train Planning Assistant, to Baddesley Colliery and the Kingsbury branch off the Tamworth–Birmingham line.

Royal Train duty

HM The Queen Mother was visiting Cadbury's factory at Bournville the following day, but the Royal Train had to be stabled overnight, so I went out there to familiarise myself with the site. It was the normal location for stabling the Royal Train, quiet and secluded but with good road access and a pub where we could gather beforehand (and shelter from the rain if necessary). The train arrived some time after midnight, and after it had been safely put away I had a drink with the railway officer in charge of the train and spent the night in a berth.

I was up early next morning to check all preparations, such as the train crew for the departure, the supply of newspapers (six copies of every paper, including the Sporting Pink), the carriage cleaners (the exterior was washed down) etc, and then had a luxurious Royal Train breakfast. After that I brushed my shoes and my bowler (I still have it) and we set off at 9.40am, arriving at Selly Oak at 10.25am. Selly Oak station had been unstaffed some time previously and was rather dilapidated, but the Palace staff who attended the recce assured us that it would be OK and that the Queen Mother did not want any expenditure on her behalf. Nonetheless, the Civil Engineer did tidy it up a bit. I did not record where the train was stabled, but it was drawn back into the station for departure at 4.15pm for Bedale. After that I went home to Nottingham.

Back to the grindstone

The British Railways Board (BRB) Signalling Principles Committee (of which I became Joint Chairman several years later) visited the area to see the new power signalboxes at New Street, Saltley and Derby. The officers' saloon was in use yet again and we finished up, very conveniently, at Nottingham. I was invited to join them for dinner at the George Hotel, which I seem to remember was Tournedos Rossini, which the George did very well. Bobby Gardiner, my old Divisional Manager, used it a lot and introduced me to the dish.

Next day the saloon was back in use, this time for a trip to Banbury. We actually travelled as far as the regional boundary at Ardley, on the Princes Risborough line, and Heyford, on the Oxford line. The line forked at Aynho Junction. It was a beautiful day in early May, and the countryside was at its best. We had lunch on the end of the old Kingham branch at Kings Sutton near a stream. It was idyllic.

The Post Office had recently opened its new sorting office, and John Pollard took me with him to a meeting with the Regional Postal Controller and his Operations Officer. In those days the Post Office was a very good customer of the railways

18

and needed looking after, so John pushed the boat out with lunch at the Midland Hotel.

After lunch it was down to the nitty-gritty. The Bescot train crew LDC was getting upset at changes to the crews' diagrams in the new timetable, so I listened to them in my best conciliatory mode and said I would do whatever I could. Crewe must have made some changes, and the trouble blew over. But all Crewe did, or could do, was shuffle work around between depots, which meant that there were winners and losers, but it kept things quiet for a while.

A pleasant interlude

On Sunday 17 May, another beautiful day, the Tyseley Preservation Group was having an open day. Quite a number of locomotives were in steam and running up and down the sidings, including No.6201 *Princess Elizabeth*, No.5593 *Kolhapur*, No.7029 *Clun Castle*, LMS Class 5 No.5428 and '8F' 2-8-0 No.8233. Pat Whitehouse was one of the leading lights in the group and he invited me into the saloon. Perhaps he wanted to make my acquaintance.

More Royal Train duty

HM The Queen was visiting Coventry in a few weeks' time, so we had reconnaissance meetings with all departments at both Coventry and the overnight stabling point. These were big meetings with a lot of people involved, including the British Transport Police, Warwickshire Police and Coventry City Council. Every detail was worked out and timed, with nothing being left to chance. The police were concerned with crowd control and road traffic issues. For lunch I had a frugal sandwich in the refreshment rooms at Coventry station.

On the day, I went to see the Royal Train arrive and be safely put away, before talking to Bob Arnott, the railway officer in charge, over a cup of tea. I had a berth in a sleeper, and the next morning brought the usual drill – checking on preparations, engine and train crew workings etc and then breakfast. The new engine arrived, was coupled up to the train, set off and proceeded in leisurely style to Coventry. I always had a Traction Inspector on board for the last leg to ensure that we arrived spot on time – not a minute early, or a minute late – which meant some fine adjustment to the speed of the train as it approached the station where the reception party was lined up waiting.

Mishaps

Whilst I was away on a week's holiday at the end of May we had a serious prang at Albion, on the main line between New Street and Wolverhampton. The driver of an EMU passed a signal at danger and ran into the side of a train of empty oil tanks that was just leaving the Gulf Oil sidings there. There were no casualties, but the involvement of a passenger train made it very likely that there would be a public enquiry by the Railway Inspectorate, then part of the DoE, the Government body responsible for overseeing safety on the railways. My first day back at work was taken up with the formal internal inquiry, but fortunately my staff had organised everything for me.

The public inquiry was held about a fortnight later by Major Freddie Rose, an officer of the Railway Inspectorate. I met him the previous afternoon and took him in the driving cab for a run over the line in an EMU from Birmingham to Wolverhampton, after which I took him to the Midland Hotel, where we had dinner with Fred Kerr, the Divisional Signal Engineer, and Laurie Taylor, the Maintenance Engineer. The inquiry was held next morning in a room at the hotel. Although it was a public inquiry, apart from a couple of bored reporters the public were absent.

It was over by lunchtime, but it revealed an interesting situation – the EMU driver had passed a yellow signal and then made a booked stop at Oldbury station. The next signal was at red, and could be seen from the station, but the driver completely ignored it, cancelled the AWS (Automatic Warning System)

without taking any action, and did not apply the brake until he saw the tank train ahead. The sideways collision took place at about 20-25mph. The driver, 53 years old and with 31 years' service, was stationed at Rugby and had a clear record. It was a reminder that AWS was only an advisory system and was not foolproof, and it was a warning that would be repeated for the next 30 years at intervals, until the belated introduction of TPWS (Train Protection & Warning System).

A significant development

The BRB had become very interested in a computerised wagon control system that was in use on the Southern Pacific Railroad, USA, and a party of railwaymen from that company had been invited to Britain to see how our railway operated and advise whether it might be of use to us. They came to have a look at the Birmingham Division, accompanied by a very high-powered group from BRB HQ – Jim Urquhart, the Board member for Operations; Bobby Howes, the Chief Operating Superintendent (COS) at the Board; Bob Arnott, the COS at Crewe; and a couple of hangers-on. We had a saloon tour of the Division and then went by car to a very new four-star hotel in Kenilworth, the De Montfort. Next we visited Stratford-on-Avon, the obligatory place to take American visitors, calling at Anne Hathaway's cottage on the way. Dinner was magnificent and we all had a very good evening. I left the party and went to bed at 1.30am. Next morning they all set off to the Liverpool Division and I went to the office to ponder about this new computerised system that the Board was interested in. It became known as TOPS – the Total Operations Processing System – which was to take up a great deal of our time over the next few years.

A new involvement – the West Midlands Passenger Transport Executive (WMPTE)

PTEs had been formed following the Transport Act of 1968, and the WMPTE was now beginning to develop its plans. I had a meeting with Dick Lord, a retired railwayman who had been called in by the PTE to advise them, and we had a long discussion about its plans for the local passenger service. This was the ground-breaking beginning of some very ambitious schemes, all of which came to pass in due course and gave a huge boost to the local railway system. The PTE was very rail-minded from the beginning, despite being composed almost entirely of busmen.

The General Election – a distraction

The General Election took place on Thursday 18 June, the opinion polls during the previous few days having predicted a

The new power signalbox at Saltley. *British Rail*

The level crossing at Bentley Heath recorded on 9 June 1976. Just one hour before the photograph was taken, a lorry had run into the crossing barriers and rendered the crossing inoperable. As a result flag operation had to be employed as in this case where a three-car DMU headed by No.M50092 makes cautious progress with the 15.02 service from Dorridge to Birmingham Moor Street. The box at Bentley Heath was to survive until 2008 when its function was taken over by the new Saltley control centre. *Philip D. Hawkins*

The signalbox at Fenny Compton seen on 3 March 1985 as an unidentified Class 47 heads north with the 13.22 service from Poole bound for Birmingham. In the foreground is the track of the truncated Stratford-upon-Avon & Midland Junction Railway that serves the military depot at Kineton. *W. A. Sharman*

Labour victory. Guildford was first to declare a result, and it showed a 5% swing to the Conservatives, a trend that was followed all over the country. The final result was Conservatives 328 seats, Labour 287 seats and Liberals four seats. Would the Conservatives undo the 1968 Transport Act? We would not have long to wait to find out.

Odds and ends

I had lunch with George Smith, the somewhat autocratic Station Manager at Birmingham New Street. I had known George years earlier when I was SM at Battyeford and he was SM at Heckmondwyke, a couple of stations down the line. He had gone from there to Berwick-on-Tweed, after which I lost track of him for a time. George was one of the old breed of SMs who stood no nonsense, but we got on well together, thanks to our previous working relationship.

A new trading estate was being developed on an old industrial site, and I went to a meeting with the developer to discuss a proposed railway layout. There was nothing remarkable about this, but we toured the extensive site in his 'H' registered Rolls-Royce. He was a typical self-made man.

So ended my first four months in the job. It had been hectic but full of interest, and I was greatly enjoying it.

PART 4: FIRMLY IN THE SADDLE

The formal approval of Saltley powerbox

Saltley power signalbox had been opened the previous year as part of a major scheme that included Trent and Derby power signalboxes, but it had not yet been formally approved by the Railway Inspectorate. All new works had to be inspected and approved by them, but in the case of schemes that took several years, such as Saltley, the plans were agreed before work began and provisional approval was given, subject to any changes the Inspectorate required. It was now time for formal approval.

On 19 February 1976, a southbound freight descends the Lickey incline after having had its brakes pinned down. Class 47 No.47378 provides the motive power. *Philip D. Hawkins*

Over the edge: an unidentified 'Peak' Sulzer Type 4, Class 46, prepares to descend the Lickey incline at Blackwell with the 08.08 service from Newcastle to Bristol on 27 February 1974.
Philip D. Hawkins

Saltley covered the NE/SW route from north of Tamworth to Barnt Green at the top of the Lickey incline (excluding New Street, which had its own power signalbox). Interestingly, it also covered the former GWR main line from Birmingham to the outskirts of Leamington, with the level crossing at Bentley Heath worked from the adjacent signalbox, which now became a crossing box. Saltley also controlled a number of branches.

The approval party, headed by the Chief Inspecting Officer, Col Robertson, together with several people from the Euston HQ Signalling Modernisation Section and a number of Signal Engineers, began their visit with lunch at the Midland Hotel on Friday 10 July, followed by an inspection of Saltley power signalbox which lasted until 7.30pm. The saloon was in use on the Saturday so that the inspection party could visit outside locations and inspect signalling and points. Fortunately, it was a beautiful day, but the inspection lasted until 7.30pm again. Then it was back again for the successful conclusion on the Sunday. It had been a very absorbing three days.

Mention of Bentley Heath Crossing reminds me of a hilarious event one day, when there was a lineside fire nearby and the firefighters laid their hoses across the rails without telling anyone they had done so. The obvious happened. A train came along and the water suddenly stopped flowing. Clearly, we needed to have a talk with the fire brigade to agree arrangements for closer liaison between us in such situations!

More mishaps

Overhead Line Electrification (OLE) is an excellent way of moving trains but it does introduce an element of vulnerability that does not apply on non-electrified lines. I had been out on the 'parish' one day (16 July) and got back to the office about five o'clock, when the Control rang to say that an express from Euston had pulled down about two miles of overhead line on the approach to New Street station. Diversions where possible had been arranged and replacement buses had been ordered, but at 5pm the roads around Birmingham were chock-a-block with rush hour traffic and all the buses were in use, so there was some delay. I motored out with difficulty to see the damage and assess the size of the problem in conjunction with the Electrical Engineers and then went back to the Control. A number of my staff had been called in to help plan an emergency service for the following morning, and I spent the night on the office floor on some cushions. I was up at 5am and had breakfast at New Street station, but normal service was not restored for some time.

The following Monday I held an inquiry into the cause of the OLE troubles and to review our response. The cause was simple – a length of rope had been thrown over the OLE at Stechford, which was the worst possible location because it meant that there was no access to the Grand Junction line for diversions. I was surprised to find that there were no contingency plans for dealing with such events, so my staff set about drawing up such plans to deal with blockages of the electrified line, producing emergency timetables and train crew diagrams. These plans were issued to all stations and depots concerned and were known as Contingency Plan 'A', 'B', etc. It was also necessary to ensure that train crews had route knowledge of diversionary routes and kept that knowledge up to date. Contingency Plan 'A' assumed that the main line to Euston was blocked at some point and provided for London trains to be diesel-hauled and diverted to Paddington, together with a DMU connection from Coventry to Leamington and back. Fortunately, we had a good supply of diesel locos at Bescot and Saltley.

Class 47 No.1544 waits in the remains of Cheltenham Malvern Road station on the line towards Honeybourne on 6 July 1971 with a Motorail service from Newton Abbot to Stirling whilst a NE-SW passenger service passes in the Bristol direction. Trains were being diverted via the Cheltenham to Stratford line as a result of a freight train derailment at Eckington earlier in the morning. *Eric Ilett*

In August 1970, ex-LMS 2-6-0 No.43106 stands at Bridgnorth with a southbound service on the Severn Valley Railway. *Andrew Muckley*

Removal day

The day of the house removal, Friday 24 July, arrived at long last. The removal men arrived at 7.20am and had finished packing by 11.30am. After coffee and a sandwich at our next door neighbour's we set off for our new home at Sutton Coldfield. We had been very happy during our five years at Nottingham but were also looking forward to living in our new home. First priority – where's the teapot? Second priority – get the beds made. Our carpets obviously had a thicker pile than the previous occupants', so I had to take three doors off their hinges and plane and chisel a quarter of an inch off the bottom. However, by Sunday night things were looking in quite reasonable order.

People can be very helpful when you move house. The lady opposite came across with offers of help, and a Mrs Anderson popped round from next door with a message about the Townswomen's Guild. Her husband, Tom, worked in Birmingham for the Halifax Building Society, which was a very respectable job in those days. I soon discovered that Tom and I had mutual interests and we have been friends ever since. So were Barbara Anderson and my wife Val.

Back to the grindstone again

Bill Bradshaw (later Lord Bradshaw, and Lib-Dem spokesman on Transport), who was my opposite number at Bristol, came to see me to have a chat about items of mutual interest. Over lunch at the Market Hotel (the office had an open 'tab' there) he

mentioned that he would like to extend the length limit between Birmingham and Gloucester from 57 to 70 wagons (57 being the limit down the Lickey incline) but his LDCs were not in favour. Would I sound mine out? They were Saltley men, and the guards were violently opposed, on safety grounds. Trials carried out with the LDCs in attendance only served to stiffen their resistance. I had to tell Bill that if we introduced a 70-wagon limit, the men at Saltley would refuse to work them, and that would lead to trouble. The game wasn't worth the candle.

Bob Arnott, the COS at Crewe, wanted to see the holiday passenger traffic at New Street, which was still quite heavy. We met at New Street at 8pm on Friday 31 July and spent the night at the Market Hotel. We were up bright and early the next morning to watch the workings; everything went well and he went off back to Crewe at lunchtime.

Level crossings once more in the news

Clattercote Farm lies on the borders of Oxfordshire and Warwickshire in the depths of the countryside, miles from anywhere except the former GWR main line between Leamington and Banbury. A farm track crosses the line at an occupation crossing just over seven miles north of the latter, and was the scene of a bump on 6 August when a train collided with a tractor and trailer loaded with hay there. The tractor fared worse – the train was virtually undamaged and carried on to Banbury. I thought that I should have a look at the site to see if there was anything that ought to be done in the interests of safety.

Having decided that the most convenient mode of travel would be a light engine, I arranged for one to run on the following Sunday and take me from Saltley to the site so that I could examine not only the tractor driver's view up and down the line but also the loco driver's view of the crossing. My son Chris, who was keen on railways, wanted to come, and seeing that it was Sunday and no one would be about, I agreed. Fortunately, it was a fine day and I saw all I needed to. We then proceeded to Banbury to reverse in order to see the driver's view of the crossing when going north. The Assistant Area Manager at Banbury, a good railwayman and very reliable, met us and gave me details of the history of the crossing. There were no particular problems, and we hoped that the farmer had learnt his lesson. The nearest signalboxes were Cropredy, two miles to the south, and Fenny Compton, three miles to the north, and a telephone would be very expensive, which we would expect the farmer to pay for or at least contribute towards the cost. There was no public inquiry.

Divisional Operating Superintendents (DOS) conferences

These were held once a month, with the COS in the chair. It was a forum for discussing matters of common interest and for raising issues. The COS also had several items that he wished to discuss. The venues rotated round the Divisions and the meetings would be held in a hotel, involving an overnight stay. It was the turn of the Preston Division to host the August meeting, and we met at the Grange Hotel for lunch. In the afternoon we had a saloon tour to Morecambe and Heysham, to look at the docks. Fortunately, it was a clear, sunny day and the Lake District hills stood out so temptingly.

Time for more road learning

Eddie Allcock took me to Crewe on the 'Midland Scot', the 08.15 Birmingham to Glasgow, then back to Birmingham on the 09.12 Liverpool to Euston. Then Traction Inspector Les Durnell took over for a trip to Cheltenham and back. I had yet to start driving! On another trip with Les on a freight train from Saltley to Gloucester, I took a very keen interest in operations at the Lickey incline. I think the Saltley men appreciated the decision I had taken over the 57-wagon length limit. We came back via the Honeybourne line, Stratford-on-Avon and the North Warwick line. It was all very interesting, and certainly not possible today.

Next day, road learning became a nautical operation. Three inches of rain had fallen within 24 hours and there were floods at the appropriately named Water Orton. All four lines were blocked at Walsall. On the Sunday I had a trip on the Severn Valley Railway behind Ivatt Class 4 2-6-0 No.43106. My son had a footplate trip, thanks to Bill Gillett, who was a man of influence on the SVR.

PART 5: GETTING DOWN TO BRASS TACKS

A new interest opens

On Saturday 3 October, the Institution of Railway Signal Engineers (IRSE) had a technical meeting in Birmingham and Fred Kerr invited me to join them. We met at Saltley power signalbox in the morning and I was then asked to join them for lunch. I had a seat of honour between the IRSE President and O. S. Nock, who was a past president, and I did indeed feel quite honoured. I had read quite a few of 'Ossie' Nock's books over the years. Arising from dinner table conversations, I was asked if I would like to join the IRSE as an Associate. Again, I felt honoured and readily agreed. It was one of my better decisions as it certainly opened a new door for me, and 30 years later I had the even greater honour of being elected an Honorary Fellow for services to railway signalling (albeit mainly in retirement).

Problems with signals

Some of the signals at the platform ends at New Street were of an unusual pattern, owing to limited overhead clearances. The three aspects – red, yellow and green – were arranged horizontally instead of the more usual vertical arrangement. From time to time we had problems with drivers reading across to the signals for the line at the opposite side of the island platform and wrongly setting off. So we had a meeting with the Signal Engineer, who came equipped with hoods of various sizes and a stepladder, and we chose one that looked as though it might be effective. I seem to remember that it generally was.

Another saloon tour

Bob Arnott asked me to organise a saloon tour for a couple of his chaps who wanted to travel on some of the less well known lines. He came too. The route went via Water Orton (a busy marshalling yard for express freight trains at one time, but now just a group of sidings gently rusting away), Walsall (reverse), Rugeley via Cannock (reverse), Walsall (reverse), Lichfield City, Wichnor Junction (reverse), Whitacre, Nuneaton Abbey (reverse) and back to Birmingham. A very interesting route, much of it freight only.

Social affairs

The DOS was a figurehead-type of job and you were drawn into all sorts of social activities. I was asked to present long-service awards at a social evening at the Bushbury BRSA club. There were 300 people present and I had to frame my speech very carefully indeed so that all the recipients went away feeling that their 45 years of service were well recognised and appreciated. Most of them were footplate staff, and I was probably becoming known as 'He who rides on the footplate', which traditionally was not something that operating staff were wont to do. You had a role to play, especially with locomen, who were now part of the Operating Department. I was always happy with locomen – they were straight up and down, and you could get on with them if you were the same.

A real emergency

One Saturday afternoon when I was coming home from New Street to Sutton Coldfield in a DMU, at Erdington station the driver was investigating an engine defect and managed to get himself covered in hot oil and water. So, in my best managerial fashion, I told the station porter to send for an ambulance, told the guard to protect the train both ways, asked a couple of onlookers to make the driver as comfortable as possible and suggested to the passengers (it was not a busy train) that there would unfortunately be some delay and they might like to use the buses nearby. I cannot remember what else, but I called to see the driver at home a few days later and found that he was recovering nicely.

Sinister visitors

One morning John Pollard asked me to help him deal with a couple of management consultants from McKinsey's who were coming to see him. He wanted me to explain to them the operating organisation and try to steer them in the right direction. They had been hired by the BRB to sort out the railway's management organisation, which we already knew had too many tiers, but the BRB was afraid to introduce changes and force them through. Hence the consultants – apparently impartial. John took me out to lunch afterwards, so I must have been helpful.

Another Royal Train event

HRH Prince Philip was visiting Birmingham, and the Royal Train was being stabled overnight as usual. It did not arrive until 2am on 12 November, but the pub stayed open, as it was raining heavily, and we all sheltered there. Job done, I motored home to bed. The chauffeur called for me the next morning and took me

A Birmingham-bound DMU recorded in wintry conditions at the picturesque station at Danzey on the North Warwickshire line in January 1970.
Andrew Muckley

A Class AL6 electric, No.E3135, flashes through Hampton-in Arden station on 15 May 1970 at the head of the 15.15 service from Birmingham New Street to London Euston. The train originally departed from Liverpool Lime Street at 13.22.
Philip D. Hawkins

The scene at Leamington Spa on 30 October 1970 as Brush Type 4 No.1694 awaits departure with the 11.54 train to Birmingham New Street from Paddington. On the left a DMU is seen arriving with a local service from New Street.
Philip D. Hawkins

One of the giant 30-ton cranes installed at Dudley Freightliner terminal. The terminal opened in October 1967 as one of Freightliner's first terminals and was hugely successful. However, following rationalisation of the Freightliner network, the terminal was closed in 1989 and all its work transferred to the terminal in Birmingham.
British Rail

A hot axlebox detector.
*Peter Barnes/Online
Transport Archive*

back to the stabled train with my shiny shoes and bowler, where I had a very nice Royal Train breakfast. I rode on the train to New Street, arriving dead on time at 9.45am. It was quite flattering, leaning out of a window to look at the signals and having people wave madly at you, thinking you were some sort of important personage. You had to enter into the spirit of the thing and wave back or it would have been in the Evening News that day with banner headlines about toffee-nosed Royals.

Closure of Tyseley train crew depot

I had a heavy day, meeting the LDCs 'A', 'B' and 'C' at Tyseley, New Street and Saltley regarding the closure of Tyseley depot and the transfer of the work to Saltley and New Street. This affected several hundred men, and my job was to explain the proposals and convince the nine LDCs concerned that the proposals were sound. However, as the groundwork had been done thoroughly and there had already been informal discussions with the LDCs, all went well. I was accompanied by the Area Managers and their assistants, the Divisional Staff Officer and one or two of my own assistants. By way of explanation, LDC 'A' covered salaried staff, such as supervisors, LDC 'B' covered train crews, and LDC 'C' covered guards and other Operating Department staff.

Remember power cuts?

This was 1970 and the electricity unions had called a work-to-rule. On the first day we had some trouble with the signals at Proof House Junction, which was annoying because we had standby diesel generators that were supposed to cope with problems of electricity supply. The next day, only a quarter of the lights were on at New Street. However, I did not note any further problems.

December was always a bad month for accidents

On 10 December I had just arrived at the office when news came through of a derailment at Tile Hill, blocking the important New Street–Coventry–Euston line, but diversions were soon in progress using our newly organised Contingency Plan 'A'. I went straight there and found that a freight train had been derailed when a journal end was burnt off on one of its wagons. After discussions with the Engineering Departments concerned, I established their requirements and it was possible to form an estimate of completion of the various stages – breakdown cranes on site, wreckage cleared, track and signalling repaired, and maybe the overhead electrified line restored and normal working resumed.

In the midst of this I was informed that there was another freight train derailment, this time between Greaves and Fenny Compton, on the New Street–Paddington line. This effectively neutralised Contingency Plan 'A', so Plan 'B' was introduced, which involved New Street to Euston trains being diverted to Coventry via Nuneaton, with diesel haulage as far as Coventry.

My notes indicate that I had a sandwich lunch in Greaves signalbox but do not record the cause of the incident. I held the formal inquiry a few days later, assisted by John McCann from the Research Department, who was extremely helpful. He was a railway enthusiast/photographer. The incident was probably a typical four-wheel, short wheelbase wagon derailment.

Hot axleboxes

From time immemorial hot axleboxes had been the bane of the railways. If the train was not stopped to detach the defective wagon the axlebox would became hotter and hotter with friction and eventually the journal end of the axle would break off, with inevitable derailment. At one time the cause was lack of grease in the axlebox, but more recently it had become lack of oil.

In the days when there was a manned signalbox every mile or two, a hot axlebox was easily detected by smoke and an unmistakable screeching noise, but when power signalboxes were introduced it was necessary to devise other means of dealing with hot axleboxes. Detectors were then placed on the track about every 25 miles, which scanned the axleboxes as the wagons passed over. The scanners compared the temperatures of the two ends of each axle, and if there was a marked difference it probably indicated a hot axlebox. The monitoring signalbox had a piece of equipment which not only sounded an alarm but also indicated which axlebox it was in numerical order from the front of the train, and whether it was the left or right box. The train would be stopped by signals and the driver informed accordingly. A member of the train crew would then walk alongside the train until he came to the vehicle indicated. After locating the axlebox he would report to the signalman its apparent state and how far he felt the train could run at low speed so that the wagon could be detached. (This is but a brief summary of the instructions, which are more detailed.)

Trouble at t'mill again

Apparently the Bristol Division (Western Region) intended to introduce the new length limit down the Lickey incline, although this had not been agreed with the staff reps at Saltley, so they were understandably a bit miffed. Indeed, so were we. On Friday evening, a call came through that the Saltley men were going on strike over the issue. My home at Sutton Coldfield was only 15 minutes away, so I was there quickly, as was my Staff Officer. I managed to cool passions and we agreed to meet again. Next morning was very eventful, with much telephoning and coming and going of staff reps, union organisers, etc. It should have been videoed as a training exercise. Finally, at 2.30pm the LDCs agreed to postpone strike action pending another meeting on Monday.

When Monday came, it was a big meeting, with Sectional Council reps and top dogs from Crewe, one of whom took the chair. Fortunately, things were smoothed over, on the understanding that trials would be held at the Lickey incline, with the Sectional Councils and the LDCs on site as observers. Privately, I was on the side of the LDCs. They worked those trains and knew what was safe and what was not. The Sectional Councils later declared in favour of the Saltley guards and the proposal was quietly dropped.

1971

PART 1: AN EVENTFUL YEAR

THE year started off well with a visit from Bob Arnott, who came in his saloon, and I met him at Saltley power signalbox. Bob was my functional boss for all operational matters, but my organisational boss was John Pollard, the Divisional Manager at Birmingham. They say that no man can serve two masters, but the Divisions had been created about ten years earlier to bring together all functions (except Engineering) at a level below HQ and provide better co-operation between the various functions. In my experience, it worked very well provided there was goodwill all round. I got on well with both Bob and John, which made the juggling act easier. On that evening, 7 January, Bob left the saloon at Saltley and I took him by car to Bescot, where he met the Area Manager/Yardmaster. We had a very productive evening followed by a meal in the quaintly named 'Dirty Duck' in Walsall and I was rather late home. But there was nothing unusual in that – railways are a 24-hour-a-day outfit, and in those days a lot of work was done at night. It was important for the boss to be seen out and about.

Back to the WMPTE

As already mentioned, the PTE had been created a couple of years earlier in order to bring together all the bus services and all the local railway suburban services in the West Midlands. It was a massive undertaking, but the PTE was determined to make it work. With regard to the local railway passenger services, the PTEs were given powers to plan the timetables and determine the fares, using grants for that purpose. So far as the buses were concerned, the PTE was determined to reduce the number of these vehicles using the city centre, and to achieve this it created hubs along the various railway routes a few miles from the city centre to which the buses were diverted. The PTE was full of good ideas, and it was a pleasure to work with; its staff, mainly busmen, were very keen to learn all about railways. For railwaymen, these were very exciting times, with the prospect of more trains and more stations and an end to the previous gloomy prospects for suburban and local train services.

A nice shot of an English Electric Type 4, Class 40, No.304 as it approaches Crewe from the north on 18 September 1971. *Chris Hall*

On 29 May 1971, Class 25 No.D7604, runs light engine through the closed Sutton Park station. This former Midland Railway line, originally from Wolverhampton, is now freight only and runs from Walsall, through Sutton Park to a triangular junction leading to Water Orton and Castle Bromwich. The Royal Mail had a depot at Sutton Park. *Chris Hall*

Long shadows in the setting sun as Class 47 No.1818 passes through Sutton Park closed station on 24 December 1971 with a Class 9 freight. *Chris Hall*

five new pence, but people fairly quickly dropped the 'new'. The penny and two-pence coins still linger on today, despite their value becoming a tiny fraction of the old penny and uselessly wearing holes in people's pockets. The strike was finally settled on 8 March.

The Corporate Plan

One day many senior managers were called to a big meeting in London to be introduced to the five-year Corporate Plan. It sounded a very good idea, and far superior to the existing system of an annual grant, the size of which was often not announced by the Government until the particular year had already started, which was not a very intelligent way of doing things. It was nice to meet old friends, but I cannot recall the plan ever being heard of again. I had travelled to London in the driving cab of a Class 86 electric, but did no driving. I was still learning, although I knew the road well enough.

Freight train derailments

These were not at all uncommon, and the steep gradients to the south-west of Birmingham were part of the problem. The former GWR line from Smethwick to Stourbridge Junction was particularly prone, and pile-ups were not unknown. I went to see a most spectacular one just north of the tunnel at Rowley Regis in which a steel train from Severn Tunnel Junction to Bescot left a heap of wreckage. I handed it over to my deputy to take the joint inquiry into that one.

Strike news

A postal strike began on 20 January, and there was no sign of it ending when Decimal Day came along on 15 February, a milestone in British history. Fortunately, the Government had the presence of mind to retain the pound sterling and the two-shilling piece (the florin, which quickly translated into ten new pence). There were 100 new pence to the pound and the shilling became

The Inspection Saloon halts momentarily for a group photograph at Langley Green station. They are some of my Trains Section staff, accompanied by the steward. *Author*

Langley Green Middle signalbox at Langley Green station. Genuine Great Western along with Western Region signals. *Author*

Below: On 19 October 1967 Class 47 No.1806 is recorded leaving the freight loop at Kidderminster with a northbound block train of 100-ton oil tankers. *Anthony A. Vickers*

Another sturdy brick-built Great Western signalbox; this is the box at Smethwick West. The rusty lines on the left used to join the line to Birmingham Snow Hill from Wolverhampton Low Level, at Handsworth Junction. The lines on the right join the former LNWR route to Birmingham New Street at Galton Junction; the latter became the normal route until the reopening of the line from Snow Hill. *Author*

A day out with my Chief Inspector

Bill Gillett was of Great Western stock and inordinately proud of having worked for the company. He must have been dismayed by the destruction of most of the GWR system in the West Midlands, a consequence of the electrification of the former LNWR line from Euston to Birmingham, Liverpool and Manchester, and eventually to Glasgow. And there he was with a boss of LMS Midland Division lineage. But we got on very well together, and I respected his judgement. Utterly dependable and reliable, he was respected by all the staff.

On this occasion, he came with me to Stourbridge and Kidderminster to look at a couple of signalling schemes, which gave me an opportunity to have a closer look at the area, of which I knew little. We had lunch in a pub, with Henry Holloway, the local Area Manager (another GWR man). I expect we had a beer, which was the accepted practice in those days, but it was forbidden in signalboxes and on the footplate. Why the distinction? Because we had no immediate safety responsibilities on what we were doing that day.

Passengers hurry to catch the Stourbridge Town railcar at Stourbridge Junction on 15 March 1969. *Roger Crombleholme*

Bill's love of the Great Western extended to the preservation of a lovely stretch of line in the Severn Valley, which ran from Kidderminster to Bewdley and Bridgnorth (and ultimately to Shrewsbury). He was one of the leading lights in its preservation. It has since prospered wildly beyond Bill's dreams, and is one of today's top-rank preserved railways.

Football specials

Saturday football specials were a regular feature of the Division, as we had several top-flight clubs, including Aston Villa, Wolverhampton Wanderers, Birmingham City and Coventry City, to name but four. On 27 February, Aston Villa was in the League Cup Final at Wembley, and the Division ran no fewer than 13 specials. Despite the ravages and cuts of the Beeching era, we were still able to find the necessary coaches, with the help of neighbouring Divisions. My notes do not indicate whether these were all electrically hauled or whether we found some spare diesels, but everything went smoothly, thanks to some careful planning by the Divisional Passenger Trains office. I had some inspectors posted at critical locations, just in case, as with 13 specials you cannot afford to have any slip-ups. Although not a football fan, I thoroughly enjoyed events like this.

Evening meetings

The Chartered Institute of Transport was very active in the Division, not just in respect of railways but also covering road haulage and buses. We had a very interesting meeting on 2 March, when Geoffrey Wilson, a BR Board Member, gave us an inspiring talk on 'The Way Ahead'. I was greatly impressed, but he seemed to disappear from view shortly afterwards. I wonder what happened to him. Perhaps he made too many enemies.

We are descended upon

The following day the London Midland Regional Board paid us a visit. They travelled on the 17.15 from Euston and stayed overnight at the Midland Hotel, where there was a private dinner for the Divisional officers. For some reason I was placed next to David Bowick who, I think, was Chairman of the LM Board. I liked David and got on well with him, but later his star deserted him. There were drinks after the dinner, of course, and we all had a merry evening. I got home at 12.15am in someone's chauffeur-driven car.

The following day I was invited to the Board's businessmen's lunch. All the local bigwigs were there, including the bishop, the town clerk and various chairmen and general managers. In the afternoon I was detailed to take a Board party on a road tour that encompassed New Street station, the main parcels depot in Curzon Street (parcels traffic was still big business) and Saltley power signalbox. The whole visit went off very well. John Pollard was at his best on such occasions.

TOPS developments

Bob Arnott, with whom I had a very good and friendly relationship, had been whisked away to BR HQ to manage its introduction as Project Manager. What he thought of the move, he didn't say. TOPS was never popular, and needed a large staff to introduce the system and then run it. And it came too late, as the days of the marshalling yard were numbered, with the ending of a way of life.

Bob visited the Division on 11 March, together with three Americans from the Southern Pacific Railroad and several people from the Eastern and London Midland Regions and the BRB in connection with the introduction of TOPS. It was obvious that this venture was going to soak up a lot of our time. The saloon became quite crowded, and I think we kept the drinks cupboard closed. In retrospect, it was all a glorious waste of time and money, but at the time the powers that be regarded it as high priority, as though it were the answer to a maiden's prayer. It was politic to go with the flow, as overt scepticism could be harmful to one's career.

A few days later, all the DOSs were called to a meeting at the Great Western Royal Hotel at Paddington for a briefing on TOPS. There was no doubt that the Board meant business.

PART 2: VARIETY IS THE SPICE OF LIFE

I become a tour guide

When the small but high-powered delegation from the Southern Pacific Railroad visited the Birmingham Division, Bob Arnott asked me if I would give one of them and his wife a guided tour of the Division. When I mentioned this to my wife she jumped at the opportunity, and so it was arranged that we would meet Ted and Jean Strong at the De Montfort Hotel in Kenilworth on the morning of Sunday 21 March, with my car. As might have been expected with Californians, they were tall, sunburnt and elegant. Having used her woman's intuition to divine what to expect, Val had dressed accordingly.

First stop was Coventry Cathedral. Now it so happened that the wife of my Parcels Officer, John Robinson, was a guide at the cathedral, so she took charge and gave our visitors the full royal treatment. She described how the 14th-century cathedral had been reduced to a heap of burning rubble during a heavy bombing raid one night in November 1940, together with much

At Tamworth High Level, on 27 March 1971, Class 47 No.1596 passes through with 6Z48, a special train of ammonia tanks. *Chris Hall*

On 1 March 1967, a year before the cessation of through services southwards, Class 47 No.D1701 stands in Birmingham Snow Hill with a down service from London Paddington. *Andrew Muckley*

of the city, and that a new cathedral, designed by the architect Sir Basil Spence, had been opened in 1962. She also mentioned the story of Lady Godiva and her famous ride, allegedly unclothed. It provided an excellent start to the tour. Lunch followed at the De Montfort Hotel, before we moved on to Stratford-on-Avon to see all the famous sights there, especially anything connected with Shakespeare. Finally, it was back to Kenilworth and its famous castle for a bit more history. I think Ted and Jean were impressed by the wealth of history in the area, not having much of their own.

Back to reality

The next day I had a meeting with staff reps regarding the final withdrawal of passenger services on the Snow Hill to Wolverhampton Low Level line. It was a sad ending to a line that had once seen 'King' class locomotives at the head of Paddington–Birkenhead services but had been reduced to a poorly patronised all-stations DMU service. The staff reps accepted it with a shrug of the shoulders. It was the end of trains on that line, and – the final indignity – Snow Hill station became a car park. *Sic transit gloria mundi* or 'From the sublime to the gor blimey'.

Derailments

A few days later, on Saturday 27 March, the Control Office interrupted my dreams at 12.30am to give me the news that the Nottingham to Swansea freight train had become derailed near Brownhills on the line from Wichnor Junction to Walsall and had been run into by the Wolverhampton to Derby parcels train. Sounded jolly! I went out there to survey the wreckage, but the breakdown cranes were on their way and so were the Engineering Departments. When they arrived we had a discussion about how long it might take to clear the line. They reckoned 24 hours, because there was quite a lot of wreckage, among which was a wagon conveying 10 tons of gelignite. I went home at 4.30am.

I woke up at 8am to be greeted by the news that the 07.12 Birmingham to Walsall EMU had been derailed at Pleck Junction on the approach to Walsall. It was a fairly low-speed derailment and fortunately there were not many passengers, being a Saturday morning. More importantly, there were no serious casualties, but as it was a passenger train there was likely to be a public inquiry by the Railway Inspectorate. I grabbed a bacon sandwich and motored out to see the situation for myself, but it was a fairly minor incident. I held the formal joint inquiry on the following Tuesday and the cause of the derailment was found to be a loose tyre on one of the wheels.

Formal inquiries of this nature were attended by all the departments involved, which in this case included, besides me as chairman (it was customary for the Operating Department to take the chair, probably because no one else wanted the work involved), the Civil Engineer (for the track), the Mechanical Engineer (for the train) and the Electrical Engineer (for the overhead electric line and the live rail). Each one put questions to the witnesses in turn, the witnesses being the train crew and the signalmen, the fitters who maintained the train, and the gang who maintained the track. The whole purpose of the inquiry was to identify the cause, and not to ascribe blame.

The public inquiry was held on 15 April. The Railway Inspectorate knew their stuff and did not mess about. The inspector took the chair, introduced himself, and stated the purpose of the inquiry, which was to identify the cause of the accident and make recommendations. Inspectors were well versed in the art and brooked no interruptions. This was a fairly modest inquiry, and there was little public interest; in fact, if I remember correctly, there was none, except for a bored reporter from the local Birmingham paper. The meeting was over by lunchtime, but the follow-up was held in private. I lunched with colleagues at the local Chinese restaurant – nothing extravagant. The report, which cost all of 32p, was not published until 20 December that year.

Football cup-tie specials

Aston Villa's ground was big enough for cup-tie matches, and on the evening of Wednesday 31 March it played host to two contenders. We had eight specials from Euston, conveying Arsenal supporters, and nine from Stoke-on-Trent. Witton station was used for disembarking as it was only a few minutes' walk from the ground. The situation was eased by the two sets of trains approaching from opposite directions, which helped with the stabling of the empty trains. Punctuality was good, and the two flows of passengers disembarking eased the situation. The British Transport Police were there in force, but there were no problems as everyone seemed to be in a good humour. We had discussed the plans with the BTP beforehand, and my inspectors were located at critical locations to ensure that the return trains left the stabling points for the short trip to Witton station in accordance with the plan. We could then relax for a short while.

It was necessary to organise the trains for the return journey and arrange for one to be in each platform before the end of the match. Succeeding trains would then gradually follow, so that there was always one waiting to enter the platform as soon at the previous one was on its way. Cup-tie matches at Villa Park were regular events, so the staff knew exactly what to do. It was a pleasure to see it all working well, and the police did their stuff in controlling the returning crowds and not allowing them on to the platforms until the previous train was on its way. I went home at 12.30am, very satisfied with the night's performance. Oh yes, and Stoke lost 2-0.

The natives get restless

ASLEF was unhappy with something, probably pay, and decided to work to rule, starting on Monday 5 April. I went to work at 7am, but there were no significant problems anywhere, except at Saltley, where some drivers were being a little difficult about cotton wool ear plugs and oil lamps. I cannot recall exactly what the grievance was. I usually found that drivers were very sensible, but something had obviously upset them. The work-to-rule was called off the following week. You might well say that drivers should always work to rule, but there was a saying that rules were written for fools, and for the guidance of wise men. A matter of interpretation?

A royal visit

On Wednesday 7 April, HM The Queen visited Birmingham, after the customary overnight pause en route. Performing my usual role of just being there to make sure all went well, I travelled

On 1 May 1974, a two-car DMU, forming the 11.27 service from Shrewsbury to Aberystwyth, departs from Shrewsbury platform 7. Standing in platform 6 is Class 08 shunter No.08816. *Philip D. Hawkins*

On 2 March 1968 the old station at Redditch was visited by a three-car DMU special organised by the Birmingham University Transport Society; this would remain the terminus for the branch from Barnt Green until 7 February 1972 when the new station was opened slightly to the north. *Andrew Muckley*

with the train to make sure we arrived in the platform at New Street dead on time. I always found that train crews rose to the occasion and could be trusted to do so – they regarded it as an honour. I believe that they received a letter of thanks from the Palace. The train left New Street at 16.00 on its way to Cheltenham, running via Stratford rather than the customary route via Barnt Green.

Another mishap

Just after 9am on Monday 19 April, a train of empty tank wagons was derailed near Great Barr, on the Grand Junction line between Bescot and Aston. I went straight there, to find half the police and

firefighters of Birmingham jumping up and down. Perhaps no one had told them that the tanks were empty. Half a dozen tanks were derailed, blocking both lines. In this respect, the West Midlands was fortunate in the variety of alternative routes available when circumstances demanded diversions for trains during any blockage. Unfortunately, my notes do not record the cause.

I called at Great Barr again on my way home, but the breakdown crews did not appear to be getting on very fast. Indeed, it took them the whole of the following day, and the line was not reopened until about midnight.

A pleasant interlude

John Pollard asked me to accompany him and the Divisional Freight Manager to a meeting with the South Staffs Wagon Co over some project that was bubbling up. I do not recall being closely involved, but I do certainly remember that the firm took us to lunch at the renowned 'Lyttelton Arms' at Hagley, where we had a marvellous meal.

A wide-ranging saloon tour

It was time to show the flag once more, so I organised a tour of some of the lesser-known parts of the Division. I took along the Divisional Staff Officer, John Whitehouse, and the Works Assistant and one or two others who did not normally have much of an opportunity to get out of the office, to have a close look at the railway. The route we followed started at Birmingham New Street, from where we proceeded nonstop to Littleton Colliery, just south of Stafford. We then retraced our steps to Wolverhampton, reversed again, and went along the Great Western line to Shrewsbury, calling at Wellington, which was quite a busy spot at that time (actually, the line from Wellington to Shrewsbury was joint GWR and LNWR, the latter having a line from Stafford). Quick reversal took us back to Wolverhampton, pausing for lunch in the saloon at Shifnal, where we parked out of sight behind some coal wagons in the goods yard. The Area Manager at Wolverhampton, Fred Smout, a splendid chap, joined us for this part of the tour. Next it was along to Bescot, where we joined the South Staffs line to Stourbridge Junction, a line full of interest at every turn and then very busy with steel traffic, but there have since been many changes and closures in this area as the industry has run down. We then carried on towards Worcester, before reversing at Droitwich for the final leg to Birmingham. But not quite – we just had time for a visit to the Redditch branch.

It had been a very full day, with so much of interest to see, yards to visit, signalbox steps to climb, and staff to meet. It took us a full ten hours, but was worth every minute. The saloon was an excellent way to meet the staff, and for them to meet us. This had been a working day, not a joy-ride.

PART 3: NEARER TO THE COAL FACE

A long saloon tour

On Tuesday 11 May, we had a visit from higher quarters: three very senior operators who wanted to visit Bescot and Washwood Heath for reasons known only to themselves.

A view of Banbury station in March 1966 taken looking towards the south, showing the once extensive sidings that existed on the up side of the station. The station itself was fully rebuilt in 1958. *Andrew Muckley*

Had news of my idea to close the humps at Washwood Heath and divert the traffic via Bescot, with big financial savings, reached the higher echelons? Or was it all to do with TOPS, which was certainly the flavour of the month? It was difficult to detect. Two of them were from Crewe, but the third, Malcolm Southgate, a very likeable and unflappable chap, was, I believe, very senior at the Board. Our paths were destined to cross again, as we shall see. They stayed for lunch, in the saloon, and then went on their way.

I carried on with the tour, accompanied by three of my staff – Peter Barlow, Bill Evison and Stan Watts. Peter was a young ex-trainee and full of good ideas, Bill was a Great Western man through and through, thoroughly dependable (as were all the Great Western men), and Stan was a former LMS man and a very experienced, hard-nosed operator. Never was the contrast between the LMS and the GWR so clearly personified. We travelled out on the Banbury line as far as Wolvercot Junction, just a few miles north of Oxford, calling at Leamington Spa and Banbury en route to discuss matters with the Area Manager and his assistant. The latter looked after the Banbury end of the area. At one time, Banbury had been a very busy junction and marshalling yard, with a large engine shed, which lasted as long as the Great Central main line stayed open. But it had closed and the junctions to the north and south of Banbury had been taken out, the traffic having been diverted mainly via Toton, Washwood

Heath and Bescot, and then down the LMS main line via Barnt Green to Bristol and South Wales, as part of the National Freight Train Plan.

The line from the Great Central diverged from the Marylebone line at Culworth Junction, just south of Woodford & Hinton, and ran eight miles to join the GWR just north of Banbury. A few miles south of Banbury another line diverged to the west and went on a long, winding route to Cheltenham, providing a route to both South Wales and Bristol. This had been a vital artery during the Second World War, as it avoided the London junctions.

It was a long day, and we were back in Birmingham just in time for me to catch the 22.00 train back home to Sutton Coldfield.

Time for some cab rides

It was a beautiful day and things were quiet, so I decided to take the afternoon off and have a trip with one of my Traction Inspectors on the 'Devonian' from Birmingham to Bristol and back. It was uneventful, but as the line speed had just been increased to 90mph from Barnt Green to Westerleigh we fairly scooted along. It was a lovely journey, with the Malverns on the right-hand side and later the Cotswolds on the left. The whole of this former Midland and LMS line would become part of the Western Region. A few days later I had another cab ride with

35

On 21 August 1972 Class 45 No.134 heads southbound on the 09.40 service from Edinburgh to Plymouth having just passed through Wickwar Tunnel to the north of Yate. *J. H. Cooper-Smith*

The 10.20 Merry-go-round empties from Didcot power station to Worksop trundles northwards at Dorridge behind Class 47 No.47315 on 26 February 1975..
Philip D. Hawkins

On 16 January 1971 the Albion-Waterston Gulf Oil empty tanks are seen passing Cosford Airfield hauled by Class 37s Nos.6990 and 6606.
At the time subsidence at Brettell Lane on the former OW&WR near Stourbridge had caused the diversion of these trains via Craven Arms
since November 1970. *Geoffrey Bannister*

Les Durnell, this time with a freight train from Washwood Heath to Banbury and back. Freight trains are better for observing the track and signalling etc than express passenger trains, for obvious reasons.

A bit of fine-tuning

The expresses from Birmingham to Euston were normally diverted into Platform 1 at Coventry because it was more convenient for passengers and avoided their having to climb the stairs. However, this diversion required trains to approach the directing junction signal preceding the station at an irritatingly low speed until it cleared, and the signal was some distance from the platform. Peter Barlow and I made a couple of trips in the driving cab to see on the speedometer the precise effect. The next step was to discuss the signalling arrangements with the Signal Engineers, and they came up with modifications to the track circuiting that allowed a higher speed at the signal by arranging for it to clear when the train was further back, thus reducing the delay. Peter had a keen brain and was very interested in signalling.

Snow Hill–Wolverhampton route up for closure

The Transport Users' Consultative Committee decided that they wished to travel over this line to assist them in their considerations, so on Tuesday 25 May we provided a special DMU. I travelled with it to answer any questions. Would this be the final nail in the coffin for Snow Hill? It looked very much like it. (Was this the revenge of the LNWR?)

A champagne lunch beckons

The large steelworks of the London Works firm, which lay alongside the Birmingham to Wolverhampton former LMS main line, was having an open day on 27 May, and John Pollard invited me to go with him. We did a great deal of business with them. I cannot recall the reason for the event, but presumably they were bringing into use an extension to the works. Steel traffic into the Division from South Wales and Teesside was increasing year on year, and indeed it continued to do so every year until I left the Division in 1977. These were halcyon days for the metal-bashing industries in the West Midlands – they were riding high and there was a feeling of confidence in the air. The open day was a most impressive affair attended by hundreds of people, with a champagne lunch and liqueurs served in marquees.

A trip to the cinema

During the Spring Bank Holiday I went with Val and the boys to see the film *The Railway Children*. We all enjoyed it, and I described it in my diary as 'An enjoyable and charming story'. Little did I know just how successful it was to become, and how it would earn many thousands of pounds for the Keighley & Worth Valley Railway over the next 30 years or so. It still attracts people who come to see where it was filmed.

Showing the flag

The Divisional Manager asked me to organise an afternoon saloon tour for a couple of guests – Charles Berridge of the

Slightly later than the date of the author's trip, but on 24 March 1978 Ruston Type 5, Class 56, No.56043 heads an MGR train towards Ironbridge power station along the section of single-track on the freight-only branch from Madeley Junction to Buildwas. *G. M. Wood*

On 19 December 1969 railcar No.M55004 stands at Priestfield station forming the 13.56 (Saturdays Only) service from Wolverhampton Low Level to Birmingham Snow Hill. *N. D. Griffiths*

National Coal Board and Denis Grosvenor of the Central Electricity Generating Board (CEGB) – to take in the Cannock line as far as Littleton Colliery, just south of Rugeley, and then across to Ironbridge Power Station, where we had a tour of the generating plant. We had a full supporting team, with Hugh Abbott (Divisional Maintenance Engineer), John Symes (Divisional Freight Manager) and a couple of my chaps. It was a very interesting tour, particularly the discussions with our two guests about all three nationalised industries. That was before Mrs Thatcher and John Major privatised the lot.

On 4 June 1975 Class 47 No.47228 passes the junction at Fenny Compton with a Cowley to Glasgow Freightliner service. *F. R. Kerr*

Busy Saturday mornings at New Street

There was still quite a heavy programme of holiday specials passing through New Street station on Saturday mornings, en route to the South Coast resorts and the South-West. Several of these trains came from Oxley Carriage Sidings, but the majority came from the East Midlands and the West Riding. It reminded me of my time at King's Cross, seeing crowds on the station waiting for their trains. I usually went to New Street or the Control Office just to see how things were going. It was history in the making.

Yet another saloon trip

It was becoming open season for saloon trips, but this one was slightly different. I went with John Pollard to Fenny Compton, where the erstwhile Stratford-on-Avon & Midland Junction Railway passed over the GWR main line on its route from Stratford to the LNWR main line at Blisworth, with a fork to the Midland at Ravensthorpe Junction, on the line from Northampton Bridge Street to Oakley Junction, on the Midland main line. I wonder if the S&MJR ever paid any dividends to its ordinary shareholders, but whilst it was open it had a lot of lovely old wayside stations. One for the artist and the historian.

The line had closed several years ago, except for a few miles from Fenny Compton towards Stratford on which the military had built a large depot with extensive sidings, probably during the Second World War. I seem to recall that we used it too, in later years, for storing surplus coaches away from vandals. However, the visit was formally to hand over to the military the whole length of the branch that remained. I cannot recall who represented the Army at the handing-over ceremony, but the act was performed by the Divisional Manager, who was a full colonel and an equerry to HM The Queen, to boot.

Ladies' Day at Ascot races

This was the highlight of the social season when all the smart society ladies, and some perhaps not quite so smart, dolled themselves up in all their summer finery, crowned by hats of considerable complexity and glamour. They certainly improved the environment at Wolverhampton and New Street on Thursday 17 June that year. Several special trains ran from Wolverhampton, calling at Birmingham New Street and Coventry. They all started from Oxley Carriage Sidings, and I was determined that we should turn them out in pristine condition. I thought it politic to be there at the start, particularly so that I could congratulate the cleaners on the high standard that they had achieved, and I knew they would not let me down. My ever-reliable chauffeur, Barry, picked me up at home in Sutton Coldfield and took me to Oxley. Everything went swimmingly, and I felt quite proud of the old firm that morning.

More about Oxley Carriage Sidings

An interesting item in the RCTS magazine *The Railway Observer* mentions in respect of Oxley Carriage Sidings that summer Saturdays saw a procession of empty stock workings. On 24 July no fewer than 16 such empty stock workings left Oxley between 05.50 and 09.00, mainly worked by the four carriage sidings pilots, all Class 25 diesels. Destinations included Penzance, Portsmouth and Weymouth. In amongst all this, four Buildwas Power Station coal trains passed, and two special freights, plus a steel special, also worked their way through.

The half-mile from Wolverhampton North Junction to the carriage sidings was being electrified so that an electric loco working an express from Euston to Wolverhampton could then proceed to Oxley for servicing and work the stock back into the station, avoiding the use of a Class 25 diesel and speeding things up.

PART 4: A COUPLE OF NASTY MISHAPS

(Neither of these mishaps occurred in the Division, but both concerned trains heading towards us and terminating there.)

Disaster to a schools seaside special

Smethwick was not one of the more favoured areas of the West Midlands, but on Friday 2 July a special train had been organised to take parties of schoolchildren from the area to the seaside at Rhyl for a day's outing. The special had ten coaches, filled with 32 adults and 380 children, and their mothers stood on the platform and waved them off with perhaps just the odd tear. It was a lovely day, and turned out to be the hottest day of the year. In the late afternoon, all the children trooped back to the station at Rhyl to rejoin the train, which set off on its return journey at 5.25pm. It passed through the junctions at Chester and headed for Crewe, which would take it past Tattenhall Junction. At the signalbox there, the signalman accepted the special train and cleared all his signals for it.

The track in this area still consisted of 60ft rails, joined together by fishplates. In normal circumstances there would have been a small gap, maybe an eighth of an inch, to allow for expansion, but on this very hot day the rails had expanded. The track patrolman, very concerned about this situation for some time, had reported it to his superiors but nothing had been done. He had examined the line that day, and in an area near to an overbridge at Tattenhall Junction he found that the gap between the rails was completely closed up. That was about 4.30pm.

The driver of the train approached Tattenhall Junction signalbox at about 70mph and, when passing under bridge 70, he suddenly saw the signalman standing at the top of the signalbox steps, waving his arms as a warning of danger. He had seen clouds of dust at the rear of the train as it passed under the bridge and realised that the train was derailed. The driver made a full emergency brake application or, as the newspapers reported it, he 'threw on all his brakes'.

The cause was immediately clear. The track had buckled in the middle of the train underneath the bridge, throwing the last three coaches sideways into a collision with the brickwork of the bridge. The accident happened at 6.8pm and the emergency services were quickly on the scene, the first ambulance arriving at 6.24pm. Eight adults and five children were taken to Chester Royal Infirmary, and one adult and 12 children were taken to Wrexham hospital.

One can imagine the scene at Smethwick as news of the disaster got round. Anxious parents rushed to the station and waited for news. A special train was quickly organised to take parents and relatives to Chester and Wrexham hospitals, whilst the first seven undamaged coaches went forward to Smethwick, crowded with uninjured or lightly injured schoolchildren and teachers. When the train finally arrived at Smethwick the scene of tearful, joyful reunion would have melted the hardest heart. Two children, a little girl of 10 and a little boy of 11 never returned home, victims of a bureaucratic bungle according to one of the Railway Inspectorate's Inspecting Officers, Major Rose, who held a public inquiry into the accident.

Motorail derailment at Oxenholme

The train concerned was the Stirling to Sutton Coldfield return Motorail train, so fortunately it was not heavily loaded with passengers. The derailment occurred at 4.30pm on Friday 10 September, and 24 of the 37 passengers on board were sent forward on another train, the 12.55 Glasgow to Euston Express, which was stopped alongside. The remaining 13 decided to remain with their cars, and subsequently continued their journey in a special train made up of the rear part of the derailed train. John Pollard swung into action and arranged a meal for them at the Midland Hotel in Birmingham on their arrival. Pulling out all the stops, he even offered them overnight accommodation there.

The derailment occurred at facing catch points some three miles north of Oxenholme, when the train was travelling on the Down line in the Up direction at about 15mph. Single-line working was in operation on the Down line between Lambrigg Crossing and Oxenholme in connection with the electrification of the West Coast main line (WCML) through to Glasgow. The locomotive and the first five coaches ran through the catch points, which were standing open, into total derailment, the locomotive and the first three coaches coming to rest on their sides down an embankment. Fortunately, all three were empty. The line was reopened two days later.

The open catch points through which the train had run had been secured in the closed position during the work that day, but owing to a misunderstanding between staff working on site a shouted message was misunderstood, the recipient of the message taking it to mean that no more trains would be passing over the single line and that he could return the catch points to the normal, open position. A very expensive error.

The railways have a new chairman
On 29 September, Richard Marsh became the new chairman of the BRB. We all hoped he would be able to obtain more funds for improvements. It was an intriguing choice – he had been Minister of Transport in the previous Labour Government.

I enjoy a day's cab-riding
I went with Eddie Allcock for a day's cab-riding around the 'parish' to show the flag. In the morning we went to Derby and back over very familiar territory, so that I could have another look at the colour-light signalling which had been installed over the whole route during my tenure at Nottingham. No more lineside signalboxes. After lunch we visited the former GWR territory from Birmingham as far as Princes Risborough on the direct line to Paddington. Beyond Warwick the line was still all controlled from manual signalboxes of typically sturdy and attractive GWR architecture with a deceptive look of permanence. The crews on

Richard Marsh, chairman of the British Railways Board from 1971 to 1976, was the son of a railwayman who worked for the Great Western Railway. Marsh grew up in Swindon and served as a minister under Harold Wilson before moving to the BRB. *British Railways*

these trains were now Saltley men since the closure of Tyseley train crew depot.

Actually, a little of the Tyseley depot still remained, as it had been acquired by Pat Whitehouse and become home to the Standard Gauge Steam Trust. It was also the home of No.6000 *King George V*. The loco had been the pride of the line in GWR days, and now it was let out occasionally to stretch its legs on the main line, hauling a special passenger train. That was on Saturday 2 October. The following day there was an open day that was reported to have attracted 15,000 people. No.6000 was joined at Tyseley by former LMS Pacific No.6201 *Princess Elizabeth*, and they ran up and down the through road, with one at each end of the train. No.6201 was a product of Crewe, but it surely had some Great Western lineage in its bones. Class 5 4-6-0 No.5428 *Eric Treacy* was also offering footplate rides. Pat invited Val and me into his private saloon and regaled us with sherry.

A spell of socialising
My wife and I were back at Tyseley the following Friday. The staff at the former train crew and maintenance depot were holding a dance at the Tyseley BRSA club and we were invited guests. They were sensible folk and felt no grievance against me for closing their depot, their home, and shunting them to a foreign (ie former LMS) depot, Saltley. I had closed a depot that had nothing much other than DMU work, and transferred them to a depot not much more than a mile away that had lots of good mainline work, both passenger and freight. They recognised it as a good deal, and the Saltley men had gone out of their way to welcome the GWR men and fit them into the rosters, according to their seniority. It was the camaraderie of the footplate at its best, and it stood me in good stead.

A word of explanation about BRSA clubs. Their full title was 'British Railways Staff Association' and they had been built during the war to provide meals for shift workers and accommodation for staff transferred there who could not find it locally. Most motive power depots had them as well as the larger goods depots, and they often provided concert halls for meetings and dances. They were run by committees appointed by the local railwaymen and were very popular for many years. They were still thriving in 1971 at several places in the West Midlands, such as Bushbury, Walsall, Monument Lane, Saltley and Tyseley, and were used from time to time for staff consultation meetings, which were often large gatherings.

The long-running saga of the North Warwick line
The North Warwick line ran from a junction near Stratford-on-Avon for 18 miles to Tyseley, where it joined the main line. It had opened in 1908, when railways were still expanding, and provided a new route for the GWR between Birmingham and Stratford-on-Avon and then on to Honeybourne, Cheltenham and beyond. Between Tyseley and Stratford it served several local stations, the largest of which was Henley-in-Arden. Although not a heavily populated area, it was a prosperous one. BR gave notice that it intended to withdraw all passenger services, but the local populace was not inclined to give in without a fight, and they had some legal heavyweights on their side. Money did not appear to be a problem.

In the latest development it was announced, on 5 August, that a subsidy of £125,000 had been granted to enable the line to continue in operation until the end of the year. The subsidy was the first since 1969, when BR applied to the Government to close the line. It was being quite heavily used, both for the suburban passenger train service and for freight trains, mainly from Washwood Heath to Gloucester and beyond. However, a few days

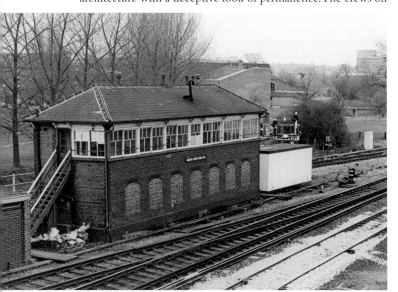

One of the manual signalboxes that controlled the line between Warwick and Princes Risborough, Banbury North, seen here on 23 April 1985, was constructed for the Great Western Railway in 1900. *C. F. Tuffs*

During the Tyseley Open Day on 11 June 1972, LMS '5XP' 'Jubilee' class No.5593 *Kolhapur* runs gently down the through line, proudly displaying its LMS parentage. *Chris Hall*

A lovely view of steam at its best on 2 October 1971: No.6000 *King George V*, the Great Western's pride of the line, is seen climbing Hatton Bank on the 'Return to Steam' special, breaking the ban that BR had on running steam specials. The next day it was performing in lighter mode at Tyseley Open Day. *Chris Hall*

later there came another announcement that the Secretary of State had approved the replacement bus service, so it was likely that there would be another long-drawn-out legal wrangle.

The subsidy had been due to end after 1971, but the DoE granted a further subsidy at the end of 1972, to be paid 90% by the Department and 10% by the West Midlands Passenger Transport Authority. The legal arguments went on and on for some years, but the line was eventually reprieved by the PTE, which included it in its plans.

We have visitors

A party of VIPs visited the Division on 4 October, including John Peyton, the Minister for Transport Industries, accompanied by

Richard Marsh, the BR Chairman, David Bowick from the BR Board, and John Bonham Carter, the LM Region General Manager. At the end of their saloon tour (I was much too junior to be invited) they expressed a desire to visit the Control Office. This was my own ground. To anyone not *au fait* with a Railway Control Office, it just looks like a lot of chaps sitting at desks and talking into telephones. I was in my element, and did my best to put on a good show. John Peyton was genuinely interested and asked a lot of questions. I was very impressed by him, although if history was anything to go by, he would be on to his next job before you knew it.

PART 5: SOME UNUSUAL ACTIVITIES

Layout changes at Banbury

I went to Banbury with Peter Barlow, my No.2, to examine the potential for remodelling and resignalling the area and simplifying the layout. This was one of Peter's strengths – he loved tackling a project such as this. There was good scope for it, as operations at Banbury were now only a shadow of their former complexity ten years ago. Since then the engine shed had closed and the former marshalling yard, which had once been a busy and important part of the railway system in that area, had lost almost all its importance. We spent all day on the project, and by evening we had enough material to go ahead and produce a firm plan for the area.

One of the items for consideration concerned the future of the train crew depot at Banbury. It was still in use for re-crewing through freights and for local trips. The work could be transferred to other depots, but Banbury depot served a very useful purpose. Owing to the rundown of the depot it was now at full strength and widely used by the Divisional Control Office in Birmingham for making up shortages of train crews at other depots in the Division. If we had closed the Banbury depot it was thought that few of the train crew there would want to transfer to the Birmingham area and we would lose them, which we could not afford to do, and the Banbury men were always willing to travel to cover a vacant turn at another depot. So there were practical considerations and we kept Banbury depot open. The priority was to keep the flow of traffic moving.

A new venture – a night saloon tour

I was not sure whether this had been done before, but it made sense. Much of the non-passenger work in the Division took place during the evening, the night, and early the next morning. Carriage depots were far busier during the night, because most of the trains were back at the depot, where they were cleaned, serviced and maintained ready for use next morning. PCDs received most of their inwards traffic during the evening and the night, and it had to be sorted and put out ready for collection by the van drivers next morning. Marshalling yards were at their busiest during the late afternoon and at night, shunting traffic for transfer to local freight depots next morning or sending it on to other marshalling yards beyond the Division. I deliberately did not ask the Area Managers to join me because I wanted to talk to the rank and file and hear about their problems at first hand. Everyone knew we were coming because a special train notice would have been circulated to all stations, depots and signalboxes concerned, so it was impossible to make an unannounced visit even if we had wanted to.

On this first occasion I wanted to concentrate on the carriage cleaning depots. Several Divisional officers took the opportunity to come with me, including Hugh Abbott, Ernie Mycock and Peter Barlow. Our saloon left New Street at 10.30pm on 4 November and the tour began at Tyseley, a recently remodelled depot that dealt with DMUs. Then it was on to Soho, which dealt exclusively with EMUs and tended not to get much attention, and then to Oxley, a new depot. I had been there in the morning to choose a site for a carriage washing machine, so it was useful to ask the supervisors for their views on where it should be built.

But now it was time for the bacon and eggs that I had ensured were on board. They were served by the steward, an engineer's man who always accompanied the saloon and was a good cook. At two o'clock in the morning they were delicious, but there was no booze – this was a 'get your hands dirty' trip. After chatting to the staff at Oxley it was time to say our goodbyes and set off for our last stop at Vauxhall Carriage Sidings, which were about a mile from New Street on the line to Aston. A very substantial LNWR building, enabling almost all cleaning and maintenance to be done under cover, it provided the stock for diesel-hauled trains on a variety of routes, including the NE/SW. We signed off at 4.45am, and I was well satisfied with our night's work.

On 1 March 1976 a three-car DMU starts away from Birmingham Moor Street station with the 15.10 service to Henley-in-Arden over the North Warwickshire line. *Philip D. Hawkins*

On 6 September 1974, the 15.10 service to Henley-in-Arden departs from Birmingham Moor street station formed of a three-car Derby DMU.
The trackbed of the line through to Snow Hill, lifted by this date, can be seen on the right of the photograph along with the portal of the tunnel that linked the two stations.
Philip D. Hawkins

A Birmingham Moor Street to Stratford-upon-Avon DMU pauses at Wilmcote station in October 1973. A quarter century on from Nationalisation, the station retains a significant number of GWR features.
Dr E. W. Fellows

The saloon was in action again a week later, but during daytime in this case. The tour began at Coventry, where we reversed and retraced our steps through New Street and on to Wellington, making several intermediate calls. I recorded that on this occasion we had pork chops for lunch. The steward was certainly pushing the boat out.

A welcome spell of socialising

Mixing socially with the staff was one of the happier parts of the job, especially as in this case we were marking the retirement of four of my inspectors. The function was held at the Monument Lane BRSA club. Val accompanied me as always, because she enjoyed it and was good at socialising. I duly made the presentations and gave a little speech, praising the inspectors for all they had done in maintaining standards in sometimes difficult and challenging circumstances. They were the backbone of the business, and my right-hand men. My ever-reliable chauffeur took us home again, just after midnight.

A few days later two of my Area Managers had organised a film show at the Walsall BRSA club, to which I was invited, together with Val and my two boys. My older boy was 16 and was very interested in anything to do with railways, so we all had a peep beforehand into Walsall power signalbox. Even Val was interested. Very naughty, of course, but what was the use of being a Divisional Superintendent if you couldn't pull a few strings?

Then, at the weekend, I went with the family to York to see an old railway colleague, Ken Appleby, who was, I believe, the Area Manager there at the time. The ladies, having no interest in signalboxes, went off to the shops, as ladies are wont to do. Ken took the boys and me first to York power signalbox and then to York South box, a more traditional signalbox. This was followed by lunch and a visit to the Railway Museum. Then it snowed and we were late home.

A novel idea

On-site arrangements for dealing with the aftermath of a mishap had always been a bit superficial, partly because they were so unpredictable. However, it was obvious that HQ had been thinking 'outside the box' and had decided that all Divisions should have a tent in which to meet on site, plus a Land Rover-

type vehicle in which to carry it. Radio equipment was also provided, and included GPO access and portable radio sets to be supplied to departmental officers etc on site, so that they could be in continuous contact both with the centre and staff on site. This was a major step forward. The tent was large enough to be the communications and command centre, and had a folding table and chairs and tea-making equipment. It would be continuously manned during an incident. The Land Rover and trailer tent were kept at the Divisional HQ.

It was obvious that we needed to have a practice to see how everything worked and whether there needed to be any adjustments. But would the different Engineering Departments, over whom we had no control, willingly participate? It was necessary to have a pre-planned exercise, and this was held at Kingsbury Station Junction, where there was road access and a suitable site. In the event, every department concerned participated and it was considered to have been a success. The ability of the command centre to contact anyone at a moment's notice was a very useful feature.

One other problem which appeared was the inability of non-participants on site to identify anybody, and it was decided that large black letters should be exhibited on the back of our high-visibility jackets, denoting our status, eg DOS, DCE, DS&TE, etc. It was a really good idea.

The festive season comes early
The annual dinner dance organised by the Chief Operating Manager's Department at Crewe was held on Friday 26 November at the Royal Hotel. Everybody of note was there, and it was quite a glamorous occasion. My wife was relieved that she had come prepared, but she needn't have worried – she looked super when she got all dressed up. We met a lot of people that we knew and had an excellent dinner, followed by a few words from the organiser before the dancing commenced. Val loved it, except for the noisy band. I had long come to the conclusion that bands went to dances to amuse themselves, which seemed to consist in making as much noise as possible so that you couldn't hear yourselves speak. I had often thought of surreptitiously taking along a pair of wire-cutters. Val commented afterwards that fur-coated wives were there in plenty.

The Wolverhampton Discussion Group
I had long thought that there was enough interest, especially among the train crews, to form a discussion group and invite speakers. The Area Manager was all in favour, and his secretary, a born organiser who stood no nonsense, set about turning my thoughts into a reality. She was an absolute gem. And so a group was formed, and I was invited to launch the project. I was delighted to do so and gave as my theme the suggestion that we are all in this together, and that staff and management ought to work more closely together for the common good. There are not two sides of the argument, only one. I was also at pains to

commend the work done by the train crew's LDC in fostering goodwill towards management. As a result, Wolverhampton was a happy depot and caused few problems. I became a regular speaker at their meetings, which continued throughout my stay as DOS. I enjoyed their company – they were real railwaymen.

Sugar beet traffic
The conveyance in trainloads of sugar beet pulp from the fields of East Anglia to sugar-refining factories all round the country was once very big business for BR. The traffic was seasonal, with several trains a day passing through the Division. There was a sugar-refining factory in the Division at Foley Park, just along the stub of the closed Severn Valley line from Kidderminster. Now Foley Park has gone and is just a piece of history, but a replacement has blossomed – the preserved Severn Valley Railway, one of the largest and, as its supporters proudly aver, the best of all the preserved railways.

An exciting new development
Various business and commercial organisations in the West Midlands had long been dissatisfied that all the big exhibitions and trade fairs were held in the London area, and they had begun to consider building their own exhibition centre on a greenfield site next to the railway on the line from New Street to Coventry. It sounded a bit unlikely, but the organisers were determined that this time they would succeed, and an important part of their plans would be a new railway station. It would be very exciting for us if it ever came about. These were very prosperous times in the West Midlands and the portents were very favourable. Regional HQ at Euston soon became involved, both with the design of the station and alterations to the track layout, and the coming years promised to be very interesting. It was something to look forward to.

Class 46 No.150 enters Cheltenham Spa Lansdown station on 7 July 1971 with the 07.10 service from Paignton to Edinburgh. Heading south is Class 45 No.69, which is waiting on the ex-GWR line from Honeybourne with a freight service. Due to a derailment at Eckington, in Worcestershire the previous day, northbound traffic was still reversing out of Lansdown station and travelling up the Honeybourne line. This flexibility was to disappear within a few years as the Honeybourne line was closed south of Stratford. *Eric Ilett*

1972

PART 1: ANOTHER EVENTFUL PERIOD

The economy drive hots up

WORD came that the BRB's annual support grant had been reduced again and everyone would have to make savings. It had become a yearly event, and I set up the Establishment Audit Circus, in which I visited each Area Manager in turn, accompanied by my staff assistant and the appropriate functional assistant. We met in the Area Manager's office and jointly examined every post on his establishment to see which could be cut out without jeopardising safety and without too much damage to the standard of service. Areas for particular attention were station staffing (there were no unstaffed stations in those days), administration, supervision, ancillary duties and parcels handling. In marshalling yards we looked for reductions in the number of shunting engines and shifts. Carriage cleaning presented a challenge, as there were several quite large depots in the Division employing hundreds of staff, but cleaning standards had to be maintained. Signalboxes did not appear to give much scope, but we had several works schemes being developed that would bring staff savings. In practice we were looking for major closures to provide most of the savings we required. But it was not as much fun as playing at trains!

A new washing plant at Tyseley

Although Tyseley had lost its purpose in life with the closure of the steam shed, it had gained a new role as the main stabling and servicing point for DMUs. The number of sets being dealt with there justified some rearrangements of the carriage sidings and the provision of a washing plant, which would incidentally bring savings in carriage cleaning staff. So it was time to decide exactly what layout we required to enable the engineers to provide

Class 31 No.5584 and its northbound freight are banked in the rear by two 'Hymek' Class 35 diesel-hydraulics up Lickey Bank in June 1972. *I. J. Hodson*

drawings and costs. Should we plan to clean DMUs as they came on the depot, or do it as they departed? I think we decided on the former, so that there was time for the vehicles to dry off before being in service again. It was therefore time to get down to work with pencil and paper, designing the best new layout,

On a fine morning with the sun illuminating the Welsh Hills; a Down Special passenger train (1Z22) approaches Abergavenny, hauled by Class 47 No.1849 on 15 April 1972. *Author*

bearing in mind that once we had decided and the work was done, it would be too late and too expensive to make changes. If there was one thing that the engineers hated, it was last-minute changes to the plan or, even worse, second thoughts once financial approval had been given, materials had been ordered and the work had begun.

The demise of Washwood Heath Yard

Washwood Heath had been one of the major marshalling yards on the old Midland Railway, and on the Midland Division of the LMS, and then on the Midland line of the LM Region. Like nearly all marshalling yards, it had a dual purpose – to receive long-distance freight trains from other yards mainly along the NE/SW axis and shunt the wagons to go forward to other long-distance yards; and to serve local sidings and depots in its catchment area, delivering wagons that had come in on long-distance freights and collecting wagons to go forward similarly. However, over the years those local sidings and depots in the area had either closed or no longer used their rail connection. Therefore, by 1972, the yard dealt mainly with long-distance traffic.

The LNWR system had an important yard at Bescot that performed a similar function. It had been modernised in the 1960s, when Dowty retarders had been installed, and still served quite a lot of local sidings and depots, mainly in the steel trade. Conveniently, it also had good access to and from the NE/SW route at Wichnor Junction to the north and at Abbotswood Junction, just beyond Worcester, bypassing the Lickey incline. Could we now produce a train plan that diverted those Midland line long-distance trains away from Washwood Heath and reroute them to Bescot? Through freights on the Midland line that did not require intermediate shunting at Washwood Heath could continue to run along that line. The prize was the closure of the Up and Down humps at Washwood Heath, with a considerable staff saving in shunters and shunt engines. The downside was that it would require a transfer of train crew work from Saltley to Bescot.

This was potentially dynamite. Despite this being 1972, Bescot was still LNWR and Washwood Heath was Midland. The staff reps (LDCs) at the two depots watched each other's rostered train workings like hawks to make sure there was no transfer of work. To attempt to force it would result in strikes, and I would get no thanks for that. One answer would be to allow Saltley men to work into and out of Bescot, but that would produce a riot at Bescot, so it was time for some very careful negotiation.

I had always found footplatemen to be pretty realistic and sensible if approached in the right way, so I began to court both depots. I was fairly well known at both depots by now as a result of my extensive footplate riding, and after several meetings I managed to persuade both depots to agree to Saltley men working into and out of Bescot, and to learn the road from Wichnor Junction to Droitwich Spa (Saltley men knew the Worcester loop). There was no loss of long-distance work at Saltley, and I had safeguarded their jobs. Saltley footplate LDC were excellent men – sensible and rational – and the scheme went in and we achieved the savings. But the writing was already on the wall for wagonload traffic, and for marshalling yards. However, the speed of the change took us by surprise. We closed both humps in May 1972.

Social events

The railway family had always been a fairly close-knit community, and the main centres still had thriving social clubs, part of the BR Staff Association formed at nationalisation to bring together the separate clubs and societies of the Big Four. They were particularly active at large motive power depots, because train driving was in many ways a lonely occupation undertaken at what are now regarded as unsocial hours. The Vauxhall BRSA club served Saltley, as well as the carriage sidings at Duddeston and the marshalling yard at Washwood Heath, and from time to time they had social evenings to which one or other of the Divisional officers might be invited.

After my efforts on behalf of Saltley, Val and I were invited to one of their social evenings. I was usually asked to say a few words, and then the music would begin. I use the word 'music' loosely, because it was pop-type stuff, played at ear-shattering volume, rendering conversation impossible. After a few rounds of jigging on the dance floor, it was usual to retire to one of the side rooms, where conversation was possible and you could get down to some useful bonding. Being plied with drinks was an occupational hazard, but it would have been churlish to refuse. The fact that you might have to disappear at any time to attend an accident was quietly overlooked. Today you would have to drink orange juice. How awful!

Incidentals

Stealing signalling cable is not new. On 3 February, 100 yards of cable was stolen at Small Heath. But there was something new – interruptions to the supply of electricity, caused by the miners'

A brace of English Electric Type 1, Class 20s, Nos.20081 and 20157 head a southbound van train past Washwood Heath Yard on 9 October 1975, after the closure of the hump yards that once served the yard. The M6 motorway is prominent on the right.
Philip D. Hawkins

In August 1972, Metro-Cammell two-car unit Nos.M51176 and M56347 is pictured at Shrewsbury station with a service to Crewe. *C. Gwilliam*

strike. New Street station was blacked out, there was no heating in the offices (in February!) and we had to make planned reductions in EMU services. It was a foretaste of things to come throughout the 1970s. However, on this occasion the Wilberforce Committee of Inquiry reported on the miners' claim and gave them an increase of up to £6 a week. The NUM were said to be talking to Prime Minister Edward Heath, but for a few more days there were power cuts and shops quickly sold out of torch batteries and candles.

Another TOPS-related visit

The BRB having felt that the West Midlands could be a useful area for a study as to the possible benefits of TOPS, we were visited by a couple of computer experts from Southern Pacific Railroad, Ron and Norma Edmundson. Norma was about 25-30 years old and was a dead ringer for Mary Tyler Moore, the American actress. Dare I take her to the marshalling yard at Bescot, among all those rough working men? Well, why not? It was time they had a bit of excitement. The Edmundsons were accompanied by a chap from the Board, and we had a very nice and not inexpensive lunch in one of the higher class eateries in the Division (the chap from the Board was paying). It was the first of many such visits.

More lunches

John Bonham Carter, a splendid chap and very laid-back, quite unflappable, came to Birmingham to meet the WMPTE people to discuss their plans, which were beginning to take shape on a large scale. It was a really exciting time, with the expansion of train services and new stations after years of cut, cut, cut. John Pollard took me along, and after the meeting we all went along to the Chamber of Commerce for lunch. Don't scoff – a lot of good work was often done over lunch, and decisions (and agreements) could be easier to reach with the assistance of a gin and tonic. The PTA/PTE people got the money for their schemes from the Government on an annual basis, which made it a lot easier for us.

Mutual Improvement Classes (MICs)

MICs had their origins at engine sheds and were a self-help movement to assist young cleaners and footplate staff to gain the necessary knowledge to qualify for promotion. Whilst they were not as active as they had been in steam days, they still performed a function at some depots. The MIC at Wolverhampton was very active and held evening meetings of a general nature, usually with a speaker. One day, when I had been at Wolverhampton, I decided to stay on and attend the meeting in order to give a bit of encouragement. It resulted in my being asked to give a talk at a forthcoming meeting.

PART 2: THE 'SPARKS EFFECT'

Major changes in the WCML timetable

When the railways were nationalised in 1948, the motive power policy was quickly decided by Robin Riddles and his team. Electrification was to be the goal, with direct changeover from steam, as had always been the practice. This remained the practice with suburban electrification, but mainline electrification posed a greater challenge. It took a long time to achieve, and was costly. There was no payback until the first electric trains ran.

There had been no money for such major ventures in 1948, except for the Manchester/Sheffield/Wath scheme on which planning was well advanced. However, a few years later, in a more favourable climate, the British Transport Commission produced its 'Modernisation and Re-equipment Plan', which included two mainline electrification schemes – Euston to Birmingham, Liverpool and Manchester; and King's Cross to Leeds (and possibly York). In the event, progress was slow, as BR's financial position deteriorated, but eventually the money was found and the new electrified service began in 1966 to Liverpool and Manchester, and in 1967 to Birmingham. It was an immediate success, as might have been expected, with new carriages, new stations and a greatly accelerated service. Passenger numbers soared, and it became known as the 'Sparks Effect'.

Train service revisions

Coventry, Birmingham and Wolverhampton were served mainly by through trains from Euston to Liverpool and Manchester, which provided a good service between the West Midlands and those places. However, it became clear that the main bulk of passengers on those trains were on the section of line south of Wolverhampton, whilst north of that point the trains were more lightly loaded. We were dragging around lightly loaded trains of 11 coaches, including a full dining car set, and it did not provide a reasonably quick through service between Euston and Liverpool or Manchester, for which other trains had to be provided along the West Coast main line. It was therefore planned that, commencing in May 1972, the West Midlands would have its own dedicated half-hourly London service, with alternate trains starting/terminating at Wolverhampton and Birmingham. All the stock would be maintained and serviced overnight at Oxley Carriage Sidings (about a mile along the former GWR line towards Shrewsbury) on the site of the old Oxley Sidings marshalling yard. Initially, work would be carried out in the open, but eventually a new carriage shed was provided.

The new train service gave us much greater control, and we gave it special attention, with regard to both cleanliness and punctuality. The trains were formed of air-conditioned carriages, which was another great advance in passenger comfort, although the air-conditioning was prone to failure in hot weather, just when it was most needed. Liverpool and Manchester were served by a revised NE/NW–SE/SW service, of which more later.

The organisation at accident sites

From time immemorial we had had a system for controlling events at accident sites. Because it had been in operation for so long, everyone was used to it and knew exactly what to do. The signalman, usually the first to know about an accident, would put all his signals to danger and tell his colleagues in adjacent signalboxes, his Stationmaster and the Control Office. The Stationmaster (or in some cases the Control Office) would call out the BTP and the fire brigade, and inform local doctors and hospitals if appropriate. Stationmasters had a chart hanging up in their offices giving details of all these contacts. The SM would then proceed to the site to satisfy himself that the safety of the line had been secured and then make a preliminary assessment of the severity of the accident, particularly the details of derailed or smashed vehicles and locomotives. He would then relay this

Class 45 No.45110 is pictured between Worcester and Pirton on 25 July 1973 heading the 10.15 service from Newcastle to Cardiff.
Philip D. Hawkins

information to the Control by the best possible means to enable them to decide how many breakdown cranes would be required and where from. If passenger trains were involved, the SM had to look after the passengers, including arranging alternative transport and dealing with all the emergency services when they arrived. He was the officer in charge until more senior people arrived from District or Divisional Office.

The Control Office would organise the attendance of breakdown cranes, and the diversion of train services from the accident site. The Head Controller would inform the Divisional officers on call in the Operating, Civil Engineering, Signal Engineering, Locomotive and Carriage & Wagon Departments, as well as the BR Research Department if appropriate. Local inspectors in some of those departments would also be notified. The SM would remain in charge on site until he was relieved by the senior Divisional Operating Officer, who would then be in overall charge.

The priorities were simple: 1 – deal with casualties; 2 – remove all the wreckage so that the line could be repaired as

quickly as possible. It was greatly simplified, because everyone knew what they had to do and got on with it, and, very importantly, they mostly knew each other too, so they quickly and easily worked as a team. There was, of course, a third priority – to discover the cause of the accident. Each department examined its own responsibilities. The operator was concerned about the signalling and driving of the trains, and each technical department examined its own equipment, and would be consulted from time to time by the operator about their findings. It was important to carry out the detective work before the evidence was disturbed, and quickly, so far as the Locomotive and C&W Engineers were concerned.

The emergency tent appears

Changes in organisation had indicated that in some ways the old-established system was no longer fully adequate, and it could no longer be guaranteed that people on site would know each other, as in most places the local Stationmaster had been replaced by an Area Manager with much wider areas of responsibility. Liaison

On 26 July 1972 the 18.17 Paddington to Banbury service is seen leaving Whitehouse Tunnel between Beaconsfield and High Wycombe behind 'Western' class, Class 52, diesel-hydraulic No.D1038 *Western Sovereign. H. K. Harman*

The platforms at the western end of Birmingham Snow Hill station following the withdrawal of the final DMU services along the ex-GWR main line to Wolverhampton Low Level on 6 March 1972. *Ian Allan Library*

and contact between people on site was more difficult and there was a need for some central point from which to control events and to which various departments could report progress. There was also a need for some form of communication to and from the site.

Following the earlier trial at Kingsbury, each Division was provided with an emergency tent, which was carried in a small trailer. One of the pool cars was provided with a trailer hook and it was arranged that, when required, one of the Division's chauffeurs (with assistance if necessary) would take the trailer to the required point, ready for the tent to be assembled at the most suitable spot central to the action and with road access. Communication within the site and to and from the site had been another problem, and we were provided with radio equipment within the tent, serving as the focal point for a number of handsets which would be distributed to the various departments on site. There was also external radio contact.

Rehearsals

We needed to have a rehearsal to familiarise ourselves, so we arranged to hold it at Harbury on the GWR line south of Leamington. All went well so far as getting the tent on site was concerned, but it was a real test to get the tent up in a gale and pouring rain. The next job was to get the radio up and running, which was achieved – eventually. This proved the value of the rehearsal.

Next, we needed a real-life rehearsal with all departments taking place, and it was arranged for the Control to send out a message to all departments that a freight train had been seriously derailed at a point about five miles north of Wolverhampton, blocking all lines, to see how well everyone responded and how the site arrangements worked. Zero hour was 5pm on a weekday afternoon. Everyone responded, but they were not too pleased when they got on site to find no trace of any derailment. However, we went through the motions of setting everything up, including the radios, so that people would know what to do when we had to use the equipment for real. I also got it in the neck from the Engineering Departments because they had to pay overtime for all their staff involved, and budgets were tight. However, it paid dividends when we had to do it for real, which in practice turned out to be a rare event, as it was only used for major mishaps (hardly any) and not for routine freight train derailments (of which there were plenty). The tent also provided some shelter in bad weather and somewhere to hold small confabs and meetings.

The end of Snow Hill

People in the West Midlands had a soft spot for the old Great Western, and many preferred its London service to that from New Street to Euston. However, the powers that be had determined to run down the former GWR service, especially north of Birmingham, in order to produce savings to help to pay for electrification. From a strategic point of view it could be argued that the old Great Western service duplicated the old LMS service, which was certainly the case so far as Birmingham and the ends of the routes were concerned, but it severely disadvantaged quite large towns on the old GWR route north of Birmingham, such as Shrewsbury, Wrexham and even Chester. They were then served by a DMU service, a poor substitute and a running sore that has existed ever since. This was recently exploited for a brief period by an Open Access operator, the Wrexham & Shropshire Railway. South of Birmingham, a limited semi-fast service was provided from New Street to Paddington, calling at main stations en route. It continued the Great Western tradition of running via High Wycombe rather than taking the far more important route via Oxford and Reading – an incomprehensible decision by the Passenger Department. The route via Oxford took longer, but the overall journey time was not of the essence. Anyone wanting a quick Birmingham–London journey went on the electric service. It took many years for this nonsense to be sorted out, mainly by the privatised train operators such as Chiltern and Cross-Country.

After 1967 there was no southern access to and from Snow Hill, but a local DMU service ran from there to Langley Green and Wolverhampton Low Level. That service struggled on until it was finally withdrawn on Saturday 4 March, leading to the complete closure of Snow Hill station and its conversion to a car park. I went there on the last day to witness the melancholy event. However, subsequent developments by the West Midlands PTE more or less compelled its reopening for local services, on a limited scale at first but later considerably expanded. The terminal station of Birmingham Moor Street was used for suburban services from Leamington Spa and Stratford-on-Avon until the Snow Hill south tunnel was reopened, when they were diverted to Snow Hill station. More recently, Moor Street station has been largely reopened with two of the bay platforms for Chiltern services supplementing the through platforms opened when services were re-extended to Snow Hill. It has also been restored

The view from the trackbed at Birmingham Snow Hill following the cessation of passenger services. The station site was used as a car park for a number of years post closure. The site was largely cleared in 1977 as a result of the dangerous condition of the structure and problems with subsidence. The new Snow Hill opened on 5 October 1987 when services to Moor Street were restored through the tunnel with the services to Stourbridge and Worcester being restored from 24 September 1995. *Ian Allan Library*

53

Class 45 No.D126 speeds down the Lickey incline with a service from Liverpool to Plymouth in July 1972. *I. J. Hodson*

to its former state as a Great Western station pre-1914 and looks splendid.

Incidentally, in 1972 the Honeybourne line was still being quite heavily used for freight trains, with 17 trains scheduled, mostly in the Cheltenham direction. I travelled over the line on a number of occasions.

PART 3: A BUSY YEAR AHEAD, AND I LEARN TO DRIVE 2,750s

Industrial disputes

Disputes were not uncommon at the time, and were to some extent understandable, considering the major changes that had taken place in the last few years and the considerable staff reductions and general upheaval. Saltley, with a long history of guards' disputes, could be quite militant, and it was important for us to respond quickly.

My phone rang at 1.30am one Saturday. 'Control here. The Saltley goods guards are on strike over the allocation of work in the new May programmes.' I rang the Staff Officer and we both went to Saltley to sort it out. They went back to work at 2.30am, on the promise of a meeting on Monday, with the Sectional Council reps in attendance. I cannot recall what transpired, but it was soon settled. The programming people at Crewe often caused problems by transferring work from one depot to another to alleviate discontent at one depot, which merely transferred the problem. That was probably how they settled this dispute.

More derailments

We had two derailments in one day on 29 March, both freight trains. In one case a journal end was burnt off a wagon, and in the other, three empty tanks were derailed (although I cannot recall why). We tried not to derail passenger trains – and were largely successful.

The May 1972 passenger timetable changes

Combined with the major changes on the Euston–Manchester/Liverpool via Birmingham route, there was also a complete rearrangement of services on the cross-country routes

from Manchester/Liverpool and from Newcastle/Leeds to the South-West. These services also included Cardiff, and Poole via Reading. It was quite a complicated timetable and demanded a high degree of punctuality.

In order to provide the maximum cross-country travel options, the two flows of traffic were timetabled to arrive at Birmingham at more or less the same time, and they occupied the two sides of the same island platform. As examples, a Newcastle to Poole service stood at New Street from 11.06 to 11.18, whilst a Liverpool to Penzance occupied the opposite platform from 11.05 to 11.15. In the afternoon a Manchester to Cardiff service married with an Edinburgh to Plymouth service. The pattern of trains, though not necessarily with the same starting or destination points, repeated every hour. If it worked, it was great, and we made every effort to make it work, although we were at the mercy of other Divisions and Regions. We kept a spare EMU up our sleeve for use if the connection to Manchester/Liverpool had to be broken.

Northbound, the pattern was similar, with timings at New Street from XX.40 to XX.55 and from XX.45 to XX.50. It should be noted that the Manchester–Cardiff services ran via Gloucester and not via Shrewsbury, and Liverpool had through services to the South-West. The train service on the former GWR line via Leamington and Banbury to Paddington was less than hourly, and trains ran only to/from Birmingham, taking two and a half hours, compared with just over one and a half hours to Euston, which was a half-hourly service. Compared with today, the service from Leeds was infrequent, with the 07.40 Plymouth, the 08.21 Poole, the 10.40 Paignton, the 12.36 Birmingham, the 14.43 Plymouth, the 16.36 Cardiff, plus a very slow 17.38 Bristol. Today's trains are much more frequent, with faster journey times, but whether the journey experience has improved is open to question.

Sleeping car and Motorail services

In the 1972 timetable there is a list of sleeping car services running to two pages, including one that I had forgotten: the 19.25 from Bristol to Newcastle. By 1976, this service had been replaced by a Bristol to Edinburgh and Glasgow service, making use of the existing service from Birmingham – a much better idea. The introduction of accelerated daytime passenger services, which ran both earlier and later than previously, led to a decline in the number of sleeping car trains.

In the early 1970s, BR had quite a good network of Motorail services. One of these, the Stirling service, is seen here at Sutton Coldfield in June 1971. There are those who believe that poor marketing and increased prices hastened its decline, but it needed stronger support from top level, which it didn't get. The improved motorway network certainly provided stronger competition, but the ability to dine and sleep on the train, and arrive at your destination refreshed, should have been strong marketing factors. *Chris Hall*

The 1972 timetable also had a wide range of Motorail services. From Sutton Coldfield one could go to Stirling and the West Country, either in a sleeper or an ordinary compartment, or motor to Crewe and catch the Inverness service. However, by 1976 the service was in decline and the Sutton Coldfield terminal had closed, but one could still go to the West Country from Worcester, and to Perth and Inverness from Crewe.

Singling of the line from Coventry to Leamington

The passenger service had been withdrawn some time ago, and not many trains were using the line, mainly MGR to Didcot Power Station. BR was approached by the Department of the Environment, which was planning a new road that would cross this line about a mile from Coventry, asking if it could be singled at this point in order to reduce the costs of the bridge. The commercial departments, both passenger and freight, saw no objection – in other words, there were no prospects of new streams of traffic using the line, so it seemed unreasonable to object. At least, that was the case at the time, but no one can predict what changes in traffic flows, passenger and freight, may come along and bring more trains to the line. It might have been wiser to have said no to the DOE's request. After all, the difference in cost between a single-track and a double-track bridge when set against the cost of a dual carriageway road is not great.

The whole line was singled on the weekend of 9/10 December, with a long passing loop at Kenilworth. As (bad) luck would have it, it was not long before more passenger trains were using the line, but that really followed on from the opening of Birmingham International station four years later and was not foreseen at the time.

I begin my driving career in earnest

I decided that it was essential for me to have a better 'feel' for the driver's job, so one Sunday in May I spent three hours at Bescot diesel depot with one of my Traction Inspectors learning to drive a Brush 2,750hp diesel-electric locomotives (later to become known as Class 47s under the TOPS numbering scheme). A couple of days later I drove an electric from New Street to Euston and back with the same inspector. It may sound a bit risky, but both the driver and the inspector were watching me, and there was not much to go wrong as long as the signals and the speed restrictions were obeyed. I kept a dust jacket for such occasions, to make it look official – not wanting to frighten the passengers.

Being at the front end is an excellent way to see the railway at work. I followed up my previous exploits with a trip to Paddington and back, followed by an MGR coal train from Littleton Colliery to Buildwas Power Station and a freight train from Bescot Yard to Banbury. My inspector then gave me a certificate to say that I was competent to drive Brush 2,750s, but I didn't take it too seriously.

The Royal Train again

On 5 July, HM The Queen arrived at Coventry on the Royal Train. It was a straightforward red-carpet job, with The Queen being met by the Lord Lieutenant. Later that month we had HRH Prince Philip, who had an engagement to open Telford New Town officially and had spent the previous night in the Royal Train. I joined the train at Wolverhampton at about 1am and we stabled the train at Trench Crossing on the erstwhile Wellington–Stafford line. Next morning I rose early and had a bath (on board) and a splendid breakfast. We had chosen Trench Crossing because it had road access and the stabling point was in a cutting. However, word must have got round locally about the Royal Train being there, because we noticed a row of heads peering over the wall at the top of the cutting. I was surprised the police hadn't kept them away, but it didn't really matter. We left Trench Crossing in time for a punctual arrival at Wellington at 10am, where cars were waiting to take the Duke to Telford. I went along to join the jamboree. Lunch was not included, so I went back to Birmingham and had lunch in the canteen.

Social events

The railway companies had always been very keen on promoting first aid, for very good reasons. In the old days, accidents were frequent and medical services few and far between. The tradition lingered on and we still wished to encourage it, hence I was invited to a buffet and dance at the Walsall BRSA club, where I made the usual speech and did the presentation of medals etc. Many of the first-aiders were very keen and took the annual exam in order to gain another bar to their medal. They also got a day's leave with pay. Val and I must have enjoyed it because we didn't get home until after midnight (in a chauffeur-driven car, of course!).

Later that year I was invited to give a talk to the Wolverhampton Discussion Group and chose as my topic 'Railways – The Political Scene'. Val came along too as the boss's wife, and we had drinks with them afterwards. It was a very convivial evening.

Class 47 No.47333 heads an up Freightliner service along the single track between Coventry and Kenilworth on 14 May 1977. *Mervyn Leah*

A VIP visit

We had a very high-powered visit one day by the Chief Executive (Railways), the BRB Vice-Chairman, and John Bonham Carter, the LM Region General Manager. The Divisional Manager and I met them and took them on a saloon tour to various parts of the Division, which was followed, needless to say, by dinner at the Midland Hotel. These dinners were usually very genial affairs with plenty of drink and everyone letting their hair down. I wish I could remember what was said, but I doubt that the Government and the Department came out of it too well. Next morning we had another saloon tour until lunch, when they all went off and I went to the canteen for lunch. The Rail House canteen was exceptionally good and was run by a staff committee.

A major pile-up and an arsonist

On 21 July, just as I was tidying up my desk before going home, the Control rang to say that there had been a major pile-up at Ryecroft Junction near Walsall. A Class 9 unbraked coal train from Washwood Heath to Bescot had got out of control on the down gradient into Walsall and had crashed into the back of the Kings Norton to Bathgate motorcar train. All four lines were blocked and six carflats had been squashed up, with nice new motorcars all over the place. My faithful chauffeur took me home for dinner and a change of clothes and then took me to the scene. Both the Bescot and Saltley steam cranes were at work all night in the pouring rain and I stayed there until my Chief Inspector relieved me at 6.45am, but the lines were not cleared until 4.30pm.

A couple of weeks later the Control Office rang me at 5.30am to say that Sutton Coldfield station was on fire. The station was of the traditional wooden-built LNWR pattern and of course it burnt well, the downside buildings being completely burnt out. Notably, the train service was not disrupted once the fire was under control. In the afternoon I took several members of my staff on a saloon tour to Banbury and Stratford-on-Avon, with tea served at Hatton, to give them an opportunity to see over the line. Next morning the phone rang at 6.50am. It was the Control Office, to tell me that the next station down the line from Sutton, at Wylde Green, was on fire. It was also a wooden-built station of LNWR design, but I cannot recall the outcome.

The 'Field' organisation

The Board had finally come to terms with the fact that the system was grossly over-managed and needed simplifying. There were four layers: at the top, the British Railways Board HQ and staff, then the Regional HQ, followed by the Divisions, then the Areas. The Area Managers were a fairly new arrangement, covering quite large areas, and had taken the place of Stationmasters.

Consultants were hired at great expense to tell the Board what any of us could have told them for nothing – that we had one layer too many. The answer was obvious. Give the top and bottom layers more work and responsibility, and merge the two middle layers with the remaining work and responsibility. Regions and Divisions would disappear and the middle layer would be called 'Territories', as though they were African colonies. It was obvious that there would be a huge amount of work to plan the new organisations down to the last position, with a detailed job spec for each post. The staff upheaval would be enormous – and very expensive in relocation and redundancy costs.

PART 4: A MISCELLANY OF MATTERS

A novel way to attack the problem of child trespass

Travelling round the Division I was unhappy with the extent of child trespass in certain areas during the summer holidays. On one occasion, on a saloon tour, we came upon a group of young trespassers, so I stopped the saloon and we all quickly decamped and caught some of them. Were they surprised! However, all we could do was to castigate them and escort them off the premises with threats of what would happen to them if they were caught again.

I discussed this problem with the local BTP chief, a very helpful police officer of the old school who was anxious to help but was finding it difficult to catch them in the act. I then put forward the idea of running 'Q' specials, using a spare diesel parcels van containing several of his officers, which would visit the usual trouble spots and when trespassers were discovered would stop alongside them, upon which his men would leap out and catch them. I went with them on the first trip and it was great fun. I hope it had some effect, and it cost nothing. The train drivers were also fed up with having stones thrown at them, so were pleased that we were at least trying to do something about it.

Railway Operating courses

When I was at Nottingham I had run Railway Operating courses for a couple of years for railwaymen who wanted to learn a bit more about the subject, and I decided to repeat the exercise at Birmingham. The sessions were held on Monday evenings in the canteen at Rail House, and the first meeting was held on 2 October, when 36 members of staff turned up. Enrolments had totalled 55, but that included quite a few shift workers who would have to rely on being given the handouts. I gave a talk entitled 'Statutory Control', followed by a film on the Beeching era. The Public Relations Office provided the film and operated the projector. I also recruited big names as an added attraction, and the following week we had Bob Arnott, who was the big chief of the TOPS outfit. Does it ring a bell? Attendance that week was 50, including the Divisional Manager and the potential 'Territory' boss when (or if) it was formed. Afterwards John Pollard took us out to the Chamber of Commerce club for a meal, together with several of the Divisional officers.

On 25 July 1973 Class 31/2 No.5686 leaves Worcester with the 11.50 service to Paddington.
Philip D. Hawkins

A change of deputy

My deputy Peter Barlow, whom I inherited when I became DOS back in March 1970, left in November 1972 to work on the Channel Tunnel project. It was just the

Seen heading through Bournville, Class 45 No.45006 *Honourable Artillery Company* makes its way towards Birmingham New Street with the 07.30 service from Plymouth to Edinburgh. *Philip D. Hawkins*

right job for him, a nice canvas to work upon with no day-to-day worries. What was more, he could speak fluent French. (This was the original Channel Tunnel project for just a single bore, with fleets of trains passing through in one direction, then fleets of trains in the opposite direction.)

My new No, 2, from Glasgow, was a splendid chap. We couldn't understand a word he said, but he was a really good and very experienced operator who stood no nonsense from anyone and just got stuck into the job. He stood no nonsense from Crewe either, which upset them a bit. Not that he cared.

On the night shift

Being a superintendent of a 24-hour railway was not a nine-to-five job. Much of the work in the Division was done at night, and that was certainly the case in the parcels business, carriage servicing and maintenance, and in the marshalling yards. It was time to pay a visit to Wolverhampton PCD, which by a cruel twist of fate was located in the old GWR Low Level station, suitably adapted. Parcels trains arrived during the night and unloaded at the old passenger platforms. The parcels were then sorted to the various delivery rounds, ready for the van drivers when they signed on at about 7.30am the next day. The aim was to have all parcels cleared out by 9am and delivered the same day, but that did not always happen. Why not? That was what I intended to find out.

On a cold November night my chauffeur, Barry, took me to Wolverhampton, with instructions to pick me up at 6am the next day (he liked the overtime). The Area Manager came out too, as well as the local NCL manager and my Divisional Parcels Assistant. A word of explanation here: NCL was National Carriers Ltd, a creation of the 1968 Transport Act, when goods sundries and goods depots were transferred to it. Parcels cartage vehicles and the drivers were transferred to it as well, which was a nonsense because they worked full-time on BR business.

There was a contract for X number of vehicles daily, but it was not always met, for a variety of reasons (or excuses?) – shortage of drivers, shortage of vehicles, etc. We had no redress, as we were unable to sack NCL and employ another firm, and we were unable to hire vehicles to make up shortages. Whoever had designed this contract, and whoever on BR had accepted it, must have lived on another planet not to have recognised the difficulties that were going to arise. NCL was part of the National Freight Corporation, whose business was road haulage, and probably saw no reason to go out of its way to help what was in effect a competitor.

NCL drivers felt no allegiance or loyalty to BR, even though they were mainly ex-BR, and they had to be watched to make sure they cleared all their parcels each day and didn't bring any back, except where there was a valid reason for non-delivery. The upshot was that we began to lose business because of the poor service, and we upgraded the Shift Parcels Inspectors to provide more clout. We also established a Joint Parcels Service Group to hold regular liaison meetings between BR and NCL. Fortunately, the local NCL manager was an ex-BR man and was keen to give a good service. That was a big help.

Problems with vandalism

On the approaches to Coventry station we had problems with vandals dropping objects on to trains from pedestrian overbridges. Having visited the sites, it occurred to me that one answer would be to completely enclose the overbridges with some lightweight material incorporating a mesh pattern that would allow the wind and light to pass through. Accordingly I took the Divisional Civil Engineer's Works Assistant to have a look at the problem and asked him for his advice. Unfortunately, I cannot recall what he said, nor whether my suggestion was eventually adopted.

More royal duties

HRH Princess Anne was beginning to take up royal duties, and used a few coaches off the Royal Train to visit Leamington Spa. I went there to see her arrive. She returned to London in a reserved compartment on the 16.34 from Coventry, and I was there to see her depart. Not to be outdone, her aunt, Princess Margaret, was in the Division a few days later, and I went to Banbury to see her safely on board the 14.30 New Street to Paddington. I wonder if she remembered me from King's Cross ten years earlier.

All this activity must have intrigued Prince Charles, because he passed through the Division a few days later on the Royal Train, pausing only for a few hours overnight when the train was stabled at Trench Crossing on the branch from Wellington. I joined the train by prior arrangement at Wolverhampton and enjoyed tea, whisky and sandwiches with the railway officer in charge of the train.

Banbury was in the news again a few days later, when Prince Philip alighted there from the Royal Train. As usual, I was there to see him arrive. He must have acquired a liking for the Division, because he was back again a couple of weeks later, on his way to Birmingham, with an intermediate overnight stabling at Berkswell between Coventry and New Street.

I went there to see the train safely put away for the night in the siding that we kept there specially for such a purpose. I had smoked salmon sandwiches with the Royal Train Officer at 1.30am, and then slept in a berth on the train. Next morning I busied myself with the usual activities and preparations for departure before having a sumptuous Royal Train breakfast. We set off punctually and arrived at New Street on the dot of 10am. It was a matter of pride to do so, but I always left it to the driver and travelled on the train. I was in communication with the front end through the intercom system on the train all the time, and had to use it only once, when we were in danger of arriving early. There was Christmas lunch in the canteen that day too.

Down to earth with a bump

The following day, ASLEF called a one-day strike for a few days hence. It was something to do with APT, the Advanced Passenger Train, although I cannot recall exactly what had upset the union. On strike days, very few trains ran.

More junketings

The Chief Operating Manager at Crewe was again holding the annual dinner dance, and he invited the LM Region DOSs and their wives. We had a thoroughly enjoyable evening, with a very good meal and music that we could dance to. Val wore a long dress, and we danced the night away (at least until 1am). We spent the night at the venue – the Royal Hotel – which was a lot more upmarket in those days.

The LM Board decided to have their December meeting at the Welcombe Hotel near Stratford-on-Avon, and the Birmingham Divisional officers were invited to the dinner. We spent a very pleasant evening in palatial surroundings, with a good dinner and plenty to drink. The Welcombe was a BR hotel at that time, and had been built in LMS days or even earlier. At one time a connecting bus ran to and from Stratford station. Next morning, some of us went back to the Welcombe to join the party for lunch, and then we all had a saloon trip to the car plant at Longbridge, where some of the Board members had discussions with the factory people about prospective new business. The two days had been quite an interesting diversion, and you picked up all sorts of gossip when the drink was flowing freely.

Halesowen Junction at Longbridge; the lines to the right headed into the British Leyland site and, until 1 September 1958, carried a passenger service between Old Hill and Longbridge although a workmen's service continued between Longbridge and Halesowen until 4 January 1960. On 23 February 1979 Brush Type 2, Class 31, No.31158 passes the junction with the 11.10 service from Plymouth to Manchester. Following closure of the Longbridge car factory in 2005, traffic over the remains of the branch ceased and the track was lifted. Redevelopment work at Longbridge has seen the trackbed removed, although the bridge immediately west of the junction remains to indicate the route of the line. *Chris Perkins*

1973

PART 1: FORWARD TO THE NEW YEAR

The WMPTE gets into its stride

THE West Midlands PTE was now busily developing its ambitious plans for making much more use of the suburban railway system around Birmingham, and one of its first objectives was to improve the service to Redditch. The town was expanding rapidly, yet the train service to and from Birmingham had dwindled to a sparse commuter service. The PTE proposed to link the Redditch service with the service to Lichfield via Sutton Coldfield and run it at half-hourly intervals. There was already a good service on the Lichfield line, and the PTE now wished to discuss with us the practicality of such a service to Redditch.

I arranged to meet Rex Faulks, the PTE Planning Officer, and take him for a walk along the Redditch branch from Barnt Green, where it left the West of England main line. We were particularly interested in the possibility of doubling the track, or at least in putting in crossing loops. The recce indicated that there was potential, so the next step was to engage the Civil Engineer and obtain his views, but I did not tell him that we had already

On a sunny, but wintry morning, Class 25 No.7608 shunts over the crossover at Sutton Park on 2 January 1973. *Chris Hall*

59

It's Sunday 22 July 1973 and a mystery excursion from Portsmouth to Shrewsbury tops the 1 in 111 gradient near Coseley, between Dudley Port and Wolverhampton, hauled by Class 47 No.1635. *Geoffrey Bannister*

The new station at Redditch seen on 6 September 1977 before the major investment went into the electrification of the Cross-City route to Lichfield City. Here a three car Pressed Steel DMU awaits departure with the 17.18 service to Birmingham New Street.

made a recce – engineers can be so touchy! Thus began the development of the cross-city service of later years, with new stations and electrification. And it was a very frequent service, which would not have happened without the PTE involvement. Thank you, Barbara Castle. Incidentally, I was to meet her a few weeks later, when she attended a meeting in Birmingham of Transport 2000, a union-backed pressure group to improve railway services, which is now known as the Campaign for Better Transport. My attendance went down well with the unions.

Rex loses no time

On 18 January we took the PTE on a saloon tour of the Camp Hill suburban line, to see what the potential was for reopening some stations, and then on 6 February we took the PTE in the saloon along the Redditch line to have a close look at it. The PTE was very keen to go forward with the scheme and had already costed it at £20 million. The Government would provide the funds directly to the PTE under the annual plans procedure, so it would not have to come out of BR's budget. BR had virtually handed over responsibility for suburban lines in the area to the PTE, which

would henceforth determine the timetable, the stopping pattern, the trains, the fares, the stations and car parking, as well as obtaining the necessary funding. All BR had to do was to run the service.

The Severn Valley Railway

As already mentioned, one of the main founders of the Severn Valley Preservation Society had been my Chief Inspector, Bill Gillett. The SVR had ambitions to reach Kidderminster eventually, but, at the time, BR served a firm at Foley Park, about a mile up the branch. As a policy, we wanted to keep the two operations separate, and Kidderminster goods yard was still a working area. We looked at any proposals from the SVR from the point of view of the benefits to BR, if any, and at that time we did not really see any. I'm afraid that I took a hard, professional line. If there were no benefits, we should not waste valuable management time on it, and Bill agreed. He was perfectly happy to run trains only as far as Foley Park. Bill was a splendid railwayman and utterly reliable, and he was a great help to me, even though I was a Midland man. I found all the ex-GWR men on my staff to be good at their jobs and thoroughly reliable.

Class 31 No.31168 coasts down the bank on the Camp Hill line in Birmingham with a train of empty bolster wagons on 9 April 1975. The line in the foreground is the loop from the ex-Great Western line into Moor Street.
Philip D. Hawkins

My Railway Operating course

I was now busy running my third or fourth Railway Operating course. We met on Monday evenings for a couple of hours and studied various aspects of the subject. Normal attendance was 40-plus – not bad for voluntary attendance – and I had the benefit of speakers from other departments. Some of the subjects we covered were rolling stock developments, modern signalling developments, the air brake and the vacuum brake, coal traffic, and the APT. At the end of the spring term I set an exam paper, but taking it was entirely voluntary. However, a good result would appear on your service history card and help your promotion, so 24 people sat the exam. I had not realised how long it would take to mark those papers, but it was well worthwhile. Some of my students went on to higher places.

More industrial unrest

The 1970s have gone down in history as a very unsettled period for industrial relations. Inflation led to increased wage demands, mainly in publicly owned industries such as gas, electricity and the railways. Oh yes, and the railway trade unions were well to the fore. Having no trains for a day was a minor inconvenience, but having no gas for five days in winter was a different matter. It was a tedious time.

A refresher

I was sent for a fortnight on a management updating course at the BR Staff College. It was almost a complete waste of time, and the subjects dealt with – none of which I can remember but all were of the airy-fairy variety – had no apparent connection with real life on the line. However, it was unwise to be seen as a rebel, so you put your head down and pretended to be interested. The management gurus who gave us lectures seemed to have come from a different planet, but no doubt it gave them a good living. We had a good living too, with snooker and drinks every evening.

The real railway family

Social events continued to be part of railway life. One Saturday evening in March we had the annual Divisional ball in one of the BRSA clubs at Vauxhall (the first station out of New Street towards Walsall). We had a very good meal, followed by the usual speeches and dancing, intermixed with socialising. It was an enjoyable family affair, but too noisy as usual.

A couple of weeks later the Wolverhampton people had their annual dinner dance, and my wife and I were invited. Again, it was a very enjoyable affair – we had been taking dancing lessons to improve our game, which helped. The Area Manager's secretary was an absolute gem, a brilliant organiser. She had been something in the WAAF and stood no nonsense. I had been in the RAF, so we got on like a house on fire. People like her make such a difference to the efficiency of an organisation.

More visits from the 'Territory' Director

Henry Sanderson, the appointed Director of the West Midlands 'Territory', paid us a couple of 'getting to know' visits. His father had been Commercial Manager of the North Eastern Region, but this was no nepotism – Henry came with a good reputation. On his first visit in 1973, we had a tour of the steel terminals by

The still busy goods yard at Kidderminster is clearly shown in the background to this view of the 14.03 Kidderminster to Lichfield City DMU running into the platform on 17 June 1975. The station was rebuilt in 1974. Today the scene is radically different, with the freight yard now converted to form the southern terminus of the preserved Severn Valley Railway. *John Glover*

On 28 January 1973 this is the scene at Ryecroft Junction, just to the north of Walsall, as the 10.20 service from Birmingham to Leeds passes. This train had been diverted to run via Bescot and Lichfield City and was headed by Class 45 No.19. It is seen passing Class 25 No.5277 with the Bescot steam crane; the latter was engaged in loading the cut-up remains of wagons derailed earlier in the month. *Geoffrey Bannister*

car. We had about ten of these terminals in the Birmingham-Wolverhampton-Walsall-Stourbridge area, which received steel in various forms by the trainload and delivered it by road to the customers on railway-owned lorries. It was very good business for the railways. We all had a very good lunch at the 'Lyttelton Arms' in Hagley, which was all the more memorable because I had not had many lunches out lately.

A short while later we took him on a saloon tour along the line to Banbury, and then to Longbridge. As we have seen, Banbury had experienced a serious decline with the closure of the Great Central and the diversion of freight trains. There was still a train crew depot there with very good staff, but it was difficult to find enough work for them. Closure was obviously on the cards, but we persuaded Crewe to diagram more work to Banbury. The extra work was transferred from other depots, but because it avoided the closure of the Banbury depot, the other depots concerned agreed to help. It was a good example of the railway family in action. The Control Office reminded me that the Banbury depot was a safety valve and its drivers 'would go anywhere' and were very helpful in covering other depots' temporary vacancies.

A very safe railway

We had had very few mishaps during the last few months, the only notable one being a bump at low speed between two EMUs at New Street. Coming from the Wolverhampton direction, the line falls quite steeply into New Street and an incoming driver was unable to stop before bumping into another DMU in the platform. The ensuing formal inquiry proved the cause to be excessive lubricating grease on the railhead, which caused the train to skid. No one was injured and there was very little damage.

PART 2: TOPS AND 'FIELD' – THE PACE HOTS UP

Out with Henry Sanderson again

Henry Sanderson was a chap who was very easy to get on with. What would be nicer, he must have thought, than to have a saloon trip to Banbury in May in order to get to know the road? He was right. A trip from Birmingham to Banbury was a very pleasant run and somehow typically GWR, with semaphore

signals that went down instead of up. The GWR people would have maintained that they were the only people in step. What was more, their signal arms went down to 60°, whilst everyone else's only went down (or up) to 45°. John Pollard came with us and we had a very pleasant day out. But it was a working day out, with Henry asking all sorts of questions, which fortunately we could answer. Lunch was taken on the stub of the old Kingham line, which turned off the main line at Kings Sutton – a quite delightful spot and serenaded by birdsong.

A few weeks later I was called to Euston to have a talk with the General Manager, John Bonham Carter, about the Territorial Organisation. Would I accept a position as Operations Manager in the new Midlands Territory, located in Birmingham? Well, it did not have quite the same ring as Superintendent in railway circles, but that honourable title, dating back to the mid-19th century, was almost extinct anyway. Nearly all my colleagues in other Regions already had the title 'manager'. It took me all of ten seconds to accept.

There was still some scepticism among the senior managers as to whether the Territory plan would actually materialise, and I went to a meeting at Kentish Town BRSA club to hear a talk about it by David Bowick, the Board's Chief Executive. He was hoping to quell the scepticism. It was 50-50.

Slipping off to watch cricket

On another May day, Yorkshire were playing Warwickshire at Edgbaston, and Yorkshire were batting. At lunchtime in the 'mess', John Whitehouse, the Divisional Staff Officer, who was a fellow Yorkshireman, whispered in my ear, 'Why don't we quietly slip off and nip along to Edgbaston?' We did. Boycott scored 88, which he would have considered a failure. That year Glenn Turner scored 1,000 runs in May – the first person to do so since Bradman and Edrich did it in 1938 (or so the papers said).

Talking of cricket and Edgbaston, I took Val to see the World Cup Final between England and Australia. The Ladies' Cup Final actually – not quite the real thing. Then, on 4 August, I went to see Yorkshire's last ever match at Bramall Lane: Yorkshire versus Lancashire. I remembered going there by tram from Sheffield station in 1945. It was quite an emotional feeling to be sitting in that ground for the last time.

Our inspection saloon, with its attendant Class 2 diesel, stands on the Down Main line at Leamington Spa, whilst passengers wait on the Up Main platform for their train. It was always a pleasure to visit Leamington Spa station when Bill Bennett was in charge. You could be sure of a cup of tea and a station up to Great Western standards. *Author*

King's Sutton station recorded looking southbound. The junction for the closed line towards Kingham and Cheltenham headed west from a junction just south of the station. The stub of the line, from King's Sutton to Adderbury, closed officially on 18 August 1969 but was still intact when used by the author on his saloon trips on the line to Banbury. *Andrew Muckley*

The TOPS revolution takes off

A trial site had been established at Radyr marshalling yard near Cardiff, and we were invited to see it in action. So off we went, with several of the Area Managers, because they would be very much involved with the implementation. They were keen to do so, as they felt it gave them more power, which it did, but the controllers in the Divisional Control Office felt that it was a potential threat to their authority, which it was. Coupled with the creation of Area Managers, who were beginning to flex their muscles, and the new power signalboxes, which had controllers and regulators, the role of the Control Office was declining, and the more perceptive controllers could see this. For half a century the Control Offices had been *the* power in the land in the day-to-day operation of the railway, but the railway was changing fast. Wagonload freight traffic was declining and marshalling yards were closing. A form of central control would always be needed, to deal with mishaps, line closures, diversions, etc, but on a smaller scale. The human relations aspect would need some careful and tactful handling. It was difficult, and the controllers expected me to support them.

Later in the year a TOPS overnight conference, the first of several, was held in Derby. We stayed at the Clarendon Hotel – apparently the TOPS budget did not run to the Midland Hotel. Lunch was not even provided; we had to fend for ourselves in the station refreshment rooms.

By October things were moving fast. The TOPS HQ Implementation Team had identified where all the TOPS offices in the Division should be located, and one day Bob Arnott came to see all the chosen sites by car. A training school for TOPS clerks had been set up at Wolverhampton in some railway coaches,

including sleepers and a dining car, and we had lunch there. In the evening I gave a talk on TOPS to the Wolverhampton Discussion Group.

Staff shortages

A shortage of staff at Bescot marshalling yard was a perennial problem. The West Midlands was booming and there were plenty of jobs available with higher rates of pay and better working conditions than those enjoyed by guards and shunters. From time to time we would run recruitment campaigns, but the standard of those who responded was often very low, and many stayed only until the end of their training, when they could go back to the Labour Exchange and sign on again. If we recruited too many, with the danger of overtime opportunities for the existing staff being reduced, we would find that new recruits were frozen out. We needed a bonus scheme to increase take-home pay without excessive reliance on overtime, but HQ would not hear of it, even though they had no bright ideas themselves. The trade unions considered bonus schemes divisive, with winners and losers, which of course was the case. So we just soldiered on.

Showing the flag again

I arranged for an afternoon saloon tour, which went to Droitwich via Kidderminster, then through to Lichfield, where we had a ham and eggs tea (in the saloon), before finally returning to Birmingham via Sutton Coldfield, where I baled out. I took some of my inspectors and office staff, and we visited a number of signalboxes. I was particularly keen on matters concerning level crossings, especially private crossings, and I made a point of checking whether the gates were closed. If not, we would stop

On 29 April 1973 Class 47 No.1716 heads north near Droitwich Spa with the 16.40 Hereford to Birmingham New Street service. *C. Plant*

The exterior of Gloucester power signalbox recorded on 23 July 1969. Control of the line between Bromsgrove and Gloucester was transferred to the new box in April 1969. *British Rail*

The back desk of the power signalbox at Gloucester; a view taken on 23 July 1969. *British Rail*

and close them, and the Area Manager would be suitably 'informed' next morning. I had some sympathy with the Area Managers, because some users just would not close the gates after them, so I told them that if users would not respond to gentle prompting, the assistance of the BTP should be sought. Open gates were an invitation to cross, and that could create a trap for the unwary – and potentially endanger trains.

The mention of safety reminds me that I was invited to give a talk to the Institution of Industrial Safety Officers on 'The Investigation of Railway Accidents'. I think they were impressed by the thoroughness with which the railway did it.

Time to relax

I was interested in visiting Western Region power signalboxes to see how they differed from those on the LM Region, so I arranged with my opposite number in Bristol, whom I had known in times past, to have a conducted tour of Bristol and Gloucester signalboxes. In between, following a nice lunch, we visited Tytherington Quarry to see the loading operations there. The visit gave the opportunity for 'a real good natter'. Gloucester box was unusual in that it directly controlled the lifting barriers at the very busy Horton Road level crossing just outside the box. I was late home again, as my wife reminded me.

The power signalbox at Bristol when new in early 1970. When opened, the box controlled 117 route miles stretching as far as Badminton, Chippenham, Bradford-on-Avon, Taunton, Severn Tunnel, Charfield and Severn Beach. *British Rail*

The parcels depot at Curzon Street in Birmingham was located on the site of the original London & Birmingham Railway station in the city. The station, designed by Edward Hardwick, who also designed the famous Euston Arch, is seen here under restoration. If plans for HS2 come to fruition, Curzon Street will again become a passenger station as the site is scheduled to become the line's terminus in Birmingham. Linford Building Group

Below: The extensive facilities available at Toton are clearly demonstrated in this track layout, which also illustrates the location of this important diesel depot. *British Rail*

The parcels business again

In 1973 we still had quite a sizeable parcels business, but we were looking for ways to speed up the sorting of parcels for delivery, and to cut costs. A new system, known as a roulette, had been installed at the Manchester Parcels Depot, in the former Mayfield Excursion station, just outside Piccadilly station, so I arranged with my opposite number in Manchester, Peter Rayner, to pay a visit. It was a very impressive operation. So far as I recall, the parcels for delivery came down a chute from the platforms, and as they passed on to the roulette each one was coded in turn by a checker. As they went round the roulette a trap door opened at the appropriate delivery round number. It all seemed so simple. Peter was (and still is) a larger than life character and full of wit. He treated me to lunch at the Grand Hotel, washed down liberally with red wine. Birmingham Parcels Depot was in the old Curzon Street Goods Depot and would have been suitable for a roulette, but the parcels business was in decline and the cost could not be justified.

The DOS conference

Once a month all the Divisional Operating Superintendents had an overnight meeting at a hotel in one or other of the Divisions. The chair was taken by the Chief Operating Manager and there was a pre-planned agenda. It was the turn of Liverpool to act as host, and the conference was held at the Adelphi Hotel, the first afternoon being given over to discussions of general interest. We also had a conducted tour of the city.

My Railway Operating course continues

I decided to run the course for another year, and was astonished when 87 members of staff enrolled. The first lecture was held on 1 October, entitled 'Passenger Station Working', and I was very gratified when 60 people turned up. This was followed by a lecture on 'Passenger Train Service Planning', when 65 turned up. The lectures were repeated the following week for the benefit of shift workers. The degree of interest was quite astonishing, and I was really pleased with the response.

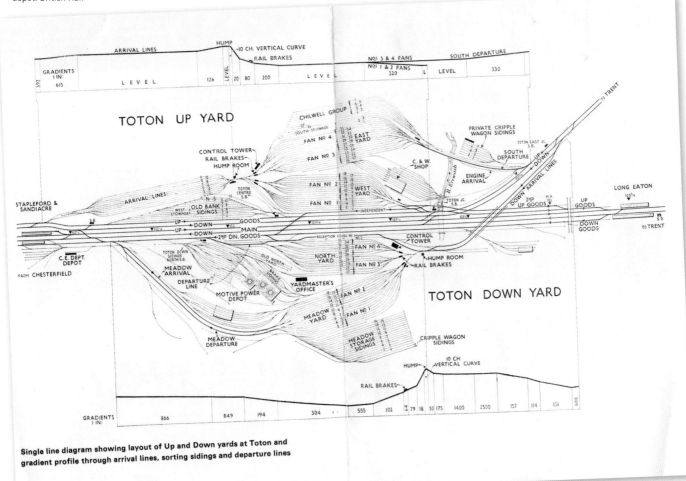

Single line diagram showing layout of Up and Down yards at Toton and gradient profile through arrival lines, sorting sidings and departure lines

One Saturday, I organised a DMU special to make a number of site visits in the Nottingham Division that I thought would be of interest and benefit to the members, and 55 came along. The first stop was Cotgrave Colliery, which had opened when I was at Nottingham and had been designed to load coal into continuously coupled MGR wagons, mainly for Ratcliffe Power Station that had opened just a few years earlier. From Cotgrave Colliery we followed the route of the MGR trains to the power station at Ratcliffe, and with the agreement of the CEGB we did the full circuit, including disembarking at the unloading hoppers to see how trains were unloaded as they passed over the hoppers at very low speed.

The final stop was Toton Yard and Diesel Maintenance Depot. The yard was still quite busy, despite much of the output from collieries now passing in MGR trains. In fact, Toton was really the last marshalling yard in the Nottingham Division, and almost all wagons which passed in less than trainloads were dealt with there. Marshalling yards were becoming redundant and closing, including some of those built at great cost under the 1955 Modernisation Plan based on the premise that one modern yard combining the traffic of several old (mainly pre-Grouping) yards would speed up transits and reduce costs considerably, as the need to trip wagons between the old yards would disappear. On the face of it, the plan seemed very attractive for a few years after

1955, but even by 1960 there were beginning to be doubts, and the decline in wagonload traffic in the late 1960s was precipitous. It seemed sensible to complete those new yards that were then well under construction but to abandon the plans for new yards that had not progressed far beyond the planning stage.

The new Diesel Maintenance Depot at Toton had been built to carry out maintenance on all the diesels allocated to the Nottingham Division, and was an eye-opener to people used to the inside of engine sheds. It was clean, tidy, warm, well lit and efficiently laid out with all the necessary facilities and equipment.

The Railway Operating course was going well. Bobby Howes, the COS from Crewe, came to talk to us, and 70 members turned up to hear him – probably a record. I was delighted with the response. A couple of weeks later we had Peter Stanley, the local signalling chief, to talk to us about power signalling. Not to be outdone, I gave a lecture on level crossings, which was already starting to become a special interest of mine.

Level crossing concerns

The installation of automatic half-barrier crossings had almost come to a dead stop following the fatal accident at Hixon in 1968. However, a scheme for such an installation at Newton Road Crossing in West Bromwich had suddenly surfaced and I was invited to attend a committee meeting of the Borough

On 27 March 1973 two Class 20s, with No.8009 leading, come off the shed at Toton. In the background a 'Peak' at the head of a coal train awaits its path.
Norman Preedy

On 12 December 1973, the first day of the railwaymen's go-slow, Class 45 No.132 drifts downhill through the disused Five Ways station with the 09.35 service from Cardiff to Manchester.
Philip D. Hawkins

Council to discuss the project. Local councils were always concerned about the safety of children, but they need not have worried; children accepted them much more quickly than adults, and behaved better than some motorists.

PART 3: TRADE UNIONS *V* THE GOVERNMENT

The Stourbridge diversion

The National Coal Board approached us with an interesting proposal. It wished to carry out opencast mining on both sides of the former GWR line between Stourbridge Junction and Dudley, and wanted the whole line to be moved to one side.

As it would pay all of our costs, there seemed no reason to object. A new line, about half a mile long, was built around the site, which became a very big hole in what seemed a very short space of time. The workings ceased about a year later and the deviation line was closed, the track being restored to its original alignment.

Government plans

In February, the Government announced a proposal ostensibly for investment in the railways, but when the Act was passed in 1974, the increased investment turned out to be for new and improved freight facilities. The main thrust of the Act was an arrangement for making grants to BR for 'Assisting the provision of facilities for freight haulage by rail in connection with loading

73

or unloading'. The grants were known as 'freight facilities grants' and a fund was provided annually to pay for approved schemes. It applied only to traffic not yet on rail, and sometimes the DoE seemed reluctant to give approval, but on the whole it turned out to be a very worthwhile scheme.

One other helpful measure was an easing of the Board's capital debt, which was reduced to £250 million, and meant that interest payments were reduced. The Board also had to make an annual return to the Government of Board members' salaries and 'emoluments'. Bonuses were unknown.

The local press looks into the future

In November, the *Coventry Telegraph* reported on BR proposals to quadruple the Coventry–Birmingham line owing to an increase in traffic. It is something that we would have liked to have done, especially as the PTE had plans to run more stopping trains on the line, but in 2014 we are still waiting. The paper also commented on the Draft Birmingham Structure Plan for the 1980s, which suggested bringing back into use Snow Hill station as a commuter station. That is something that did happen.

Trade union strife

It was now December and some of the trade unions were being difficult. ASLEF was working to rule, or going slow, which was much the same, with some effect on the train service. But the political situation was becoming grave. Edward Heath, the Prime Minister, broadcast to the nation (I cannot remember what he said, but it may have been on the lines of 'Who governs the country?'), and Anthony Barber, the Chancellor of the Exchequer, delivered an Emergency Budget (which was a damp squib).

It seems incredible now, but when I went back to work on 27 December, there was neither light nor heat in the office. The following day there was heat but no light. Then the electric power engineers settled their dispute, but the miners and the engine drivers were still causing problems. TV closed down at 10.30pm to save electricity.

Christmas festivities

John Whitehouse, a genius at organising events, arranged at the Divisional Manager's request for a dinner to be held at the Birmingham Chamber of Commerce for the Divisional officers and their wives. We had a private room, and I recorded that we had a very enjoyable evening indeed. John Pollard was very polished at that sort of thing. And by the way, my memory tells me that we paid for it all ourselves.

A couple of days later I was invited to a Christmas lunch by George Smith, the Area Manager at Birmingham New Street. George was almost the last of a long line of traditional stationmasters stretching back a hundred years. He ruled his station and stood no nonsense, and understandably resented any interference from anyone, high or low. I could get on with him because we had both come up the same way and we respected each other. He retired a couple of years later and was replaced by someone 20 years younger and of a quite different breed – the new managerial breed. Some specimens were beginning to appear, and of very high calibre as it turned out.

An unidentified Class 86 electric runs into Platform 3 at Coventry with a service from Euston to Birmingham/Wolverhampton. The half-hourly expresses were the pride of the Division; punctuality and cleanliness were the order of the day. *Author*

1974

PART 1: THE YEAR OF THE TOPS INVASION

Would 1974 be any better?

THURSDAY 3 January was a dull, cold day. No lights were allowed in the office, but at least we had heat. Night schools were cancelled to save electricity. Six days later, BR announced that it was going to take a tougher line with ASLEF, starting at midnight, and on 15 January, ASLEF held a one-day strike. John Whitehouse and I went to Banbury by car, to get out of the way, and a couple of days later John Pollard took me to the Chamber of Commerce for lunch, probably for the same reason. The pound slumped to its lowest level ever, and there was talk of an election. A few days later, it was announced that the election would take place on 28 February in view of the continuing miners' strike, and ASLEF decided to call off their action in view of the forthcoming election, which was a relief. I had cab trips to Euston and to Crewe to attend meetings. It was nice and warm in the cab, and fortunately it was a mild January.

We cheered up when Henry Sanderson, the Territory Director-designate, came to talk to an audience of 75 on the Railway Operating course. I was over the moon with the success of the course, which was completely optional for everyone,

including me. It was clear that there were many good railwaymen around who wanted to further their careers, or just to learn.

The General Election

The final result was Labour 301 seats, Conservatives 297 and Liberals 14. However, the Conservatives had polled more votes than Labour, and the Liberals had polled six million, so it looked like there would be another election fairly soon. The following Monday, 4 March, Edward Heath resigned and Harold Wilson became Prime Minister again. Would he do any better? A couple of days later the miners were bought off, for £100 million.

TOPS again

It was definitely coming, and I was sent on a week's TOPS course at the BR Staff Training College at The Grove, Watford. There were 12 of us on the course, all senior operators like

Looking south at Tyseley on 6 March 1974 as the 06.53 Paddington to Birmingham service heads towards its destination behind Class 47 No.1610. *Philip D. Hawkins*

The computer room at the heart of the TOPS scheme; the project was officially launched by the then Minister for Transport, John Gilbert, on 27 October 1975. *British Rail*

The sharp end of the TOPS system: a terminal located at a freight yard into which data on freight services was sent and received. *British Rail*

myself, and in fact I knew all of them except two. The Grove had been a large country house set in extensive grounds a couple of miles from Watford, and had been requisitioned by the LMS as its wartime HQ. When HQ moved back to London it became a training college, and I had already been there on courses several times over the years. It was very comfortable and you were well looked after. We had evening sessions, but they finished early enough for a drink or two and a game of snooker (or table tennis for the more energetic). It was a sensible and practical course, and well run.

It was clearer than ever that TOPS would have a big impact on the Divisional Control Office. TOPS, not the Control Office, would direct the flow of empties. Area Managers, flexing their muscles, would also have an impact. The Control organisation sprang from its roots at Rotherham in about 1908, when it was set up to reduce the long hours incurred by goods train drivers. In fact, the main work of the Control had always centred on freight traffic and the working of freight trains. However, the pattern of freight train working had altered considerably and needed less attention from the Control. Some 'streamlining' (ie job cuts) was on the cards and I could feel the tension growing in the Control Office. They could feel their authority being reduced.

TOPS had been building up quietly for some time, but now it accelerated throughout 1974 in the Birmingham Division,

reaching a crescendo at cut-over, when the system went live (or 'on-line' in modern parlance). The amount of management time devoted to it had been immense, and even after cut-over on 16/17 November, it still had to be managed carefully until everyone knew what to do and did it efficiently. The number of people who needed training, and the time and energy absorbed, reached stratospheric proportions.

The whole scheme was managed and administered, including the planning and training, by a special BRB HQ team who had been seconded for the purpose. Each Division went on-line in a planned succession, beginning in the South-West with the Exeter Division, then into South Wales, and moving north, so it had been in operation for some time before our turn came. In conjunction with the Divisions, the team decided where the TOPS offices should be located (usually in marshalling yards and goods depots) and how many staff would be needed in each office. The Divisional Control Office had several machines through which they could access the information files, and all the controllers had to be trained. I had a machine in my office, which allowed me to snoop on what was going on in the Areas, with the potential to make the Area Managers' lives a misery. I had to train myself.

There was a succession of meetings throughout the year, including fortnightly progress meetings held in London, and it absorbed a lot of our time. Whether it was all worthwhile, given the rapid decline in the less-than-trainload freight business in the 1970s, is certainly questionable, but once the juggernaut began to roll it was impossible to stop it. The whole thing was masterminded by Bob Arnott. We got on well with each other, but his place as the COS at Crewe was taken by Bobby Howes, who was a horse of a different colour. Bob Arnott told the Divisional Manager that the TOPS cut-over had gone better in the Birmingham Division than anywhere else, so I was understandably gratified. But there was no bonus.

However, there was one useful spin-off. Locomotives were brought into the scheme, which enabled the Mechanical Engineering people to see where they all were and to direct them to maintenance depots when necessary. It also enabled BRB HQ to see where there were surpluses of locomotives, and move them to areas with a shortage.

Transporting new cars by rail

For several years now the car factories in the Coventry and Longbridge areas had been sending away trainloads of new cars

A train of Austin/Rover cars from Longbridge passes through Kings Norton station on 25 February 1986. The car factory at Longbridge closed in 2005 with the collapse of its then owners; much of the factory site has now been redeveloped although a residual car factory remains, producing MGs for the marque's Chinese owners. *Gary Grafton*

An up Pullman service, diverted from the Trent Valley line, makes for Euston at Berkswell on 14 May 1974 behind Class 86 No.86028. *Philip D. Hawkins*

A pleasant function: the Divisional Manager, John Pollard (third from the left) had just presented certificates and cheques to members of a Banbury traincrew for dealing with a wagon on fire between Berkswell and Tile Hill on a Bescot to Eastleigh freight train. It was good policy to reward such mishaps. I am on the extreme left. Bill Bennett (second from right) radiates Great Western pride. Such men were invaluable. *BR*

on railway flat wagons. This was good business for us, and a new terminal had just been opened at Bell Green, Coventry, which was initially sending three trains a week to Dagenham. An existing terminal nearby at Gosford Green was already in operation, sending cars to Liverpool.

Attending funerals

Sadly, attending funerals was part and parcel of the job – the human side. I had two in one week: one of my Signalman's Inspectors, and the Area Manager/Yardmaster at Bescot. Quite properly, it was expected that the boss would be there at the funeral, together with the Divisional Welfare Officer, who would help the widow if necessary through all the formalities that follow bereavement. It was all part of the 'railway family'. It was also Denis Healey's 'soak the rich' budget day.

Another level crossing meeting

As previously mentioned, the modernisation of level crossings was proceeding very slowly, because expensive changes following the Hixon crash in 1968 had made it difficult to produce a financial case. However, one morning I attended a meeting at Langley Green about a TV control system, which would allow the crossing gates there to be replaced by barriers controlled remotely and the crossing to be monitored by CCTV. This type of development was to become very popular in locations that were unsuitable for half-barriers.

Mishaps

Accidents were now called mishaps, and freight train derailments were quite frequent. On 28 March, there was a derailment of tank wagons at Portobello Junction, between Bescot and Wolverhampton on the original Grand Junction line, in which the signalbox was demolished, but my notes do not record what happened to the unfortunate signalman. Next day, two 16-ton mineral wagons in a Toton to Reading coal train were derailed at Kingsbury, on the former Midland line between Tamworth and Water Orton. It was referred to in the Railway Inspectorate's annual report as being caused by three reversals of cant gradient within the space of 20 sleepers in straight track.

The following day was a Saturday, but the phone rang at 8am about a SPAD (signal passed at danger) incident at Wolverhampton North Junction, where the lines from Stafford and Shrewsbury meet at a trailing junction. As it was a beautiful sunny morning I motored across there, to find a debate going on as to whether it was the driver's fault or whether there had been a technical failure of the signalling equipment worked from Wolverhampton power signalbox. I therefore arranged for the same driver to drive the same train from the carriage sidings at Oxley to Wolverhampton a couple of days later, and I sat in the secondman's seat. I asked the driver to explain to me as we went along at about 15-20mph exactly what signal aspects he had encountered and how he had reacted to them. After we stopped in Wolverhampton station I looked across at him a little quizzically and he admitted a little shamefacedly that he must have passed the junction signal at danger. I thanked him for being honest about it.

On Wednesday 24 April, just as I was thinking of getting ready for bed, the phone rang (again!). It was the Control, informing me that a goods train had run into the back of another on the Down Goods line at Castle Bromwich, near Washwood Heath. The first train, with two Type 2 diesels, was carrying a block trainload of steel; the second was a loaded MGR coal train en route to Didcot Power Station. I went straight out there and found quite a pile-up. It had been a bad collision. As soon as the breakdown cranes had arrived and started work I went to the Control Office, having asked the Engineering Departments for an estimate of the time that the various tracks could be returned to traffic. This information was needed by the Control Office to enable it to plan the necessary diversions, as the main lines were blocked by the breakdown cranes. Then I went home for breakfast and a few hours' sleep.

Collisions on goods lines, where trains were allowed to follow each other with the driver looking out for the tail lamp of the one in front, were not uncommon, but the practice was being phased out by then. It was no longer necessary at most places, and I seem to recall that we withdrew it from this section of line. It was a relic from days long gone when goods trains used to queue up, waiting to enter Washwood Heath yard.

A couple of days later I went out to Long Eaton to join a Didcot-bound MGR train running at about the same time as the

Retaining just a trace of the Great Western, Hall Green station plays host to the 15.20 DMU service from Stratford to Birmingham Moor Street on 6 June 1974.
Philip D. Hawkins

On 7 August 1974 Class 86 No.86205 pulls into Lichfield Trent Valley with the 06.34 service from Holyhead to Euston. At the time this was the only weekdays express service from Lichfield to London.
Philip D. Hawkins

one that had crashed, having arranged that it would run along the Down Goods line from Water Orton. I needed to have a close look at the signals, and also see if there were any lights in the area that might have distracted the driver. However, I drew a blank, and there was no Railway Inspectorate inquiry.

Disciplinary procedure after SPAD incidents

If a driver was considered to have passed a signal at danger, the disciplinary procedures were automatically invoked and he was sent to the Divisional Medical Officer for an eyesight test and a general report on his fitness to drive. His Area Manager would then issue him with the appropriate discipline form (known as Form 1), on which the driver could either state his case or ask for a personal hearing. Normally a driver would ask for a hearing, and I made it a rule that I personally took all hearings for SPAD incidents. At the hearing, the driver was entitled to be represented either by a colleague or one of the staff reps.

In the case under notice, the driver had already admitted that he was in fact guilty, so it was only a question of the punishment to be meted out. The options were a reprimand, a severe reprimand, or a suspension from duty of varying duration – or even a reduction in grade for repeated offences. I was guided by the man's age and service history, and by the opinion of the driver by his Locomotive Inspector, who sat in with me at the hearing. This driver was in his late fifties and had a clean record, as was so often the case. Punishments, other than a verbal warning, were recorded on the man's service history, and I debated long and hard with myself. The driver had over 40 years' service, a clean record, and was well thought of. He had made an error, but had not done it on purpose, and I felt that he had already punished himself more than I could do. So I explained to him that the least punishment available to me for such a serious offence was a reprimand, and why I was being lenient in his case. It was not to be taken as a standard. I knew that the drivers at his depot would be waiting to see what I did. There were other cases where a driver was being a bit too careless and had to be put on shunting duties for a period. In steam days he might be put on shed shunting, an option which was no longer generally available. But each case had to be judged on its own merits. Those were the days of what I regard as 'the grown-up railway'.

The driver in this case accepted my punishment, but there was a second stage in the machinery by which he could appeal against either the findings or the punishment, or both, and the

appeal would be heard at a higher level. The trade union representative, usually the district organiser, could attend at this stage. The disciplinary machinery worked extremely well, and had built-in safeguards. I believe it dated from 1919, when a number of agreements were made with the trade unions concerning such matters as conditions of employment, the role of the unions and the whole machinery of negotiation.

Another football cup-tie

On Wednesday 3 April, there was an evening FA Cup semi-final replay between Liverpool and Leicester City, held at Aston Villa's ground. Being a midweek match, many of the spectators were expected to travel by train, and we had many specials to deal with. All the arrangements for dealing with the passengers were made in close co-operation with the BTP, and we again chose Witton station as the loading and unloading point of the passengers.

Not the 'Footex' described by the author as departing from Witton, but a similar service operated from the Birmingham Division during the 1973/74 season. On 2 March 1974, Wolverhampton Wanderers played Manchester City in the League Cup Final at Wembley; pictured at Bentley Heath on the line from Birmingham to Leamington is a football special carrying Wolves' fans heading for the match. The train was hauled by Class 47 No.47088. The fans would have returned happy as Wolves won the match 2-1. *Philip D. Hawkins*

At Hatton on 7 August 1974 a Metro-Cammell three-car DMU awaits departure with the 16.06 service from Leamington to Stratford. *Philip D. Hawkins*

Everything was carefully planned in advance, down to the finest detail, and I had inspectors and my assistants on duty at critical locations. Trains were closely regulated so that a second train could be waiting to enter the platform as soon as the previous one had disgorged all its passengers and departed empty. The police shepherded the passengers down the stairs (the station was on an embankment) and along to the ground. All the trains were on time and everything went well.

That was the easy bit. After the match, the crowds surged back to the station and there was soon a massive queue of several thousand fans. We wanted to avoid any accidents – the platforms were fairly narrow. All the empty trains were lined up, one at each signal, waiting to enter the station, and the police controlled the queues at the foot of the stairs at each side of the station, allowing only one trainload of passengers at a time on to the platform when the empty train had arrived. Fortunately, it all went according to plan and the police did a good job.

PART 2: THE REORGANISATION FIASCO

A new express passenger service to Glasgow

Birmingham had had a through service to Glasgow back in LMS days, and train-spotters all along the line will remember that the appearance of the Birmingham–Glasgow train, identified by its roofboards, meant that the 'Royal Scot' would not be far behind. But now that the line through to Glasgow had been electrified, Birmingham had a new starting service, departing at 08.10. It came into operation on 6 May, and I saw it depart punctually with modest ceremony that day. Two days later there was greater celebration when the Divisional Manager escorted a large party of travel agents and businessmen all the way to Glasgow and back so that they could sample the new service. Several of us went along to help out with the guests. The train had now been named the 'Midland Scot', but it seems to have lost its name the following year. The speed of the train was impressive, and there were plenty of free drinks for the guests (and the escorts!). Lunch was served in the Station Hotel (still under BR ownership), after which the Scottish Tourist Board had organised a coach tour to Loch Lomond, particularly for the travel agents. Then it was back to the

station for the return train, on which dinner was served. The journey time was about four and a half hours, at a maximum speed of 100mph, and I arrived home at 11.30pm after what had been a long but very successful day.

I am called to London for a special meeting

On Sunday 13 October, all the Divisional functional officers from the whole of BR were called to a special meeting in the Great Eastern Hotel at Liverpool Street, where we were addressed by the BRB Chairman, Richard Marsh, and the BRB Chief Executive, David Bowick, on financial affairs and the current investment programme. Labour had been returned to office in the second election that year, and the Board was bracing itself for demands for economy. Nothing new there! It was quite apparent that Richard Marsh, who had been Minister of Transport in the Labour Government in 1968/69, was fed up with governmental interference, and he made his feelings and frustrations very plain.

However, the real purpose of the meeting became clear when David Bowick began to speak to us about the 'Territorial'

The Great Eastern Hotel, opened originally in 1884 and designed by Charles Barry (junior) and his brother Edward, was extended in the late 1890s by the addition of a new wing, the Abercorn Rooms, designed by Robert Edis. The hotel was to survive the redevelopment of Liverpool Street station and underwent a major upgrade in the late 1990s. *British Rail*

A brace of electrics (a Class 86 and a Class 87) and an EMU (Class 310) line up at Birmingham New Street on 19 June 1974. The headcode 1A40 indicates a service to Euston. Chris Hall

At Small Heath, Birmingham, on 15 May 1974, a three-car DMU forming the 14.55 service from Birmingham New Street to Leamington Spa leaves the station — visible in the background — as the 14.11 service from Leamington Spa to New Street approaches the station. *Philip D. Hawkins*

Viewed at St Andrews Junction, Birmingham, on 21 August 1974, a pair of Class 47/4s, Nos.47535 (leading) and 47532, provide high power for the 11.30 service from Poole to Newcastle upon Tyne. *Philip D. Hawkins*

On 7 August 1974, a Derby three-car DMU glides into Gravelly Hill station with the 07.45 service from Birmingham New Street to Lichfield City. *Philip D. Hawkins*

reorganisation. Whilst there had been no outright opposition to the Territory proposals in the Divisions, it was clear that there was considerable unease, especially in the Regional offices, and a feeling was growing that it would never happen. David Bowick was keen to settle all doubt on the issue. 'Just get used to the idea,' he said. 'Territory is coming.' I think that none of us was reassured, but in fact it never did happen. What a huge waste of money, time and effort.

New accommodation

In the meantime, planning went ahead for the Territory organisation, with job descriptions being prepared and accommodation planned. A brand-new office block was built at Birmingham to a very high standard, quite appropriately named Stanier House, and until Territory began, we all moved in there from the adjacent offices in Broad Street, which were leased. I had a plush new office, twice the size of my previous one, and my secretary occupied the adjacent room. Access to me was now via my secretary! I suddenly felt a lot more important, but people who had been accustomed to 'just dropping in' now had to face my protective secretary. Naturally, there was a drinks cupboard. We even had an 'Executive toilet suite', complete with shower, with access restricted to selected keyholders – very USA!

Messing arrangements were also upgraded. At the Broad Street offices there was just one big canteen, run by a staff committee and serving very good conventional meals. I sometimes used it if I was in the office at lunchtime because it was convenient. However, at Stanier House, the dining arrangements were let out to contract and there was a private dining room for senior managers. All departments had transferred to Stanier House, and lunchtime was a very convenient occasion for meeting other departmental chiefs quite informally, including the local chief of the BTP, the Estate Surveyor and all the Engineering Departments. It was a rule that you did not 'talk shop' during the meal, but afterwards, with coffee etc, a lot of very effective business was done.

One other advantage of Stanier House was that it was air-conditioned, and that became very useful during the hot summers of 1975 and 1976. We even had a uniformed commissionaire at the door, although there was no such thing as showing passes or wearing name tags. At the Broad Street offices there had been unchecked access from the street. Now the pendulum had swung a little the other way, but that is the way with pendulums.

David Bowick is proved wrong!

I had met David Bowick on a number of occasions. He was really a very nice chap and had risen through the operating ranks, but

had allowed himself to become mesmerised by the consultants who devised the Territory Organisation. It was too sweeping a change and created immense opposition in the Regions, who could see their powers and functions being split between the Territories and the BRB. The unions, although not opposed to the changes in principle, demanded a high price for their agreement and co-operation. However, the price was too high, especially with the Government demanding a reduction in the annual financial support payment, so the proposals were shelved. In a way, it was a pity, as reform of the organisational levels was desperately needed, not only to save money but also to speed up decision-making.

We still had four levels – the Board, the Regions, the Divisions and the Areas. The laws of physics demand that there should be a top and a bottom, so that left the Regions and the Divisions. Rather than having a Big-Bang reorganisation, changes should have been done piecemeal over a period of time. Some work should have been moved from the Regions to the Board, then some from the Divisions to the Areas. The Divisions should then have been merged into units covering larger areas, and finally amalgamated with the remains of the Regional offices.

In the event, nothing was done, and the existing cumbersome and expensive organisation continued almost unchanged for the next ten years, during which reductions in freight traffic and the shedding of some activities further simplified the administrative workload. Economies were made at the workface, rather than in administration. However, it was concluded that further economies had to be achieved somehow, and it was decided that the Stoke and Birmingham Divisions should be merged and be based in Birmingham. The Divisional offices had been located in Stoke for commercial reasons, whereas most of the operational activities were at Crewe and on the West Coast main line, which the Stoke Division controlled from just north of Rugby to north of Crewe. I had a whole series of meetings with my opposite number at Stoke to determine where Area Managers should be located and the areas they should control, and the staffing of the Divisional office. It was then left to the staff people to work out the detail. However, I left Birmingham before the merger took place, and cannot recall if it ever happened.

Derailment at Cropredy
In 1974 we continued to be free from serious accidents, but we still had the usual run of freight train accidents. However, we did have one Railway Inspectorate inquiry during the year, albeit in respect of a quite minor passenger train derailment. This occurred at Cropredy on 5 November, when a DMU from Leamington Spa to Oxford became derailed on a broken rail. The derailment took place just a few hundred years south of the closed Cropredy station, about three miles north of Banbury.

On 6 March 1974 Class 47 No.1694 comes off the Camp Hill line at Saltley with a Freightliner train for unloading at the adjacent Freightliner terminal. A Birmingham to Euston service can be seen heading southbound in the distance. *Philip D. Hawkins*

At Acocks Green on 6 June 1974 the 08.05 Paddington-Worcester-Paddington via Birmingham service is headed by Class 47 No.1585. *Philip D. Hawkins*

Just before 7am a freight train passed through Cropredy, and both the driver and guard felt an unusual movement in the train that was sufficiently strong to cause them to report it on arrival at Banbury. The following train, the DMU, was stopped at Claydon Crossing signalbox, where the signalman explained the circumstances to the driver and warned him to proceed with caution. The DMU had just passed through Cropredy, travelling at about 25mph, when the driver saw a piece of rail about two feet long missing from the line immediately ahead. The train passed over the gap and became derailed. Talk about an 'own goal'! Fortunately, there were only seven passengers in the train, none of whom was injured.

The track on the Up line consisted of 113 lb/yd flat-bottom continuous welded rail laid in 1971. When the site was inspected by the various departments, it was found that a piece of rail about 12ft long had broken out of the rail, and sections were sent to the Research Department at Derby where the existence of several 'tache ovale' defects were discovered in the rail. These are faults that develop within the rail over a period of time and result from faulty manufacture.

It has to be admitted that BR did not shine in this derailment. The guard's report to the supervisor at Banbury was not handled as expeditiously as it should have been, and the driver of the DMU was travelling too fast in the circumstances. He had jumped to the conclusion that the 'bump' referred to a well-known 'wet spot' just before Cropredy. Nor did the Civil Engineer's Department come out of the inquiry with credit. The previous

annual track inspection, with equipment capable of locating tache ovales, had been missed because the equipment was not available, and the examination prior to that, in 1971, had discovered several tache ovales. The sections of rail affected had been removed, but the implication that there might be other developing defects was not followed up. So black marks all round.

Unusually, I did not attend the accident myself, but asked my assistant to go. The Inspectorate's public inquiry was held in the Divisional Office on 10 December by Major Freddie Rose and was concerned entirely with the quality of the rail and the examination procedures. It was over by lunchtime, so I took them all to lunch at the Birmingham Repertory Theatre. By tradition, the Operating Department always took the chair at inquiries, even when the cause of a mishap lay with a technical department. When I went to the Board in 1977, I had many dealings with Freddie Rose, and we always got on very well together. That close working relationship disappeared in 1990, when the Railway Inspectorate, which had enjoyed 150 years of autonomy, was taken over by the Health & Safety Executive.

I was disappointed by the extent of the Operating Department's shortcomings in the Banbury area, because I had a high regard for the standards set by the GWR and its successors, so I sent my Chief Inspector to read the Riot Act. He was a splendid and utterly conscientious railwayman of the former GWR, and I knew that he would feel that he had been let down.

1975

PART 1: INTERESTING DEVELOPMENTS, VIPs AND CRASHES

VIPs

I was invited to join the LM Regional Board for lunch when it was holding one of its meetings at the prestigious railway-owned Welcombe Hotel near Stratford, and David Bowick invited me to sit next to him. Having come up through the operating grades, he liked to have an operator to talk to. We got on very well, which should have boded well for my future – but didn't – as a result of his fall from grace over the Territory fiasco. He later resigned and went to live in Malta, which was a great loss to the railway industry, but the moral for me was 'Don't hitch yourself to a falling star!'

The following day the Board members decided they would like to visit the TOPS office at Bescot, which was working very well. Everyone was pleased (and relieved). Had we been a bank, we would have been in line for a big bonus. It was only one of a succession of VIP and high-level visits to Bescot.

A few days later David came back to Birmingham to address the Midland Section of the Chartered Institute of Transport, of which I had just been elected vice-chairman (and was in line to be chairman in a couple of years' time). He brought sensational news – the Territory concept had been abandoned – the reason put forward being that it would have been too expensive to implement. We suspected that the real reason had been the intense opposition from the Regional General Managers to the dissolution of the Regions. However, we all welcomed the return to stability. David also announced the abandonment of the Channel Tunnel project.

Birmingham was within easy reach of London and Board members seemed to like visiting us as a form of relaxation. One evening in February, the BR Chairman Richard Marsh came for dinner at the Midland Hotel, accompanied by David Bowick.

Class 52 No.D1051 *Western Ambassador* stands at Birmingham New Street after arrival with a service from London Paddington in January 1975. *I. J. Hodson*

On 12 April Class 87 No.87017 arrives at Birmingham New Street with a train from Glasgow and Edinburgh.
David A. Flitcroft

Class 25 No.25289 pictured at Cradley on 17 June 1975 with a pick-up freight.
John Glover

It was a most entertaining and illuminating evening, and I wish I could remember what was said, but it soon became clear that they both wanted to let their hair down. As the wine flowed, their frustrations with the Government became ever more apparent. It was an astonishing and very instructive evening. I cannot imagine what they would have thought about how the railway is run today, but in 1975, by comparison, we had a great degree of freedom in its running. The main areas of contention were the level of financial support and investment in future projects.

More mishaps

We had a particularly bad freight train derailment on Friday 14 February near Fosseway, on the freight-only line from Wichnor Junction and Lichfield (City) to Walsall, which resulted in three 100-ton tankers becoming derailed and turning over on to their sides. They were the last three vehicles on a train of eight. The cause was a rail that had broken in two places under the wagon and caused a six-inch piece to become detached, the breakage being the result of a wheel burn. Rerailing was planned for Sunday, when two breakdown cranes could be assembled.

The tankers had apparently not been badly damaged, and it was hoped that they could be turned upright and rerailed without trouble, but it was not to be. The Water Board were also in attendance in case there was a danger that watercourses might be contaminated by spillage, and unfortunately quite a lot of oil started to be spilt during rerailing. The horrified Water Board officials quite rightly demanded that work should be stopped, and eventually the oil in the derailed tankers had to be pumped out into road tankers brought as near as possible to the site.

On a cold, misty Sunday morning, 16 February 1975, two massive breakdown cranes set about the task of rerailing the now-empty 100-ton bogie tank wagons at Fosseway, between Lichfield and Walsall. The derailment was caused by a broken rail. *Author*

Before and after at Hartlebury level crossing. The wooden gates have been replaced by four lifting barriers and road traffic signals whilst the station footbridge has been removed. *Author (both)*

What a mess! I went along to witness the débâcle and took some photos, but unfortunately it was a typical murky February morning so they didn't come out very well.

Three days earlier, the telephone had rung at 1.45am. A block trainload of zinc ingots from Cardiff to Walsall had been derailed at Hartlebury on the former GWR line between Kidderminster and Worcester. Some zinc blocks weighing approximately 15cwt each had been loaded on to bogie plate wagons instead of ordinary 'Hyfit' wagons, and some of them had fallen over and crashed through the floorboards. Two fell on the track, derailing three bogie plate wagons and the brake van and damaging a quarter of a mile of track. I motored there through the inky darkness to assess the situation. On my way back home at 7am I called into the Control Office, who had already arranged diversions. They were very good at that sort of thing.

Aston Villa again

This time Aston Villa themselves were playing at Wembley, and we ran 20 specials from different parts of the Division. It was quite a job to work out the train plan and stopping patterns in conjunction with the club, and to arrange for the necessary coaching stock to be in position ready for Saturday morning. Locomotive and train crew rosters also had to be prepared.

On the day itself, I hung around at New Street station and in the Control to see how things were, and was gratified to see everything going according to plan.

We had an even busier day on Saturday 5 April. Ipswich were playing Fulham in a semi-final match at Villa Park, and Birmingham were playing at Sheffield. There were special trains in all directions, but unfortunately I didn't record the details for posterity. I spent my time between New Street and the Control Office, and everything went well, thanks to careful preparations. Handling 20 football specials was routine in those days because there was a good organisation to deal with it, having been honed and polished over many years. And by the way, it was the third successive day of snow showers.

PTE developments

The PTE was now planning to run a frequent service of DMUs between Lichfield and Redditch, and it was necessary to see whether and to what extent the signalling arrangements would have to be modified to provide the necessary line capacity. The Signalling Section people from Euston, and the Signal &Telecoms (S&T) people together with the PTE representatives, attended a meeting to work out the detail, which proved to be a very interesting exercise. It was clear that more capacity would

Left: As part of the scheme to improve services between Lichfield City and Redditch, a number of stations south of Birmingham were rebuilt and reopened. These included Five Ways, seen here under construction, which finally reopened in 1978. *British Rail*

Below: A new station was also constructed at Longbridge; it is seen here on 11 May 1978, four days after the start of the enhanced DMU service, with a recent arrival from Four Oaks in one platform as a northbound train waits to depart in the second. *Les Bertram*

This wasn't a trip to see steam engines, but I did take one photo of a German-built 'Kriegslok' 2-10-0 resting between Kulata and Sofia. *Author*

be needed at New Street, and it was decided to convert Platform 12, a parcels platform, into a passenger platform. That required a separate meeting with the Civil Engineer, the Architect and the Station Manager, and in the end it was quite a large meeting. But it was good to see that things were buzzing, and it was the prelude to much more activity.

Royal Train visits

It was beginning to look as though we were going to be busy. Preparations for dealing with the Royal Train followed a very familiar pattern, beginning when we received news from various quarters (Crewe, the local authority concerned, or the BTP) of a proposed royal visit. This came several weeks in advance and allowed us plenty of time to make very detailed preparations, including the selection of an overnight stabling point (there were a number of these which we used from time to time), the destination station (including which platform and which exit, in which we were guided to some extent by security issues) and where to stable and service the train if it was to be used again that day. This required a considerable number of site visits and meetings.

The site visits took place first and normally consisted of just me and my Chief Inspector and the local Area Manager. Having made our plans in outline, it was then necessary to hold site meetings with all concerned. They were quite big meetings, including the BTP, the county police, the local authority, staff from the Palace, possibly the Civil Engineer, and the S&T people if structural changes or telecommunications questions were raised, together with someone from Crewe, who would be Royal Train Officer on the day, the Area Manager(s) and me, plus Bill Gillett, my Chief Inspector. Quite a crowd, and we tried not to congregate in full view of the public, which might have caused adverse comment!

On 26 March, I went with the Area Manager at Leamington on site visits to Fenny Compton (halfway to Banbury and a potential overnight stabling point) and Stratford-on-Avon in preparation for a royal visit in June, which turned out to be a major affair. Bill Gillett and I went to the Stratford area again, on 1 April, with the Area Manager and a chap from Crewe, Frank Sykes. We had two more days of site visits on 10 and 11 April to Berkswell (a regularly used overnight stabling point between Coventry and New Street), to Moor Street (the former GWR suburban terminus in Birmingham), to New Street, and to Kings Norton (a few miles south-west of New Street on the former Midland line to Bristol). On the second day it was back to Stratford-on-Avon for a more detailed recce, and then on to Milcote, a few miles south-west of Stratford on the former GWR line to Honeybourne and Cheltenham. It looked as though there were a number of royal visits in the offing.

Royal train events were always enjoyable because there was scope for a bit of initiative in choosing the most appropriate way to deal with a visit, and then the opportunity to be present on the day and standing back to see it all work out to perfection (you hoped!). You were also relatively free from interference from either Crewe or Euston. And on the day of the visit the Area Manager took all the glory, as the Stationmaster had done in days of yore.

A Trip Abroad

A friend and I took a remarkable trip in April 1975, travelling from Greece through Bulgaria, Rumania, Hungary, Czechoslovakia and into West Germany. Fortunately, my friend apparently had some influence in those countries and had managed to wangle first class tickets and sleepers throughout, with the result that we were treated with some considerable respect. The Brotherhood of the Rail? No. I should have written a book about that trip, but I was too busy working. Perhaps now's the time.

One of the two locomotives involved in the fatal accident at Nuneaton on 6 June, No.86242, is seen is seen on 12 July 1979 at Camden with the up 'Manchester Pullman'. *John Glover*

Seen at Coventry station on 5 November 1975, Class 86 No.86007 arrives with a service from Euston to Manchester. *Brian Morrison*

Aftermath of an accident: on 14 August 1975 Class 86 No.86238 observes the 10mph speed restriction as it passes the ill-fated platform 3 at Nuneaton with the 13.45 Euston to Glasgow Central service. The platform was in the process of being rebuilt after the June accident.
Philip D. Hawkins

PART 2: ROYAL TRAIN EVENTS

First – a bad crash

On Thursday 5 June 1975, the 23.30 Euston to Glasgow night sleeper, formed of 12 sleeping cars, two vans and a buffet car, left on time, hauled by a Class 86 electric loco, No.86242. However, just beyond Kings Langley the locomotive broke down and another one, No.86006, was put on the front, the whole train starting off again 75 minutes late. Despite the increased trailing weight of the train by hauling the failed locomotive – 667 tons – No.86006 reached full speed and was running at about 80mph as it approached Nuneaton at 1.54am. Just south of the station there was a 20mph temporary speed restriction whilst the track layout was being altered, but the express hit the speed-restricted section of line at unchecked speed and rushed headlong into disaster.

No.86006 left the rails almost at once and smashed its way into the station for several hundred yards; No.86242 actually mounted the platform and came to rest touching the station awning. The sleeping cars at the front of the train were scattered in all directions, some on their sides, whilst those at the rear remained upright and fairly well in line. Looking at the wreckage, you would have expected many fatalities, but in fact there were just six. All the passengers, of whom there were about 100, were in sleeping berths, which would have cushioned them from the impact, but ten of them were detained in hospital with serious injuries.

Newspaper photographs taken at the time were pretty horrifying. The West Coast main line belonged to the Stoke Division, and my area finished at Nuneaton Abbey station, where the former Midland Railway line went over the top of the WCML to join the former LNWR line from Nuneaton Trent Valley station to Leicester. I had never in my railway career seen a serious railway accident, so decided to go and have a look. It was a terrible sight. I never saw another one.

I then went back to the Control to see how all the diverted WCML expresses were being dealt with. They were running mainly via the Grand Junction line between Bushbury Junction, north of Wolverhampton, and Stechford, south of Birmingham New Street, and avoiding both cities, so they were not being seriously delayed. Plans were then being made for dealing with the following day's diversions, which was a little easier as it was a Saturday. I spent the morning in New Street power signalbox watching all the expresses and specials. There were 28 Up expresses in two hours – one every four minutes! On the Sunday I went into the Control to oversee the planning for a reduction in the local passenger services on the Monday to provide paths for all the WCML diversions that day. Oh, and by the way, Thursday had been EEC Referendum Day when almost 70% voted 'Yes'.

The burning issue was why the driver of No.86006 had not reduced speed to 20mph. Both the driver and his secondman had the usual printed notice, and knew of the slack at Nuneaton because the driver had been over it at the slow speed required on the previous night on a similar train. There was also a trackside system for warning drivers that they were approaching a temporary speed restriction. This consisted of a warning board with a speed indicator at braking distance and a second speed indicator at the commencement of the speed restriction. They were both illuminated at night by bottled gas, but on the night in question the bottle was empty. The permanent way staff who were responsible for changing the gas bottles before they ran out had failed to do so. That was error No.1. The driver and the secondman both stated that they had looked out for the warning board but, unable to locate it, had assumed that the speed restriction had been removed. However, they were not entitled to assume that, because if a restriction had been removed before the advertised date, the warning board would have remained in place, with normal line speed shown. So that was error No.2. But a very sorry state of affairs was also revealed. Drivers were expected to stop and report to the signalman if a warning board light was out, so that other drivers could be informed, but although several drivers had passed the board with one or more lights out in the preceding two hours, none had stopped to do so. That was error No.3. It emerged that they had become tired of stopping to report lights out when it happened so frequently and nothing was done.

A couple of months later I asked my assistant to travel in the cab from Euston to Birmingham, both in daylight and darkness, and report on the condition of warning boards etc. His report was quite frightening. There were many cases of warning boards missing, or at the wrong distance, or with no lights during darkness. It revealed slackness all round. I sent a copy of the report to Crewe, which was not a very clever thing to do really, because they should have kept an eye on this sort of thing and done something about it. I also sent a confidential copy unofficially to the Divisional Civil Engineer, who thanked me unenthusiastically. Fortunately, my predecessor at the BRB decided to actually do something about it, which was to arrange for a portable permanent magnet to be placed in the track on the approach to a warning board and thus alert the driver even if the lights were out, or if vandals had tipped the board down the bank, which happened sometimes. But it was a struggle even to achieve that, and it was still in the gestation stage when I went to BRB HQ a year after a report by the Railway Inspectorate was issued, following a public inquiry. As a postscript, the driver of the Inter-City sleeper was charged at Birmingham Crown Court on 9 June 1976 with six counts of manslaughter. After a three-day trial he was found not guilty and discharged.

Threatened strike

On 2 June, the NUR announced that its members were going to strike on the 23rd of the month if they did not receive a 30% pay rise instead of the offered 27½%. This was a period of terrible inflation following the 'Barber Boom'. In 1973, inflation was running at 19.6% and in 1974, 22.3%. The NUR called off the strike on 20 June, which was a relief all round, and settled for the increase on offer.

The Royal Train visits

Thursday 26 June was a very hot day – it was said to be 100°F (38°C) at Wimbledon. Barry, my faithful chauffeur, called for me and took me to Berkswell to wait for the arrival of the Royal Train at 1.45am. After it had come to a stand just beyond the points, a light diesel came through the crossover from the Up line on to the rear of the Royal Train and drew it back into a long siding which had been retained specially for the purpose. This was the stub of the former line to Kenilworth and Leamington Spa. (It was not the practice to propel the Royal Train when it was occupied by royalty.) The locomotive that had brought the Royal Train was then dispatched to shed. I joined the railway officer in charge of the train in his saloon and shared a nightcap with him before retiring for a few hours in a first class sleeping berth.

I rose at 7.30am after a cup of tea and then had the Royal Train breakfast – grapefruit, a full fry-up and toast. The new train engine arrived promptly and was attached to the front, and we set off at 10.2am for a stately progress to New Street, arriving dead on time at 10.30am. Having disembarked our royal party, the train then went ECS to Tyseley Carriage Sidings for cleaning and servicing, which included a supply of dry ice for the air-conditioning in the royal vehicles. We had lunch in the train before travelling empty to Birmingham Moor Street to pick up the royal party and depart at 2.45pm for Stratford. There were more crowds, more cheers and more waves as we trundled gently through the pleasant countryside. After the royal party had left the train at Stratford, it was drawn back into the carriage sidings to await its next trip, which was to be the most exciting one.

After HM The Queen had rejoined the train at 5.20pm we moved slowly, with a loco at each end, down the line towards Honeybourne, stopping after a few miles at the closed station of Milcote, where only the platforms remained (it having closed in 1966). We now awaited the arrival of the Duke of Edinburgh, who was coming from Newcastle by helicopter, and as we were now standing in mid-section, the standard safety precautions had to be applied. Bill Gillett had arranged for a handsignalman to be appointed a mile in rear of the train with detonators on the line, while he himself remained in the signalbox as an extra precaution. We were in telephone contact, thanks to the S&T Department. Afternoon tea was then served while we awaited the sound of an approaching helicopter.

Eventually it came and landed in the field next to the railway. The Duke jumped out, went through a field gate into the road, ceremoniously opened by the farmer, and then to the level crossing and on to the platform. As the road was a very minor one, the police closed it whilst we were there. There were no houses in the vicinity and, so far as I was aware, there were no eyewitnesses, which was unusual for the Royal Train. I telephoned my faithful inspector, said that we were now ready to return wrong road to Stratford station, received the OK, and then walked up to the locomotive at the front of the train and told the driver that we were now able to return. After that short journey, the royal party disembarked for the third time and the train proceeded into the carriage sidings once more. Then it was time for tea and, as we had plenty of time to spare, three of us had a stroll round Stratford whilst HM The Queen enjoyed herself at the Shakespeare Memorial Theatre.

After the last passenger train of the day had arrived, the Royal Train was drawn back into the station and another engine was attached to the rear for the final departure via Leamington. The Queen finally came back to the train half an hour late at half past midnight (a royal prerogative, but I bet she was really tired by then), and there were still plenty of people around to see her off, including the Area Manager covering Stratford, a genial, grand old ex-GWR man who was in his element that evening. They don't make them like that any more! And then we set off to take HM back to London, accompanied on the train by the Western Region Royal Train Officer, who had now joined us. I left the train at Banbury after smoked salmon sandwiches and whisky en route, as a sort of celebration that everything had gone smoothly after months of careful planning. Barry, faithful as ever, met me at Banbury and took me home.

Shildon 150

On 31 August I went to see the Cavalcade of Steam in connection with the 150th anniversary celebrations at Shildon commemorating the opening of the Stockton & Darlington Railway in 1825. There were 30 steam locomotives altogether, including LNER 'A4' and 'A3' Pacifics, LMS Nos.6201 *Princess Elizabeth* and 5690 *Leander* and several from the GWR and the Southern. The steam parade was spectacular, as the locomotives travelled slowly along the line for all to see. The day was blessed with glorious sunshine.

BR builds a big new station

As previously mentioned, the West Midlands motor manufacturers had ambitions to hold their annual motor show nearer to home and as there was no suitable venue locally that was large enough, they had set their sights on building their own exhibition hall. Things now rapidly began to take shape, and it was time to design a new station, which I believe the scheme paid for. Money seemed to be no object, and the result was a fine,

Above and below:
On 31 August 1975 I went to see the Cavalcade of Steam in connection with the 150th Anniversary Celebrations at Shildon.
There were 30 steam locomotives altogether, including LNER 'A4' and 'A3' Pacifics, LMS Nos.6201 *Princess Elizabeth* and 5690 *Leander* and several from the GWR and the Southern. The Steam Parade was spectacular, as the locomotives travelled slowly along the line for all to see. The day was blessed with glorious sunshine. Here are views of LNER No.4771 *Green Arrow* (above) and the Midland Compound No.1000 (below). A very nostalgic day for those deprived of steam and a delight for everyone. *Author*

modern station. The airport authorities may well have contributed to the cost, as they were also keen to have rail access.

Naturally, there were many meetings at various levels during the planning and construction periods, and in order to provide for the crowds and the number of special trains expected two island platforms were built on either side of the main lines, with loop lines at each side. All the usual facilities were provided in a very spacious hall above the platforms, with escalator access to the road entrance and to the island platforms. There was then a very wide footbridge giving direct access to the exhibition halls, and also direct access to Birmingham Airport by means of an elevated Maglev-type tramway, together with ample parking both for the station and the exhibition halls themselves. After a great deal of deliberation, it was decided to call the station Birmingham International, after the airport, rather than Birmingham National Exhibition Centre, which was a bit of a mouthful. As a spin-off, most of the NW/NE to SE expresses were diverted from New Street to run via Coventry instead of via Solihull in order to serve the new station.

With construction of the new National Exhibition Centre visible in the background, a down electric service from Euston towards Birmingham New Street heads through the future location of Birmingham International station.
British Rail

On 16 May 1975 Class 25 No.25122 is pictured at Bentley Heath in Warwickshire having just passed through Dorridge station (visible in the background) with the 06.05 Redhill to Crewe parcels train.
Philip D. Hawkins

1976

PART 1: ANOTHER EVENTFUL YEAR

Birmingham International opens

BIRMINGHAM International station opened on 26 January, and my chauffeur took me there to see the first train arrive and depart just after 6am. It was truly a momentous occasion, but it went off very quietly with no fanfare of trumpets and no VIPs of any sort. Barry and I stood on the platform and watched the first train arrive and depart. There were very few passengers and just a few railway enthusiasts.

The first exhibition at the National Exhibition Centre took place a few days later, and we had six special trains from Euston. Everything went well, and I had arranged for all the train announcements to be in French and German as well as English. One of the clerks at the station came from Germany, so she was ideal for the job, and we found someone who could do the French bit. It is, of course, common practice on the Continent to give train announcements in several languages, but higher authority was not amused. But it didn't matter, as we only did it on the first day for a bit of a lark – after all, it was an international station.

Gradually the number of exhibitions increased – the Ideal Home Exhibition opened on 22 October – as did the volume of passengers. On 5 May, 5,000 passengers were recorded. The official opening came rather belatedly, when Peter Parker, the new BRB Chairman, came to perform the honours on 27 September. In the afternoon he addressed senior management in Stanier House, our new Divisional HQ in Birmingham, and

The fine new Birmingham International station, with the people-mover that connected it with Birmingham Airport. *Author's Collection*

Below; New, at the time, Class 312 EMU No.312202 is pictured at Birmingham International station having just arrived with the 17.00 Birmingham New Street to Birmingham International service as Class 310 No.310061 arrives with a service from Euston to Birmingham New Street via Northampton. *Philip D. Hawkins*

Wolverhampton power signalbox – the interior. *Author*

he came across very well. He was a very good front man and I was impressed. Perhaps he would be able to woo the Government and get some more money, and maybe he could use his talents to improve relations with the railway trade unions.

The National Exhibition Centre turned out to be a great success, and the station, with its two island platforms, worked extremely well. I spent a lot of time there that year, and it was pleasing to see such crowds of passengers.

Night-time inspection saloon tours

These were an excellent way of getting around and meeting the staff on nights. The train timings were advertised beforehand as

The view to the south of Wolverhampton station on 16 March 1965 showing the then new power signalbox. Visible on the extreme left is the route into the Wolverhampton Low Level station, which was still open at this date. *British Rail*

usual, so that signalmen knew our route and staff on the ground were aware that we were coming. I was not a believer in snooping, and I relied upon my inspectors, whom I regarded as my eyes and ears, to keep me informed. They did a good job. The timings of the saloon tour were flexible once we had started, leaving New Street at 22.25. Several Divisional officers elected to come with me, including the Staff Officer, my Glaswegian No.2, and the Maintenance Engineer.

1. The Wolverhampton area

We had a full night's work ahead of us. First stop was Oxley Carriage Sidings to see the night shift at work, cleaning the London trains for next morning. I used to tell them that their depot was the best in the Region and that their trains were the cleanest. They believed it, and so did I. We took a pride in the London trains.

The next stop was the parcels depot at Wolverhampton in the old GWR station, which had been suitably converted. The night shift was the busiest, with parcels trains and vans to be unloaded and the contents to be sorted into the delivery rounds.

2. Bescot Marshalling Yard

Then it was on to the marshalling yard at Bescot, which was also very busy on nights. I was particularly interested to see the new TOPS system at work and to try to assess to what extent it had made the working more efficient. I gained the impression that it had not done much, other than create a need for more staff, both in the office and in the yard. It was more useful to staff in the goods depots, who could ascertain what traffic was en route for them and help them to plan their delivery operations more effectively. They could also keep their customers informed and up to date. Staff shortages were endemic at Bescot, and we were always short of shunters and goods guards. Rates of pay and working conditions were inferior to those in surrounding industries, so it was an uphill task. However, staff shortages meant that there was plenty of overtime available, which helped to offset the relatively small basic wage.

3. Supper, then Duddeston Carriage Sidings

Next stop was some quiet little spot where we could have our great fry-up supper away from prying eyes. At two o'clock in the morning it tasted good. Then it was on to Duddeston, which was the first station on the LNWR line from New Street to Walsall and Lichfield. The LNWR carriage shed serving New Street was located here and was still in good condition. It supplied coaching stock for loco-hauled train services from New Street, excluding the Euston trains. EMUs were dealt with at a new depot at Soho, between New Street and Wolverhampton, whilst DMUs were dealt with at Tyseley, but those two depots were not on our itinerary that night.

4. Curzon Street PCD

The final stop was at Curzon Street PCD, which was in the former goods depot and was reasonably well laid out for dealing with the traffic. These parcels depots were known as PCDs because they had been set up to deal with parcels traffic for a wide area and to greatly reduce the number of stations that dealt with collection and delivery. In theory it worked well, but the problems were the same as at Wolverhampton – shortage of staff and failure of National Carriers Ltd to provide the contracted number of delivery vehicles. They were short of drivers, but had powers to hire vehicles and drivers. However, that would have pushed up their costs, so they didn't do it.

A View of Bescot Marshalling Yard. It was mechanised with Dowty retarders. *Author*

A meeting of electrics just south of Rugby on 4 March 1976 with Class 86 No.86261 in the foreground heading the 10.55 Euston to Manchester express about to pass a sister locomotive on an up express. *Philip D. Hawkins*

On 20 June 1976 Class 86 No.86228 heads the 12.59 service from Wolverhampton to London Euston out of Wolverhampton station. Also visible are a pair of '08' shunters and two Class 25s in the distance. *Andrew Pallett*

On 31 March 1976, Class 50, No.50004 is seen at St Andrews Junction, Birmingham, with the 10.25 service to Paddington. The locomotive, only the second of the class to operate a service over this route, had headed north on the 06.45 from Paddington. *Philip J. Hawkins*

The insoluble problem

The problem created by the transfer of all BR's parcels collection and delivery vehicles, together with the staff, to the newly formed National Carriers Ltd (NCL) under the 1968 Transport Act has already been touched on. NCL was part of another new publicly owned organisation, the National Freight Corporation (NFC), which was expected to collaborate with BR, but it did not happen. NFC was a road haulage firm in competition with the railway, and such a forced marriage was doomed to fail. Worse still, the contract between NCL and BR for a fixed number of parcels vehicles daily was too rigid, and there were no sanctions

available to BR when NCL failed to deliver on the contract. NCL had the same problem with staff shortages as we had, and those shortages were endemic, but the contract did not allow us to hire vehicles from outside contractors. Relations between BR and NCL locally rapidly soured, to the benefit of no one, and the standard of service in the parcels business deteriorated, leading to a loss of business. It was the start of a long decline that ended with BR getting out of the collection and delivery business altogether. However, the parcels business was changing too, and the mail order firms that supplied a lot of BR's parcels traffic were in decline. I thought to myself that the next time the General Manager wanted a tour of the Division, we would do it on nights so he could see the problems for himself at first hand. However, the Divisional Manager did not think much of the idea and I suspect he secretly thought that we were enjoying ourselves too much, swanning around at night. But we saw a lot and had the opportunity to debate

On 20 March 1979 the Oxford University Railway Society organised a tour over a number of lines north of Oxford. Amongst the routes visited was the surviving section of the Stratford-Honeybourne-Cheltenham line and here No.W55035 is seen alongside Honeybourne West Loop signalbox. At this date, track lifting on the line, which had closed as a through route three years earlier, had yet to commence but from later in 1979 the demolition of the route was undertaken. *Peter Waller*

Following closure of the line from Stratford to Cheltenham via Honeybourne the track was lifted despite interest from a preservation society. Today, following restoration by the Gloucestershire & Warwickshire Railway, it's again possible to take a train from Toddington station — a far cry from the scene of dereliction portrayed in this April 1980 view looking southwards at Toddington. *Andrew Muckley*

the issues among ourselves in the peace and quiet of the saloon. We had another night tour later in the year.

The GM visits
The General Manager came down from Euston on 16 March to have dinner and a talk with the Divisional Manager and his officers. These were always very pleasant and interesting occasions and, as was customary, everyone relaxed after dinner. The General Manager liked to get away from Euston from time to time, and we were very conveniently situated, only an hour and a half from Euston. He stayed overnight. Harold Wilson had announced his resignation as Prime Minister that day, and Richard Marsh had resigned as BRB Chairman the previous day, so we had plenty to talk about.

The GM was back again on 12 August, and this time we had dinner at a Wolverhampton hotel. It must have been a good evening, because my chauffeur didn't take me home until 1.30am. The following day we took the GM and his party around the Division in the saloon. The main topic of conversation was probably Viv Richards scoring 291 in the test match. (West Indies declared at 687 for 8.) In the evening my wife and I went to the Alexandra Theatre to see a performance of Arms and the Man. It was very well done, with an excellent cast. Birmingham was a very good centre for the arts.

The weather
After the driest winter for 100 years we had the predicted water shortage. We also had the hottest summer in Birmingham for 33 years, which peaked at the end of June and the beginning of

July. It caused a lot of problems with buckled rails, points failures, DMU and locomotive failures, and air-conditioning failures. We were grateful for our new air-conditioned offices, which fortunately did not fail.

My Chief Inspector retires
Bill Gillett had been my Chief Inspector ever since I took up my post at Birmingham in March 1970. Bill was a splendid Chief Inspector who was universally respected, even by LMS men, and was utterly reliable. I could give him a job and leave him to it. He was, I think, the last of his generation, and exemplified complete loyalty to the railway service (and to me). He had his farewell 'do' at the BRSA club at Saltley, accompanied by his wife, and I made a presentation and a little speech.

Closure of the Honeybourne line
This was part of the former GWR route from Birmingham to Cheltenham, via Stratford and Honeybourne, where it crossed the GWR line from Oxford to Worcester. The latter had been originally the Oxford, Worcester & Wolverhampton Railway (the OW&W), once known sarcastically as the 'Old Worse & Worse' owing to its inability to pay satisfactory dividends. The Honeybourne line continued in use for freight after the passenger service had been withdrawn, but the number of freight trains using the route had declined to a level where the continuance of the route could not be justified. It was listed to close on 3 November, but a derailment hastened its end on 25 August. Part of it now forms the preserved Gloucestershire & Warwickshire Railway.

PART 2: A BUSY AUTUMN

The Railway Operating course begins again

My evening classes in railway operating did not run every year, but they had proved very popular so I decided to run the course again during the autumn and winter of 1976/77. Although I gave a proportion of the lectures myself, I was also able to call on the services of a whole range of speakers, mainly from within the railway industry but also from industries with railway connections.

The course began on 4 October, when there was an attendance of 40, but the following week 65 attended, which was very encouraging indeed. The subject, 'The Railway Parcels Business', was delivered by the Regional Parcels Manager. These lectures were the forerunner of similar courses that I was to run many years later, to a rather different and older audience.

The National Exhibition Centre and the International station

The name 'International' had been chosen because the station also served the nearby airport, but most of its business consisted of passengers visiting the National Exhibition Centre. Traffic levels had been increasing throughout the year since the station opened, and on Saturday 23 October, 12,000 passengers disembarked at the station for the *Daily Mail* Ideal Home Exhibition, setting the pattern for a very busy period indeed. The station had been designed very well to cope efficiently with such crowds, many passengers arriving on normal timetabled services, but for busy exhibitions special trains were run, mainly from London but also from Manchester and stations in the north of England. Fortunately, we still had enough spare locomotives and coaches to enable us to run all the specials that were needed.

Special trains were usually run to the outside platforms, Nos. 1 and 4, leaving the main lines clear, and the empty trains were then sent forward to some convenient point for stabling and servicing. The more critical operation was to ensure that the specials arrived back in the platforms at the appropriate time, and this required very careful watching. I had my inspectors posted at various points to be on hand if anything went wrong. If it had, we could have had several thousand passengers milling around in no time.

The West Midlands itself produced plenty of visitors to the exhibitions, and the booked local services were usually adequate, although they were strengthened when necessary. However, passengers coming from Birmingham often travelled in comfort in the London trains and returned the same way, which quickly revealed a problem that had not been foreseen. The London trains had two or three first-class coaches and a dining car at the London end, but when the trains stopped in the station those coaches were opposite one of the two entrances to the platform. Law-abiding passengers struggled along the platform to the second-class coaches, but, as passengers are wont to do, they all tried to join the train through the first available door beyond the dining car, causing some delay. The less law-abiding contingent invaded the first-class accommodation for the short journey to Birmingham, which rather destroyed the peaceful atmosphere for which passengers had paid good money, and was naturally undesirable. Drivers normally stopped well down the platform, so we quickly had to erect '10/11 car stop' notices and instruct drivers to stop at them. That was the best solution. Loudspeaker announcements telling passengers to move down the platform were not always very effective, especially if the platform was crowded. Persuading passengers to spread themselves evenly along

Class 87 No.87013 *John of Gaunt* arrives at Birmingham International with the 13.40 service from Euston to Wolverhampton on 13 July 1978. *C. J. Tuffs*

Cradley Heath was one of the stations where the West Midlands PTE funded the provision of a road-rail interchange. This view, taken on 21 July 1984, shows a Class 116 DMU on the 14.00 Stourbridge Junction to Birmingham New Street service in the rebuilt station with the bus shelters and a West Midlands PTE bus visible behind the footbridge. *John Glover*

that part of the platform at which the second-class coaches would stop was an art form, and they objected to being shoved around. A study of crowd behaviour can be fascinating.

Bus/rail interchanges

By now the WMPTE had become very active indeed, and its policy of establishing bus/rail interchanges at suitable suburban stations at which buses from outlying areas could terminate in order to enable passengers to transfer to trains was an example of transport planning at its best. It was only possible because the PTE controlled all bus operations within its area. Visiting these locations, I saw how well the interchanges had been laid out and how successful these arrangements were. Full marks to the PTE.

One other measure, of an egalitarian nature, introduced by the PTE was the withdrawal of first-class accommodation on suburban trains, which had been underused, to provide additional seating for commuters.

Educating the emergency services

It had become apparent that the emergency services and the county police forces knew very little about the workings of the railway, and we had had one or two silly incidents, such as the occasion referred to earlier when the fire brigade had laid their hoses across the line without ensuring trains that were stopped, or when the police, who were chasing some miscreant or other, arrived at a level crossing when the gates were closed across the road and demanded that the gates be opened. Fortunately, the signalman stood his ground, and I wish I had seen the faces of those police officers when a train roared through. It was clear that some education in the working of a railway, and how to get in touch with us in an emergency, was required.

As an ice-breaker we decided to stage a mock accident, to be held in the carriage sidings at Oxley, and invited all the emergency services – the police, the fire brigade and the ambulance service. The local BR first aid groups joined in enthusiastically, and with ghoulish delight. Injured people, both conscious and unconscious, with labels showing their supposed injuries, lay in various postures, groaning realistically in a carriage that we had purposely (but carefully) derailed. It was all filmed so that lessons could be learned.

We then had a meeting to discuss our conclusions, and were at pains to help the various authorities to understand the railway organisation a little better. This included giving them contact numbers as first call, with priority being to phone the Control Office, who could then take the necessary action from a railway point of view. Everyone thought it had been a very useful exercise, and privately I wondered why I had not done it earlier. It also emphasised the need to have the trailer tent on site as soon as possible, to act as a communications centre and point of contact. In the event, we never needed it whilst I was at Birmingham because we never had a sufficiently serious accident, but it was best to be prepared.

Cab-riding

During the tail-end of the year, I managed to find time for a couple of driving trips – one from Oxley Carriage Sidings to Euston and back with an electric loco, and one from Saltley to Didcot Power Station with a train of MGR coal wagons and a Class 47. On each occasion, I was accompanied by one of my Traction Inspectors, who enjoyed it as much as I did.

Class 47 No.47233 approaches Oxford with an empty merry-go-round train from Didcot power station on 21 June 1978. *Les Bertram*

The upgraded DMU sidings at Tyseley, with good modern facilities. *Author*

The 12.36 Birmingham to Leicester DMU prepares to dive under the main line to Euston at Grand Junction, Birmingham, on 11 November 1976 shortly after having left New Street station. *Philip D. Hawkins*

They considered, quite rightly, that I should know as much about driving trains as I did about signalling them. The Operating Department had been responsible for drivers for only about ten years, and it was important that they felt part of it.

The fact was that I spent as little time in the office as possible. I felt that it was more important to be outside, seeing how things were going, meeting the Area Managers to hear their concerns, looking round their 'parishes' and showing the flag.

Another night-time saloon tour

This was an unusual way of showing the flag, but it was important not to be branded as part of the 'nine-to-five' group. As usual, about five of my staff were sufficiently interested to accompany me, and our first stop was Tyseley. This once important GWR steam depot now belonged to one of the mainline preservation groups, but the extensive carriage sidings were still there. It had become the main depot for maintaining and servicing DMUs

and had recently been equipped with good lighting and a carriage washing machine. Its busiest shift was undoubtedly the night shift, when all the units were on the depot and were being cleaned and serviced for the next morning's trains.

Most of the DMU services were crewed by Saltley drivers, although New Street had a share. After Tyseley we visited the other carriage cleaning depots, pausing at about two o'clock in the morning at Oxley for a good fry-up. No alcohol, though – this was a working trip.

The Chartered Institute of Transport

Railway engineers all had their own institutions, but there had been none for the railway traffic departments. Therefore, just after the First World War, a group of senior officers of the railway companies decided to found their own institute, which resulted in the formation of the Institute of Transport. The new institute also welcomed members from road transport, mainly from municipal bus companies. Lorrymen were in the minority, mainly because of the nature of the road haulage industry, it being formed in small units.

The institute, which received its Royal Charter in 1926, was mainly an educational body, and to become an Associate member one had to pass exams in a number of courses, twelve in all, in groups of three. Some of the ones I recall were statistics, English, commercial geography, the law of transport, common and statute law, and the principles of railway operating. I opted for postal tuition and took the exams at two-yearly intervals from 1957, qualifying as an Associate member in 1965, which entitled me to put the initials AMInstT after my name. I have to say that I learned an enormous amount about the wider elements of transport, which has been extremely useful ever since.

The institute was directed from London, but the country was divided into sections which had their own committees and held regular meetings, mainly with speakers. I found myself on the committee for the West Midlands, and it became my turn to be chairman. That was really great fun and made a change from railway work.

1977

PART 1: CHANGES AHEAD

The break-up of the Divisional team

THE seven years since my appointment as Divisional Operating Superintendent at Birmingham had seen the establishment of a very settled team of Divisional and Area officers with very little change. Such an environment had created an efficiently run Division and a successful and happy team that worked well together. But it all came to an end in 1977 when John Pollard retired. He ran his Division with a very light touch and left me to get on with my job, which suited me. His main responsibilities were with the commercial and business interests in the West Midlands, and with the various public bodies, of which there were quite a few, including the West Midlands Passenger Transport Authority. John had begun his career before the war as a junior clerk at Ramsbottom, but any trace of a Lancashire accent had been polished away by his Army service, in which like so many other young railwaymen he became a lieutenant-colonel. It was whilst he was at Birmingham that he had become a full colonel and an equerry to HM The Queen.

My great friend John Whitehouse retired from his post as Divisional Staff Officer at about the same time. John hailed from the Sheffield area but had also lost his local accent, and had spent five years of the war in India and Burma with the Worcestershire Regiment, rising to the rank of major. As a true Yorkshireman, John was a keen supporter of the Yorkshire County Cricket Club, and if the team were playing at Edgbaston we would sometimes sneak off during the afternoon to watch them. John excelled with people, and could charm the trade unions and the local staff reps – hence the generally good staff relationships within the Division. He and I were the fire brigade that was called out whenever trouble loomed. He would phone me up and say, 'There's trouble at t'mill' and off we would go. The 'mill' was Saltley, which had two very militant staff reps, and I always admired John's skilful

Below: On 9 July 1977, Class 46 No.46053 heads a north-east/south-west train as it approaches the junction at Water Orton heading towards Birmingham New Street. *David J. Hayes*

handling of tricky situations. He had more patience than I had. John and his wife retired to Norwich, but we kept in touch and met regularly until he died a few years ago.

I also lost Tom Gibson, my excellent Scottish No.2. He succumbed to the lure of Transmark, which was the consultancy wing of the BRB specialising in commissions from overseas railways, and went off to sort out the railways of Bangladesh. His was a difficult act to follow. Tom had a very strong Glasgow accent, and the Bangladeshis must have wondered what had hit them.

There was a wave of retirements that year, including Ernie Mycock, the Divisional Passenger Manager, and Fred Smout, the Area Manager at Wolverhampton. Later that year I too joined the exodus, but not into retirement. More on that later.

A Railway Operating course outing

One Saturday in January we had a course outing, beginning with the 08.15 from New Street to Euston, and thence to King's Cross, where we were met by Don Wyman, my opposite number, who had been Area Manager at Bescot and in charge of all the freight terminals. First stop was the power signalbox, recently opened, followed by a trip on the new electrics on the Moorgate service to visit the new EMU depot at Hornsey. The icing on the cake was a trip on one of the new HSTs from Paddington to Bristol Parkway, before returning home direct to Birmingham. It was a very successful day out. At the following Monday meeting we saw a number of films, including Peter Parker, German Computer Applications, and the new Italian High Speed Line. This was 1977!

Back to the NEC

I spent a lot of time at the National Exhibition Centre, mainly in the position of an observer but on hand if needed, and when a toy fair was being held there I took the opportunity to visit the fair itself. There was a marvellous mouth-watering display, and lots of excited children. A few days later we were busy again with the International Spring Fair traffic. Earlier that day, I had taken a footplate trip to Paddington on the 08.35 from New Street, and hopped off at Birmingham International on the way back. The next event to be held at the venue was the Boat and Leisure Show.

Looking after the new General Manager

At one time, the person holding such a figurehead position as the General Manager might have expected to remain in office for a good number of years, but now they seemed to change with the seasons. In the eight years that I was at Birmingham we had at least four. The new man, David Binnie, followed the usual pattern. Dinner at the Midland Hotel and lots of chat lasting until after midnight (I wish I had recorded some of the conversations), and a saloon tour the following morning, followed by lunch at the Midland Hotel again – no slumming it in the saloon.

Back to The Grove, Watford

I had been to the BR Staff Training College on quite a few occasions over the years, and this time it was a week's Computer Appreciation course. There were 15 of us, most of whom I knew, and it was all very leisurely, with plenty of coffee breaks and good cuisine. The bar was well patronised in the evening, as were the snooker tables as usual. I cannot recall whether I appreciated computers any better afterwards, but it made a change. Keeping awake during the lectures was probably the most difficult part of the course.

Still on the education front, I went to a one-day teach-in at Euston entitled 'Health and Safety at Work'. It was all about personal safety, not operational safety, which was the responsibility of the Railway Inspectorate. I was distinctly underwhelmed by the bureaucracy of the whole thing.

With Stourbridge Junction North signalbox, a GWR box of 1901 that closed in 1978, in the background, the 13.03 Kidderminster to Lichfield service has just departed from Stourbridge Junction station en route to Birmingham New Street on 10 November 1977. *Kevin Lane*

The interior of the then new power signalbox at King's Cross recorded in 1977. In the foreground is the King's Cross station announcer whilst the three signalmen are at the Wood Green (left) to Finsbury Park (right) section of the panel. *British Rail*

A close-up of the control panel at Kings Cross power signalbox, showing the busy Finsbury Park section. *British Rail*

On 1 October 1977, Class 313 EMU No.313011 stands in the wheel-turning shed at Hornsey depot. The rubber cover surrounding the EMU was designed to keep heating within the building. *Keith Grafton*

Moorgate station on 15 January 1977 as Class 313 EMU No.313010 awaits departure with the 14.50 service to Welwyn Garden City. *Brian Morrison*

A new Area Manager at Wolverhampton takes charge

Brian Simpson, the new Area Manager, had arrived at Wolverhampton, and I spent a day taking him all round his area, which included Wellington, Kidderminster, Stourbridge and the Black Country. Brian was a first-rate railwayman and I was glad to have him in the Division. I noted that I did not get home until 10pm, so it was a long day – a not unusual event.

We had had a mishap on the half-mile long Stourbridge branch, which ran on a steep falling gradient from the Junction station to the Town station (a dead-end). It was worked by a diesel railcar, which had somehow got out of control and ran through the buffers at the end of the line and almost into the street below. No one was badly hurt, but the reason for the runaway was a mystery. The railcar made the journey without difficulty a dozen times a day.

It was, of course, necessary to find out what had gone wrong, so we did some tests one Sunday morning when there were no booked trains. We took along the same driver, plus his Locomotive Inspector and several Mechanical Engineers. The answer soon emerged, and concerned the driver's operation of the vacuum brake handle. Put simply, instead of making a firm brake application on the way down, he was making short, light applications, which had the effect of using up all the vacuum in the brake chamber and not replacing it – hence no brake. This should have been obvious from the brake gauge on the dashboard. My son Chris, by now 22 and working for BR, came with me. At the time of writing, he is working as an inspector in the Rail Accident Investigation Branch (RAIB).

Another Royal Train visit – a big one

It was HM The Queen's Silver Jubilee year and she was carrying out a series of visits. We had a very interesting one, which began as they usually did with the Royal Train being stabled for the night in a siding at Berkswell so that they all had a good night's sleep. They were going to need it! Barry, my chauffeur, called for me at 11pm and took me to Berkswell, and after the train had been safely 'put to bed' for the night I had a whisky with the Royal Train Officer.

After returning home for a few hours' sleep, Barry then picked me up again at 6.45am and took me back to Berkswell in time for the Royal Train breakfast, which would probably last me all day. We left at 9.5am and moved gently to a special platform that had been erected in some sidings on the northern outskirts of Bushbury. It was planned for The Queen to alight there and use a newly built wooden walkway to an opening that had been made in the wall of the Goodyear factory alongside.

Class 25 No.25169 arrives at Bescot with a short van train from the Walsall direction on 27 June 1977. *John Glover*

We had adopted this method of delivering The Queen because the police wanted to avoid HM having to alight at Wolverhampton station and be conveyed by car through the town centre. The IRA was quite active at this time, hence we adopted what we thought was a very ingenious stratagem. The sidings that we used had lain unused for several years and the Civil Engineer was not at all amused when we told him our plan. However, he did what was required (maximum speed 10mph) and also built the wooden platform and walkway.

It looked fine when it had the red carpet on it, but it was only 20 yards long.

There was now a critical issue. The door through which The Queen would alight had to be in the centre of the platform when the train stopped. A few yards out either way would have been a disaster. It was therefore necessary to calculate very carefully the distance from the centre of the driver's seat to the centre of the door through which she would alight, and a marker was put on the ground at the precise spot where the driver should stop, after having been very carefully measured out. The railway officer's coach was some distance back from The Queen's coach, and I was looking forward as we approached Bushbury. I saw the locomotive turn off the main line into the sidings and then carefully and slowly draw the train through the connections giving access to the appropriate siding. Hearts were in mouths at this stage, and the relief when we saw The Queen alight was

An involvement with the Royal Train was one of the highlights of the job and I have many happy memories of such events. 27 July 1977 was a red-letter day for us, and this shows HM the Queen, having just returned to the Royal Train at Coventry after a walkabout, smiling radiantly at one of the officials who had been accompanying her. The Duke of Edinburgh is saying farewell at the other window. I was hovering somewhere nearby, anxious to get the train away the few miles along the line to Birmingham International. For the first time in my recollection we had a late departure of the Royal Train — of 25 minutes. We weren't doing things by halves! *Author's collection*

The second picture shows the Royal Party leaving the train at Birmingham International for an evening function, by a rather unorthodox route. Nothing is too much trouble on such occasions. But the day wasn't over yet. *Author's collection*

Below: Class 47 No.47529, in immaculate condition, hauls the empty coaching stock from the royal train past Stafford Road Junction on 27 July 1977 en route for stabling at Oxley carriage sidings during HM the Queen's visit to the West Midlands for the Silver Jubilee. *Andrew Bannister*

Sir Peter Parker, chairman of the British Railways Board from 1976 until 1983, is seen at Euston station on 16 May 1977 at the official hand-over of the new Royal Train to HM Queen Elizabeth II and HRH the Duke of Edinburgh. This was the year of the Queen's Silver Jubilee and saw her visit the West Midlands on a number of occasions. *British Rail*

palpable. We were spot on – and we were dead on time. But there was more excitement to come.

We went to Oxley Carriage Sidings for stabling and servicing, with a loco on each end, and remained there until mid-afternoon before setting off for Coventry, where The Queen was to rejoin the train prior to departure at 5.26pm. There were huge crowds at Coventry and The Queen was doing one of her walkabouts, shaking hands and receiving bunches of flowers from children. At about 5.15pm a harassed policeman almost ran to me and said, panting, 'The Queen's running late.' 'How much?' I asked. 'I don't know,' said he. 'Well, let me know when she's ten minutes away, because I'm going to open the railway and the level crossings again.' I had just closed it to avoid the station being used by passengers whilst HM was just passing through it on her way to the train.

Fortunately, it all worked out well, and we got the Royal Train away about 25 minutes late. Next stop was Birmingham International station where The Queen alighted at 8pm, looking radiant, fresh and regal, to attend an evening function nearby. The royal party returned at 11pm and I went with the train as far as Bescot on its way to overnight stabling at Old Dalby in Leicestershire. The ever-faithful Barry brought me home after what had been a super and memorable day during which we had served our monarch faithfully.

PART 2: THE END OF A PERSONAL ERA AND A DIGRESSION

More footplating

I had no idea, on 3 August, that the end of an era was approaching for me, although I had already had offers of two jobs at Crewe, neither of which I wanted. I was now 51, so it was time for a move – perhaps the final one. However, I was looking forward to a day's footplating (actually cab-riding) with one of my inspectors, Arthur Bullock. The first leg was the 07.13 passenger train from New Street to Paddington with a Class 47, which I drove as far as Banbury. Then we doubled back to Wolverhampton via Coventry before taking an EMU (very mundane) back to Coventry, thence to Stafford for a lunch break, and finally to Birmingham. This sounds a bit like joy-riding, which it was, but it was also an opportunity to talk to drivers and get their angle on things.

Out of the blue

I was phoned by Crewe to see if I wanted to go on a year's Transmark assignment to Botswana to sort out their signalling. It sounded very inviting, but what sort of a job would I get when I came back? Once you got out of the mainstream it was difficult to get back in again. I declined, but a friend of mine took it on and spent a year there with his wife, putting in a new signalling system. Apparently he was very well looked after and even dined with the President.

The end is nigh

Tuesday 11 October began like any another day, until Euston phoned to say that Bob Arnott wanted me to be his Signalling Officer at the Board. Signalling was certainly one of my main interests, and it would not be just an office job. Indeed, the offer sounded very attractive. I knew I would enjoy working with Bob again, but it would be a major change for me. However, there would still be plenty of opportunities for getting out and about, but throughout the length and breadth of the system rather than being confined to one Division. I went to see Bob a few days later and arranged to start in a couple of weeks' time. Whilst I was in London I went to a lecture at the Railway Marketing Society by Peter Parker, the BRB Chairman, at the Great Western Royal Hotel in Paddington.

My colleague at Reading very kindly agreed to lend me his car and chauffeur for the day, so I spent it visiting all the estate

On 16 October 1977, with my departure imminent, Control called me out to a derailment of an express just north of Aston Junction, on a Sunday diversion. I lived not far away at Sutton Coldfield, so I was quickly on the scene to assess the situation. It was not a serious derailment, but several bogies had been derailed. Vandals had wedged open the trailing catch points with a couple of concrete troughing lids. The train was 1S27 Plymouth to Edinburgh. My last bit of excitement!
Author (all)

I had formed a real bond with the staff at Bushbury, and they turned out in force to wish me farewell. *Parting is such sweet sorrow. Author*

The Birmingham Repertory Theatre — a fitting symbol of a fine city. Unfortunately, it wasn't to last. There were dark clouds ahead. *Author*

A fitting symbol — the ubiquitous 350hp diesel shunter, based on a pre-war LMS design. I'm standing left of centre, next to Harold Hook, a very good railwayman. Bescot Yard was in good hands. It was goodbye with a touch of sadness. I was going to miss all these chaps. *Author's collection*

agents in the area. I already had my sights on the lines into Paddington and Marylebone, and there seemed to be more scope in the Reading area, where house prices were a little nearer those in the Birmingham area. There was also an excellent train service between Reading and Paddington, including HSTs running nonstop in half an hour.

No respite yet

The following Sunday I was called out to an incident involving a passenger train at Gravelly Hill (on the Birmingham–Sutton Coldfield line). A diverted NE/SW passenger train had become derailed, fortunately at low speed. Two bogies were off at some catch points, which had been wedged open by some vandals. There were no casualties, and as soon as the C&W people had confirmed that there was no damage to the coaches in front of those derailed, we moved all the passengers forward to the front portion and sent it on its way. The undamaged coaches in rear were taken back to Birmingham, giving the breakdown people a clear run. The BTP were very helpful, but I doubt if it could be done today.

Farewells

On the Friday following, my wife and I went to a social evening at the Bushbury BRSA club for the presentation of first aid awards. Having been there a number of times over the years and having got to know everyone, we were made quite a fuss of, and I was rather touched. I was sure that nothing like that would happen in my new job.

My last week at Birmingham was mainly spent visiting all the Area Managers and saying farewell, followed by all the staff in the offices at Stanier House, as well as my inspectors and the Control Staff. There were 13 of us for the final lunch in the mess. I provided wine and cigars, and then there was a final round-up of the offices. I was last out, at 6.30pm. I knew every inch of the Birmingham Division and several hundred people within it, who all reported to me directly or indirectly, and I was really going to miss that personal contact. And I would miss the prestige of being a Divisional Operating Superintendent and all the trappings of that office.

It really was the end of an era for me, but it had to come some time, and I was looking forward to the new job. It would need quite a mental adjustment – most people went to BRB HQ from a Regional HQ and knew the routine in such offices, but I was making a bigger leap. For 34 years I had been near the action, closely involved with the day-to-day railway, but from now on it would be no concern of mine. What I had to do was to bring my outdoor experience into the corridors of power, where the knowledge I had gained would be of enormous value.

A new life begins

On Monday 31 October, I walked through the doors of 222 Marylebone Road, the headquarters of the BRB. I had been there quite a few times before, on matters concerning TOPS and the development of MGR working of coal traffic, so it was not entirely strange. I had also been there 23 years earlier for the final interview stage of the Traffic Apprentice Management Training Scheme. I was fortunate enough to be selected, which altered my whole career with accelerated promotion.

The building was the old Great Central Hotel, facing the front of Marylebone station, and therefore contained several hundred bedrooms with large public dining rooms and function rooms. The bedrooms were now offices, and in some cases interior walls had been knocked down to make larger offices. It was not entirely satisfactory, and it seems strange that the BRB had never contemplated building a proper office block. It had been necessary to build overflow offices just across the road for several departments, including the S&T, with whom I was destined to have frequent meetings. Fortunately, I was already an Associate of the IRSE and knew several of them through institution meetings and conventions. That was a great help.

There were four separate messes at '222' (as it was usually called). The directors and Board members had their own mess,

Built by the Great Central Railway, 222 Marylebone Road, headquarters of the British Railways Board, served as a hotel until 1939. Following privatisation of the railways, the building has reverted once again to a hotel. *British Transport Commission*

then came the senior officers' mess, of which I was a member, followed by the management staff mess, and at the bottom of the heap was a mess for the clerical staff etc. The senior officers' mess was a grand affair. It opened for lunch at 11.30am, and there was an ante room area for pre-prandials, of which there was a large selection. Wine with the lunch was a regular feature, and there was always an excellent menu. We lived like lords, and it was not a good idea to hold afternoon meetings.

My staff

At Birmingham I had had a secretary, but at '222' I had a shorthand typist, whom I shared with the Chief Traction Officer, John Powell, along the corridor. She did not maintain my drinks cabinet as I did not have one, nor did I really need one considering the ample supplies of booze in the mess. John, who was very easy to get along with, presented me with an all-line cab pass that I was to make good use of.

Within my small section I had five assistants, all quite senior and all experts in their own fields. We had no dealings with the outside day-to-day railway. Our job was twofold: firstly, to maintain operational standards and amend them when required; and, secondly, to liaise with the technical departments concerning new developments, mainly in signalling systems.

Involvement with the Railway Inspectorate

We worked closely with the Railway Inspectorate, now part of the Department of Transport, and implemented the recommendations in their accident reports, where appropriate. They would send us draft copies of their reports and recommendations so that we could check the reports for any factual errors, and this would be followed by a meeting to discuss the recommendations, for which there was always room for manoeuvre. Working with the Inspecting Officers, splendid fellows who were realists and down-to-earth, was one of the happiest and most rewarding parts of the job. They were all Army officers with experience of military railways, particularly at Longmoor, and had joined the Inspectorate in mid-career, and their reports were held up as models of report writing. They really knew their stuff and were universally respected (well, almost – sometimes they upset the engineers, which was not difficult!).

Standing committees

I was chairman of the BRB Signalling Committee and joint chairman of the Signalling Standards Group (jointly with the S&T Department). The Signalling Committee met for two days each month, and from time to time the meetings were held at Regional HQs (Paddington, Crewe, York and Glasgow). The Regional representatives put items on the agenda that were of general concern, especially of lessons learnt from accidents, and the need to discuss amendments to the Rules, etc. The Regions, not the BRB, were responsible for ensuring that all accidents were investigated and that reports were sent direct to the Railway Inspectorate (note – not to the BRB). The Regions were also responsible for making all the necessary arrangements for any public inquiry that the Railway Inspectorate might require. These arrangements dated from nationalisation and worked well.

I was now the grand custodian of the British Railways Rule Book, the Train Signalling Regulations Book and the General Appendix, which I regarded as quite an honour. Nothing in those venerable publications was added, deleted or amended without the assent of the Signalling Committee. I was told with some pride that the Signalling Committee was the oldest standing committee in railway history, dating back to the mid-19th century when the superintendents of the larger railways met to discuss items of mutual interest.

Looking back to the Hellifield rail crash

A reminder of how the railways reacted to accidents in days gone by.

The 7¾-mile stretch of line from Stainforth Sidings signalbox to Hellifield South Junction signalbox has seen several fairly serious accidents since the Second World War. One of these occurred at 4.43am on 22 December 1955, whilst the 9.5pm St Pancras to Edinburgh train was standing in the Down platform at Hellifield. It was run into at 25-30mph by the following Glasgow sleeper, the 9.15pm from St Pancras. The double-headed Edinburgh train was formed of seven vans and five coaches, including two sleepers, and there was some derailment and damage to the train, but fortunately the brakes had been released ready for departing. The 9.15pm had ten vehicles, four of which were ordinary coaches and three were sleepers, and was

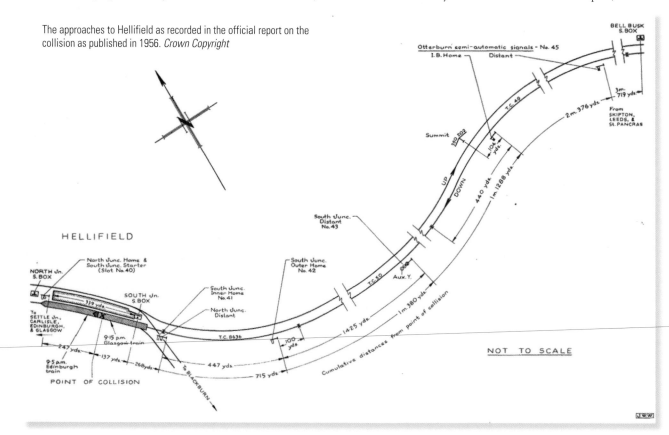

The approaches to Hellifield as recorded in the official report on the collision as published in 1956. *Crown Copyright*

The interior of Hellifield (South) box pictured on 16 July 1967. *D. A. Idle*

headed by a Class 7P 4-6-0, probably of the 'Royal Scot' class. The locomotive was derailed and heavily damaged, but all the coaches remained on the rails and were more or less intact.

Immediate calls were made for assistance, and doctors, an ambulance, the police and the fire brigade were quickly on the scene. Fortunately, their services were hardly needed, as only two passengers needed treatment and they were allowed to continue their journey. It would have been much worse if the driver of the Glasgow train had not reacted so quickly when he saw the tail lamp of the Edinburgh train. Also, the parcels vans bore the brunt of the collision.

The signalling

Hellifield South Junction box was situated at the Skipton end of the platform, and the line was track-circuited throughout from Bell Busk. The signalling arrangements on the Down line between Bell Busk and Hellifield were of particular interest to aficionados of railway signalling because between the two signalboxes there was an additional intermediate block section at Otterburn worked from Hellifield South box, consisting of a semaphore home signal and a semaphore distant signal. The system dated from 1910 and was not common – intermediate block sections were usually worked from the signalbox in the rear.

The signals approaching Hellifield were as follows: 1 – a colour-light distant signal (lever 43); 2 – a semaphore outer home signal (lever 42), 440 yards in rear of the semaphore inner home signal; 3 – the inner home signal (lever 41). The tail lamp of the Edinburgh train was 400 yards beyond this signal, underneath which North Junction's distant signal was located.

Events as the Glasgow train approached the station

Driver Blakemore of Holbeck shed took over the Glasgow train at Leeds. He had a clear run after Skipton and was running at 55-60mph at Bell Busk. The Otterburn signals were clear and he almost closed the regulator to coast on the falling gradient through Hellifield. He saw Hellifield colour-light distant at clear but missed the outer home signal. He relied on his fireman seeing the inner home signal. His fireman was looking out and shouted 'One off', meaning that the inner home signal was clear, but the North Junction distant signal under it was at caution. The driver immediately braked, then looked out and saw the tail lamp of the Edinburgh train.

The signalman at Hellifield South Junction broke the rules by not replacing Otterburn intermediate block signals after the Edinburgh train passed them, resulting in the Glasgow train passing them in the clear position. He was also slow in replacing his distant signal and the outer and inner home signals, with the result that the Glasgow train probably passed them in the clear position before he did so. The driver was criticised for failing to see the outer home signal (owing, he said, to smoke drifting down the cabside) and relying solely on the distant signal having been at clear, and expecting a clear run through the station. However, it was likely that the outer home signal was still at clear before he passed it. Incidentally, at one time there had been another intermediate block section – known as automatic signalling – at Ingber, between Gargrave and Bell Busk.

Just as an aside, the official Ministry report into this accident cost 9*d*. And purely as a matter of interest, the two trains had ten parcels vans between them, carrying mail, parcels and all manner

A three-car 'Pressed Steel' suburban DMU stands at the modernised Redditch station having formed the 17.18 service from Birmingham New Street on 6 September 1977. *Les Bertram*

Class 45 No.45056 is pictured about to pass through Craven Arms on 10 September 1977 hauling the Saturday 08.45 service from Newquay to Manchester Piccadilly. *Les Bertram*

On 3 January 1977 Class 45 No.45047 turns towards Birmingham with the 07.01 service from Newcastle upon Tyne to Poole having just passed through Saltley. *C. R. Davis*

Class 86 No.86226 approaches Wolverhampton with the 10.29 service from Euston on 2 April 1977. *David A. Flitcroft*

of traffic, indicating the huge quantities of such traffic carried by the railways in those days.

PART 3: NEW HORIZONS

The outings begin

I had a lot of road learning to do. I was fairly well acquainted with the LM Region and most of the Eastern, but much of the Western Region would be new to me. I had travelled extensively over much of the Scottish Region in the previous 30 years, but not on duty. And the Southern Region, the most complex of all, was a closed book. It looked as though I would be out of the office quite a bit.

I did not consciously set out to travel in the driving cab over all the main lines in Britain, but that was how it eventually worked out. On every occasion, I was accompanied by a Regional Traction Inspector, arranged beforehand, and sometimes by one of the Regional Signalling Officers, who usually welcomed the opportunity to have an excuse to get out of the office for a day.

A visit to London Bridge power signalbox

Apart from road learning I needed to learn about the different signalling arrangements in the Regions. Despite British Railways having been in existence for 30 years, power signalboxes built during that period showed marked regional differences. One of the newest was London Bridge, a major NX signalling system on a grand scale (see below). It covered most of the suburban lines on the old South Eastern Section of the Southern Region, a veritable cat's cradle of lines carrying intensive passenger services. I was there for the evening peak and marvelled at the quiet skills with which the signalmen went about making the whole thing work, quickly and efficiently dealing with any minor problems that arose. Those chaps were experts in their own field and were top-grade signalmen, as would be expected.

The NX system

The letters 'NX' stand for 'entrance-exit', a route setting system in which the signalman sets a route by pressing a push-button at the beginning (the entrance) of the desired route, and another button at the end (the exit) of that route. If the route was available, ie if parts of it had not been given to another train, the points would automatically be switched to the desired route and locked, and the signal at the entrance to the route would automatically be cleared (the actual signal aspect displayed could be either green, single yellow or double yellow, depending on the state of the line ahead). During rush hours, trains often travelled for miles on double yellows, as I was to discover when I travelled with a driver at a later date.

The NX system was actually first used in 1937 at Brunswick, Liverpool, on the Cheshire Lines network, but later development was based on a turn-switch system, known as 'OCS' (one control switch), which was widely used until the 1960s.

The fish tank

There was a large fish tank in London Bridge signalbox, which had been provided deliberately to relax the signalmen with 'visual refreshment'. This was no psychological wild-goose chase but a recognition of the very considerable change from the environment in which signalmen had traditionally worked, alone or in small numbers and seeing every train. Now they were cooped up in a signalling centre with no view of the trains, except from a window in the corner. Of course, it was not necessary for them to see any train in order to carry out their signalling duties – all the information they needed was provided on giant control and information panels all along one wall so that everyone could see where all the trains were. The signalmen sat at desks that had all the control buttons etc they needed to carry out their duties. There is no way of knowing whether the fish tank helped to relieve tension, but things could get a bit fraught at London Bridge if there were a mishap or line blockage in the rush hour.

As a matter of interest, when the power signalboxes at Trent, Derby and Saltley were built in the late 1960s they were provided with windows at the corners that gave some views of the world outside, and the signalmen were free to wander over and have a look at passing trains during quiet moments. The windows also allowed some natural light to enter, and were provided with blinds

The occasion, on 9 June 1976, of a royal visit to the signalbox at London Bridge. Tony Ball, the project engineer for the London Bridge resignalling scheme is seen explaining the working of the South East side panel to HRH the Duke of Edinburgh. In the foreground is Brian Hamment-Arnold, the Southern Region's South Eastern Division Movements Manager. *British Rail*

Derby power signalbox, showing a close-up of the panel. The signalman is just setting a route. *Author*

A typical course in progress at the Staff Training Centre at Crewe; this view slightly predates the author's involvement with training of staff at Crewe but was typical of the ambience of staff training during the period when he did courses for trainees in Nottingham, Birmingham and during his time with the Board. *British Rail*

to guard against low sunlight affecting the displays on the control and indications panels. However, the York power signalbox, which opened in 1951 and was said to be the largest of its type in the world, was on an upstairs floor in the station buildings and had no windows.

The educational side of the business

Residential courses on Signalling and Safety of Operations were regularly held at the Staff Training College at Crewe for supervisors and junior managers, and it was part of my brief to visit them and deliver a talk on the subject. I was no stranger to the task, as my Railway Operating courses at both Nottingham and Birmingham had been running for a dozen years. I was also honing my skills for more demanding presentations to U3A (University of the Third Age) classes later in life, although I was not to know that at the time. (The U3A was not born in the UK until about 1982/83.) I had another such duty a few weeks later for staff on a course for Assistant Area Managers.

I enjoyed visiting the college at Crewe, which had previously been part of the Webb Orphanage. Francis Webb was Chief Mechanical Engineer of the LNWR in the late 19th century, and was both an autocrat and a philanthropist – not an unusual combination in those days, I believe. Such a provision was necessary in Webb's time. In 1874, the worst year, 788 railway staff were killed, but ten years later the figure had fallen to 500.

Cab-riding begins in earnest

I next turned my attention to the Western Region, and met Chief Inspector Jack Temple at Paddington for an HST cab trip to Cardiff and back. Jack was one of the old school of GWR men – loyal to the railway tradition and proud of his GWR heritage – and a positive mine of information. The railway was fortunate to have such dedicated men. He was enormously helpful, and I found him a very valuable contact if I needed to discuss signalling matters unofficially with someone knowledgeable. I had a number of excellent trips with Jack.

The GWR had been pioneers in the introduction of an automatic train control system in the first decade of the 20th

century, and it was extended throughout the system in the 1930s, helping to give the GWR an enviable safety record. The BR AWS system was now being installed throughout BR and was replacing the GWR system at the time. This had to be done in order to enable traction units fitted with the BR system to work over Western Region lines.

Into the stratosphere …

From time to time, meetings were held at high level between the Railway Inspectorate and the heads of the main departments – Operations, Civil Engineering, S&T Engineering, and Mechanical Engineering. The chair at these meetings was taken by the Board member for Operations, which was an indication of the importance that the Board attached to them. There was no fixed agenda and it was just a general get-together with the Inspectorate so that they could raise any issues that were of concern to them. I was probably roped in to take notes and found these discussions of great interest. The meeting was held at the Great Western Royal Hotel at Paddington, and was followed by a splendid lunch – fillet of beef. It was also the first of my many

A British Rail AWS inductor as installed on the line between Salisbury and Wilton. *British Rail*

meetings during the forthcoming years with Inspecting Officers, which were always interesting.

… and off out again

An old colleague of mine from the Birmingham days had become the DOS at King's Cross, and I arranged to meet him so that I could visit the power signalbox there, which had opened a few years earlier. After that we visited the new Hornsey depot for the EMUs that operated the new electric service. This was followed by lunch at the Liverpool Street mess and a cab trip from King's Cross to Peterborough and back, which brought back many memories of my days at New England as Yardmaster and at King's Cross as Deputy Stationmaster.

Back to the Signalling Committee

The December meeting was held at '222' and lasted the usual two days. The Signalling Committee meetings were not large –

just one representative from each Region, plus London Transport, two of my chaps, and me. The London Transport representative was a member in order to cover issues that might arise at locations where LTE used BR signalling equipment at shared stations. I soon got to know them all and found that they were experts in their own field. We all got on together very well, which was essential. I cannot recall the agenda, but any changes that we might make to the Rules and Regulations etc had to be very carefully thrashed out in order to avoid any doubt or ambiguity. The general rule of things was that the Signalling Committee had the last word.

The minutes were in two parts. Part 1 included significant changes for confirmation by the Operating Committee. Part 2 contained the other items, 'for noting only'. The Operating Committee was the next layer upwards, and its members were the Chief Operating Superintendents/Managers of the five Regions, plus the Chief Operating Superintendent of the Board. In other words, the top brass. I usually attended those meetings if there were any Part 1 items, and in order to ensure as far as possible that these items had an easy passage through the Operating Committee it was customary for the Regional Signalling Officers to use their wiles to persuade their Superintendents where possible to support the changes. It was also necessary occasionally for me to exercise all my tact and ingenuity at the Signalling Committee meeting to achieve unanimity there, but there was a bit of give and take.

As this was the December meeting, we had the customary Christmas lunch at the 'Portman Arms', with 'a bottle of Andre Simon Graves AC', according to my notes. The second day we had the usual buffet lunch in the office, provided by the Catering Department.

Next day I had a visit from a Mr Patterson of CIE (the Irish Railways) who wished to discuss some signalling matters with me, and later resulted in my having a tour of CIE and its signalling installations. Away from the Dublin area, it was like turning the clock back 100 years, and CIE were anxious to modernise.

Class 87 No.87028 has arrived at Birmingham New Street on 6 September 1977 with the 15.10 service from London Euston. *Les Bertram*

1978

PART 1: OUT AND ABOUT AT HOME AND AWAY

Off at a gallop

THE New Year had hardly begun when I was out again. This time it was a tour of the level crossings in Liverpool, Birkenhead and the Wirral to examine the possibility of automation and unstaffing. I was met there by three colleagues, from the BRB S&T Level Crossing Section, the LM Region Chief Operating Superintendent's Office at Crewe, and the LM Region HQ at Euston, plus one of the Railway Inspectorate's Inspecting Officers. We toured around by minibus visiting level crossings, which were plentiful in that area, ending at Hoylake

where we all spent the night in the appropriately named Stanley Hotel (named in honour of Lord Stanley, not me). In view of a lack of inviting restaurants there, we took the electric train into

Below: Sutton Coldfield was home for the duration of the author's period in Birmingham and so the station there became very familiar. This view, taken on 7 August 1974, shows the station as the 08.08 service from Lichfield City to Birmingham New Street arrives. The train is formed of a three-car Derby set with No.M50833 leading. *Philip D. Hawkins*

Liverpool and had a meal in a Berni Inn. Very popular in those days, Berni Inns were the beginning of the dining-out revolution. Next morning we continued our visits, finishing with lunch, after which I went straight home to Sutton Coldfield. (We had not yet moved home, not wanting to do so until my second son had sat his 'A' Level exams in the spring/summer.)

An interesting diversion

As already mentioned, I had previously become chairman of the West Midlands section of the Chartered Institute of Transport after a stint as vice-chairman. There was quite a good following in the West Midlands by the 1970s and every year in January we held a one-day conference on a topical subject. This year it was

entitled 'Transport in the European Economic Community – Towards Europe'. These one-day conferences were very popular and would attract audiences of over 100 people. We had three very good speakers, covering the various forms of transport – road, rail and air – and the conference went off very well, so needless to say I was very pleased (and not a little relieved) especially as the national president was also there! It was pleasant to meet old colleagues and reminisce. My term of office did not finish until about Easter, so as I had to chair the meetings in Birmingham until then, I could spend more nights at home. HQ were very good about this, as they wanted to encourage senior railwaymen to represent the railway interest in the institute.

A general view of Swansea station taken on 5 April 1983 sees, on the left, Class 08 No.08898 shunting stock for the 17.15 service from Swansea to Milford Haven (including TPOs that will return as part of the 19.32 Milford Haven to Cardiff service), whilst HST No.253029 forms the 15.35 Swansea to Paddington and Class 47 No.47509 Albion awaits departure with the 15.21 Swansea to Paddington extra. *Stephen Miles*

Below: On 11 September 1979, a three-car DMU, with No.W50705 leading, approaches Milford Haven with the 11.15 service from Swansea. *Brian Morrison*

On 12 September 1981 Metro-Cammell two-car DMU Nos.M51179 and M56358 depart from Shrewsbury with the 16.43 service for Aberystwyth. *Brian Morrison*

Back and forth

The following Monday, I went straight from home to the former Webb Orphanage at Crewe to give the usual safety lecture on the course for Assistant Area Managers. I was there all day and came back home instead of going to London. My faithful old chauffeur, Barry, picked me up at New Street, a facility I still enjoyed courtesy of my friendly successor at Birmingham.

A couple of days later I took the sleeper to Milford Haven, which left Paddington at 00.50 and arrived at Milford Haven at 08.46. It was a beautifully crisp and clear day but with a bitter north wind. At that time, Milford Haven was a typical small port in West Wales, but I managed to find a café open, which was a relief. Then it was time for more road learning. I retraced my steps as far as Swansea on the 10.30 DMU, a fascinating journey and very enjoyable, and then on an HST to Cardiff, where I met an old colleague who was Divisional Operating Manager for South Wales, and we had a discussion about the signalling of the Central Wales line. Finally, it was back to Swansea to spend the night in the Grand Hotel, just opposite the station, with dinner at the hotel – it was another ubiquitous Berni.

The following morning, after a big breakfast of kippers, I caught the 09.59 DMU to Shrewsbury. The Assistant Area Manager at Llanelli met me, and travelled with me as far as Llandrindod Wells where we had lunch in a pub together. I carried on as far as Shrewsbury on the next train, and then it was back home again for the weekend.

The station at Llandrindod Wells on 19 July 1983 as the 12.27 service from Shrewsbury to Swansea enters the station. *B. Perryman*

To the Continent – an introduction to the UIC

BR was a member of the UIC – the Union Internationale des Chemin de Fer – which had its HQ in Paris. Historically it had dealt mainly with cross-border matters, such as through rates and fares, international train timings, etc, but it was now looking at standardisation and developments of common interest in technical and operating fields. A new UIC sub-committee had been formed to consider ways and means of working branch lines more economically instead of just closing them, and the BRB thought that it might be useful to be a member of this group to see if there was anything practical that we could adopt. Being the

On 16 February 1980 English Electric Type 3, Class 37, No.37190 waits to depart from Milford Haven with the 09.40 service to Swansea. The station buildings were subsequently demolished. *Stephen Miles*

The power signalbox at Feltham pictured on 28 August 1974. *J. Scrace*

A close-up, taken on 22 August 1974, of one of the five panels in the then new power signalbox at Feltham, showing the track diagram with its push buttons to operate signals and points. On the lower left is one of the CCTV monitors used to control level crossings, in this case one of those at Egham. The section of track directly in front of the signalman shows the line between Sunningdale and Ascot. *British Rail*

BRB's Signalling Officer, I was nominated to be that member, which over the next few years led to some very interesting meetings. The meetings were supposed to be held in the UIC offices in Paris, but my continental colleagues were having none of that nonsense, and every alternate meeting was held in a host country. That led to some very interesting gatherings! Eventually it would be our turn, but that was some time in the future.

Many European countries had joined this new sub-committee, and at my first meeting I met the delegates from DB (West Germany), DR (East Germany), SNCF (France), ÖBB (Austria), MAV (Hungary), CFF (Swiss), RENFE (Spain), SNCB (Belgium), NS (Netherlands) and NSB (Norway). The inclusion of a couple of railways from behind the Iron Curtain was interesting, but indicated the continuing pan-European influence of the UIC. The chairman of the group was Dr Büsch from DR, a splendid chap who clearly had not been brainwashed and was certainly not a card-carrying communist.

The official language for proceedings of the UIC was French, but owing to the number of German speakers in attendance, the meetings of our group were conducted in both French and German – not English. I had a working tourist-knowledge of both languages but certainly not enough to cope with a railway

meeting, so I took an interpreter with me. The BRB had an International Office that supplied interpreters for this purpose, and mine was an excellent chap who knew where all the best (but not too expensive) restaurants in Paris were, away from the tourist hot spots. It was a wonderful experience. We had the best beef bourguignon I have ever tasted. It was ladled out of a great big pot at the table – with wine, of course.

On the second day of the meeting an excellent lunch was provided at the UIC offices, and the table was awash with wine. I thought that this was really what the high life was all about, the continentals really lived it up, and I kept pinching myself to see if I was awake. After the meeting I met an S&T colleague at his hotel and we had dinner together – a very tasty cassoulet – and then it was home in a sleeper on the night ferry, first class of course, but not before the interpreter had taken me to a little parfumier whom he knew where I could get a little present for my wife Val that wouldn't break the bank.

What did the conference achieve? Very little, although the conference secretary (also from DR) produced a voluminous and very impressive report and recommended more meetings. I looked forward to them. As did Val, because it was the practice to take wives on meetings away from Paris. Watch this space!

Back to reality

After the usual safety lecture at Crewe on Monday, the following day I took the early train to London to spend a day in the office, catching up with the paperwork. I was out the next day, visiting signalboxes at Barnes, Feltham, Streatham and Victoria, escorted by the Southern Region's Signalling Officer. The following weekend there were reports of the worst snows in north-west Scotland for 20 years, and a train was trapped in a drift at Forsinard in the wilds of Caithness. The newspapers were full of dramatic stories of the rescue of the trapped passengers – no mobile phones in those days. This led directly to the development of RETB, the Radio Electronic Token Block system.

The birth of RETB

The next Monday I came home for an Institute meeting, but not before a good lunch in the mess washed down by a Sancerre. The Forsinard incident had really stirred up a hornets' nest and a meeting was hurriedly arranged at Preston with the Scottish

Region about the signalling communications north of Inverness that had been damaged in the recent snowstorm. Apparently, over 20 miles of overhead telegraph wires had been blown down and the hawks were saying that it was too expensive to replace them. If a cheaper alternative could not be found, the line would have to close.

This was undoubtedly my finest hour. It had occurred to me that if we could no longer send messages about the electric tablet signalling system by wire, why couldn't it be done by radio? Could the Railway Technical Centre at Derby develop some form of interface between a radio message and the tablet instruments in the signalboxes? But hey, could we bypass the token signalling system altogether and send a radio message directly to the train driver in his cab? Could we devise suitable safeguards? As a by-product, we would save all the staffing costs of the signalboxes. And so the electronic token was born. Instead of the driver being handed a physical tablet or token by the signalman, an electronic token would be sent to him through the ether by the signalman at a radio control centre to a receiving instrument in the driving cab. The instrument would display the 'from and to' of the electronic token.

The essential thing was that it had to be affordable, and if the procedures for receiving and giving up the electronic token by the driver and the signalman took a short while at each crossing point it was thought to be a small price to pay for keeping the line open. There was also a significant safety aspect to this. In the Forsinard incident, there was no means of knowing exactly where the train was stuck, as there was no communication with the driver. All that anyone knew was that the train had left one crossing point but had not arrived at the next one, and they were quite a few miles apart. With RETB, the driver would always have radio contact with the signalman, and it was a very useful by-product that helped with the Scottish Region's decision to keep the line open. In the meantime, a system of signalling was adopted as a stopgap, using post office telephones.

PART 2: LONG-WELDED RAILS AND BR HQ

The beginnings

The LMSR carried out trials with flat-bottom rails of the standard 60ft length before the Second World War. One such site was Cricklewood in 1936. The rails were laid on baseplates which had a type of bolt fastening at both sides of the rail to hold it firm, but the war put an end to such experiments. The railway companies resumed their trials with flat-bottom rail after the war, and 260 miles had been laid by the time of nationalisation in 1948.

After British Railways was formed following nationalisation, the new organisation decided almost at once that flat-bottom rail would be the new standard. The new rails, weighing 109 lb/yd, were considered to be much stronger than the 95 lb/yd bullhead rails and more suitable for higher speeds and heavier axle-loads.

Problems emerge

However, the mix of the two types of rail was not without problems. Saturday 8 August 1953 was a particularly warm and sunny day in the Scottish Lowlands. The Down 'Royal Scot' that day consisted of 13 coaches hauled by a Class 8 Pacific, No.46231 *Duchess of Atholl*, and was coasting down easily from Beattock

Stanier Pacific No.6231 *Duchess of Atholl* pictured at work during pre-Nationalisation days; this was the locomotive derailed at Abington on 8 August 1953. Ian *Allan Library*

Heading north over the sinuous curves of continuous welded rail, a BR Derby 'suburban' three-car DMU has just departed from the newly-opened station at University with a service for Birmingham New Street on 27 May 1978. *John Glover*

when it became derailed near Abington. A buckle had developed in the rail underneath the train, causing the last seven coaches to derail. Fortunately, there were no serious injuries. The derailment occurred only 30 yards beyond the end of a section of 113lb/yd flat-bottom rail, the heavier and stronger rails having been pressing against the weaker bullhead section, causing it to buckle. There had already been a number of incidents of this nature, and they continued to occur.

By the late 1960s, the use of flat-bottom rails on main lines had become common and the practice had developed of welding the ends together to form one continuous rail, known as CWR. The advantages are many. For example, joints between rails have always been a source of problems, as the track is less firm vertically at joints, causing 'wet spots' and rail end breakages. CWR is stronger and gives a smoother ride, and less maintenance is required.

Dealing with expansion

The expansive forces are contained in the rail itself, except for short portions at the ends which have special tapering joints. In order to contain the stresses of the expansive forces, a greater depth of ballast is required under the sleepers. The ballast must be extended sideways beyond the sleeper ends and extra ballast must be placed beyond the sleeper ends, creating a 'ballast shoulder'. Tight gripping rail fastenings must be used. Finally, the rails must be free from stress when they are in the mid-temperature range. This only became the standard after a bumpy learning curve and took some years. In the meantime, the track resembled an outdoor laboratory.

Stressing is a technique which is applied to track when it is laid and is intended to produce an absence of stress at a rail

temperature of 27°C. When track is laid at a temperature below that level it will have shortened through natural contraction and must be stretched to the length it would have been at 27°C. The stretching is done by hydraulic rams, and when the rail has been stretched it is welded to the adjacent rail. It is now under tension in a stressed condition and can safely contain the forces of expansion up to a rail temperature of 27°C, at which level it will be stress-free.

Experience

By 1968 there were 4,000 miles of CWR and considerable experience had been gained in handling the problems involved, but two accidents that year showed that things could still go wrong. On 12 June, a fine, dry day, the 12.40 freightliner 3E46 from Ardwick to Harwich became derailed on buckled track at speed near Berkhamsted in Hertfordshire. The area had been relaid the previous December but had not been stressed, the work having consisted of removing a redundant crossover and replacing it with new plain track. For various reasons, the stressing work was postponed and had still not been done before the date of the derailment.

The other derailment took place on the WCML at Auchencastle on the descent from Beattock summit two days later. It was another hot and sunny day, and a freightliner train running at 75mph became derailed when the track buckled beneath it. The track had been stressed in June 1967, but 170 sleepers had been changed in the weeks preceding the derailment, and on the Sunday before the derailment the track had been tamped, inducing incorrect stresses.

However, the learning process was still incomplete. In 1969 it was much worse. On 13 June an express passenger train travelling at nearly 80mph between Paignton and Paddington became derailed near Castle Cary, and ten days later the 'Tees-Tyne Pullman' from King's Cross to Newcastle was derailed at over 90mph on CWR near Sandy. In each case the driver saw the buckle as he approached it and casualties were light in both cases. In the same month there were two CWR derailments of freight trains at high speed.

The Chief Civil Engineer, under considerable pressure from both the public and railwaymen, immediately established an emergency programme to add extra ballast along the shoulders of the track. This was a large-scale operation and was given high priority by both engineers and operators. In addition to this, special precautions began to be taken in very hot weather to impose speed restrictions if rail temperatures rose over a certain limit. These measures were very successful, as the number of track buckles – only a few of which resulted in derailment – went down from 48 in 1969 to nine in 1970. By 1975, the mileage of CWR had increased to 8,000 and the state of the art of CWR maintenance had become very refined. After that there were only occasional lapses.

Lecture in progress, and days out

I seemed to be spending at least one day a week giving in-house lectures on safety and associated subjects, mainly at Webb House, Crewe, but also at The Grove, Watford. These were primarily to managers at various levels, but every so often there was something different. Traffic management trainees, now mainly from the universities, went to The Grove for four weeks to learn the Operating Rules and Signalling Regulations etc and I went along once a week to see how they were getting on and to have a nice lunch. They were all young and a bit brash, and I had to have my wits about me. They would pounce with glee on anything that wasn't spot on because they had yet to realise that life on the railway would be quite a change from life at university. A couple of Operating Inspectors were seconded to me for these courses, and soon knocked them into shape. They said that I would notice quite a change in the attitude of the students by the end of the last week, and I did. I was surprised to see four girls among them. In truth, I was astonished, as women on the railway at that time hardly ever progressed higher than secretary, except in some specialist departments, and certainly never in the Traffic Department where rough men used rude language. But I was very impressed with these girls. They came across as very sharp and it did not surprise me to see them rising rapidly up the promotion ladder.

Slightly down to earth a day or two later, I went visiting signalboxes on the Sussex coast with Gerald Summerfield, the Southern Region's Accidents & Signalling Officer. It was a bit of a swan really, with lunch in a nice little café near Littlehampton.

The Operating Committee had its next monthly meeting at Scunthorpe, a somewhat unlikely place, but the purpose was to see a demonstration of a radio communications system. Scunthorpe was, and still is, the centre of a large steelworks complex. After the evening meal we worked on until 10.45pm, the meeting finally finishing before lunch next day and I went off to Scotland, calling in at home on the way. The route was Grimsby, Lincoln, Nottingham and Sheffield to Sutton Coldfield, for a few hours at home, and then on the 23.50 sleeper from New Street to Glasgow.

A short Scottish safari

After being woken in my sleeper with a cup of tea, I got up and had breakfast in the station restaurant, after which I made my way through the busy Glasgow streets to the Scottish Region headquarters in Buchanan Street (next to the site of the cosy old station of the same name, which was the gateway to the excitements of the Highlands and brought back happy memories). At the offices, I met Andy McCaig, a true, braw

The carriage sidings at Craigentinny, Edinburgh, recorded on 19 April 1977, showing work in progress in upgrading the facilities. *G. A. Watt*

The interior of the new power signalbox at Edinburgh. *British Rail*

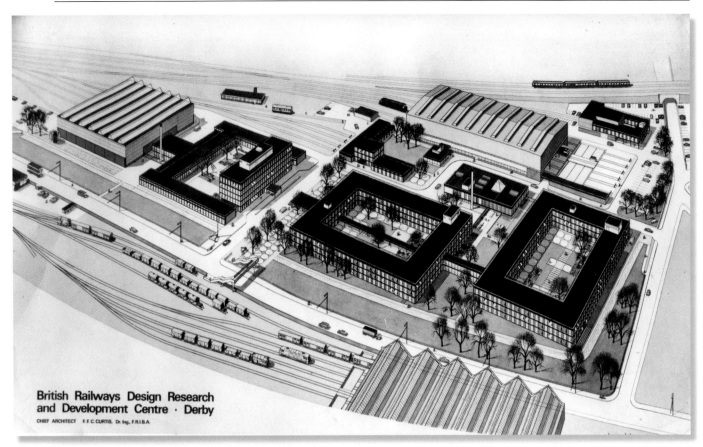

British Railways Design Research
and Development Centre · Derby

CHIEF ARCHITECT F.F.C.CURTIS, Dr. Ing., F.R.I.B.A.

Work in hand at the Railway Technical Centre on the development of computer simulation of trains. *Ian Allan Library*

The extensive facilities offered by the Railway Technical Centre at Derby. The facility originally dated from the early 1960s and was on such a scale that BR was able to claim that it was the 'largest railway research complex in the world'. This is an architect's drawing showing the expansion of the site. *British Rail*

was greatly to the credit of the impecunious BR that money had been found for it. Doing all the research in-house was much better than wasting millions on consultants from outside the industry. I went to a meeting there to discuss the design of the automatic warning system (AWS), my concern being with the signalling side of it. There was no question at that time of progressing to a more modern system of train control, which would have been slightly premature in any case, as large chunks of the Southern Region had yet to be equipped with the homespun AWS.

The meeting had attracted some big names, including the Head of the Research Section, the Assistant Chief S&T Engineer and the BRB Chief Traction Officer, John Powell, who had an office next to mine. Needless to say, we had a good lunch in their excellent facilities.

PART 3: LIFE AT THE BOARD

Official duties

My term of office as chairman of the West Midlands section of the Chartered Institute of Transport was coming to an end, but not before I had chaired a meeting at which the speaker was Frank Higgins, the chairman of the Transport Users' Consultative Committee. Whilst I was in Birmingham my old boss, John Pollard, had his retirement 'do', so I was able to go along and join in, and there were plenty of old cronies there, of course.

Level crossings again

Level crossings seemed to have been high on the agenda for ever, and I had an all-day meeting with Lt-Col Tony Townsend-Rose, one of the Railway Inspectorate's Inspecting Officers, on the

Scotsman. For starters, we had a cab trip to Dundee, visiting the signalling centre there before going on to see those at Perth and Cowlairs. The Scottish Region had carried out a lot of signalling modernisation. Next day we had a cab trip to Edinburgh to visit the new signalling centre and the new carriage servicing depot. Proud of all that the Scottish Region had achieved, Andy was anxious for me to have another visit, and sooner rather than later, and I looked forward to it. Being Friday, I came straight home from Glasgow Central to Sutton Coldfield on the 16.10 departure, travelling with the driver as far as Preston.

The Railway Technical Centre (RTC)

Built to bring together all the technical departments, the RTC at Derby had splendid facilities and a lot of pretty good boffins. At that time, the RTC was probably the best in the world, and it

One of the BR ferries allocated to the Harwich to Hook of Holland route from the mid-1970s was the *St Edmund*, seen here heading from Harwich on 14 May 1978. The *St Edmund* was to have a relatively short life in BR service as the ferry was requisitioned by the Ministry of Defence in 1982 and sent to the Falklands. The ship stayed in the South Atlantic until early 1983 and, on her return to home waters, was bought by the MoD and then served as HMS *Keren*, again largely in the South Atlantic, until the summer of 1985 when the erstwhile ferry was sold on for further service. *G. R. Mortimer*

subject, although I cannot now recall exactly what we discussed. Tony was a splendid fellow who had been involved in bomb disposal in his military career, and we got along very well, eventually having meals with our wives at our respective homes. It would now be regarded as fraternising with the enemy, and the close relationship he and I formed, both on the job and off it, would horrify some people today, but it worked because we respected each other's points of view and experience (and practical common sense). I cannot recall him ever asking for anything that was not fully justified, and site meetings with him were a joy. These were still the days of what I fondly remember as the 'grown-up railway'.

A European rail tour
This was about the last vestige of my time at Birmingham. Having discovered a member of staff who had been in the BR International Section but now worked at Wolverhampton, I asked him if he could organise a rail tour for the students on my Railway Operating course. He had all the right contacts and readily agreed, so we went ahead with the tour. Wives and girlfriends could come too, and he even arranged alternatives for those who would rather visit shops and cafés than marshalling yards and engine sheds.

Val and I travelled across from Harwich to the Hook of Holland in a two-berth cabin, and after a big breakfast on board we caught a train to Utrecht where we had a slide show and a visit to the signalbox. The tour had begun! Then it was off by

A member of my staff at Wolverhampton had organised a study tour of Swiss Railways for my Modern Railway Operating course. He obviously had good contacts. The tour began at Hook of Holland in April 1978, where NS No.1311 awaits departure. First stop Utrecht for a visit to the signalbox, then on to Amsterdam for lunch as guests of Dutch Railways. We had a very tasty buffet, then a visit to the carriage sidings. We were treated as honoured guests. Then overnight to Basel. *Author*

The modern Muttenz marshalling yard at Basel. It occupied a huge site and, like most such yards, it was quiet in the mornings. *Author*

This ingenious device, known as a Robotug, was fitted between the rails on each track, and its purpose was to follow the last wagon of a 'cut' along a siding, to ensure that they were all buffered-up. *Author*

The attractive concourse at Zurich station. *Author*

A spectacular trip up the Jungfrau. I'm standing with my back to the summit, but not really suitably clothed for mountaineering expeditions. *Author*

A beautifully turned-out, and massive, 4-8-2 steam locomotive at Zurich locomotive depot. Needless to say, the place was spotless. *Author*

A view along the Aletsch glacier from the some location. Later that year I was to view the glacier (and the Jungfrau) from the far end. *Author*

A view along the Upper Rhine valley from a train on the Lötschberg Line (the Bern-Lötschberg-Simplon) during an excursion. *Author*

train to Amsterdam for lunch as guests of the Dutch Railways, a very tasty Indonesian dish of rice, kebabs, pineapple rings, etc, which I can remember to this day. After that we visited the carriage sidings to see modern Dutch rolling stock at close quarters. The Dutch railway authorities treated us as honoured guests, and it was really very flattering. Then followed a canal tour where we saw 'ladies in windows', also at close quarters. Wives hastily covered their husbands' eyes! Finally, after profusely thanking our guides, we caught the 21.18 to Basel, with couchettes. My Wolverhampton friend was doing us proud so far. Was there no limit to his ingenuity?

We arrived at Basel at about 6am and went straight to our hotel, conveniently situated just outside the station. After breakfast, bearing in mind that this was an educational visit as well as just a holiday, we spent the morning at Muttenz marshalling yard, a huge modern affair and very impressive. Then it was back to the station for lunch, followed by a signalbox visit. On the following morning we went to Zurich by train and spent the morning at the locomotive depot. This was very interesting indeed and well organised. The depot was spotless, and the people there had even put on display for us outside the building a superbly clean 4-6-2 steam loco.

The afternoon was free, so most of us had a look round Zurich with our wives. Then, finally, we returned to Basel and our hotel. Those of us who had not yet had enough of railways for one day went to the station after dinner to see the international trains and the complicated shunting. Interestingly, the border of Switzerland and Germany cuts Basel station in two.

Next day the holiday began. We were up early for the 07.54 train to Interlaken on a beautiful sunny morning, from where we caught a narrow-gauge train to Kleine Sheidegg, with a superb view of the Jungfrau. The more adventurous (or wealthy?) went further, on the Jungfrau Railway, to the summit at 11,333ft above the clouds in a world of eternal snow and ice. The last four miles are in a tunnel inside the mountain. It was a wonderful experience and the views were absolutely stunning. Then it was back to Interlaken and time to go home.

We caught the 20.42 train to Paris, with couchettes again. After a couple of days on the loose in Paris, we finally made our way home. However, the excitement was not yet over. It snowed heavily (on 11 April!) between Boulogne and Calais and the telegraph wires were down, all the telegraph poles leaning over at crazy angles with the weight of snow. We therefore missed our planned sailing, but it had been a very enjoyable break – and educational too. I had learned quite a lot about Swiss railways and looked forward to the next visit.

Another UIC meeting in Paris

I accompanied Val on the boat across to Dover, then said *au revoir* and came straight back on the same boat and on to Paris for a two-day UIC meeting about reducing the cost of working branch lines and other secondary routes. They had not had the Beeching experience! I cannot recall exactly what the meeting was about,

A cable car up the Eggishorn, and a novel way in which to transport the rubbish lorry. *Author*

The view towards the Jungfrau along the Aletsch glacier. Once again, I wasn't dressed for mountaineering. *Author*

The UIC party (left to right) Herr and Frau Gerber; Herr Gerber was my opposite number on Swiss Railways, and he probably earned twice as much. The lady in front is the wife of the newly-retired Chief Operating Manager of Swiss Railways, who was taking the photograph, then the West German representative, then me. I can't recall who the others were. The Swiss were hugely hospitable. *Author*

The power signalbox at Motherwell. *British Rail*

On 30 September 1978 the 13.46 service from Stranraer to Glasgow Central departs from the loop at Dunragit. *S. J. Turner*

Above left, above, below left: What became known as 'Bridge Bashing' was becoming too prevalent for comfort (as in this incident at Oyne in Aberdeenshire), but the Department of Transport couldn't be prodded into action. The civil servants didn't seem to regard it as potentially very dangerous, even when faced with the evidence. *Author's collection*

Noises in driving cabs

I went to a meeting at Derby to sort out the various noise signals in driving cabs. These had traditionally been given mechanically, but now it was intended to reproduce them electronically, although to sound like the mechanical noises as far as possible. In addition to the AWS clear and warning sounds, there was the DVD (driver's vigilance device) and the fire alarm. We listened to a variety of electronic noises, which all sounded the same to me, but eventually, with a bit of fine-tuning, it was all sorted out and I was able to spend the night at home again, albeit with an early start next morning for the Signalling Committee meeting.

Off to Scotland again

It would seem that Scotland exercised an irresistible fascination for me, and a few days later I was on my way to Carlisle on the 08.10 from New Street, where I was met by a Traction Inspector by the name of Craigie for a cab trip over the mainly scenic G&SW Section to Glasgow. There I met another inspector, George McLellan, who took me to Motherwell power signalbox.

These outings did have a purpose. I was getting a feeling for the entire railway system and, more importantly, I was getting feedback from inspectors on matters of concern to them that I and the Signalling Committee might be able to do something

but it cannot have been very exciting. Eventually I came back to England in a sleeper on the night ferry and spent the next day in the office catching up. Then I finally went off home for the weekend.

Another industrial dispute

The late 1970s and early 1980s were a time when you got used to folks being on strike, with railwaymen being in the vanguard as usual. I was still living at Sutton Coldfield and was unable to get back to London as the signalmen on the line to Euston were having a one-day strike. However, I was able to get to Paddington, as the loyal Great Western men were at work as usual.

I left King's Cross in 1963, but I couldn't resist including this splendid shot of 'Deltic', Class 55, No.9005 *The Prince of Wales's Own Regiment of Yorkshire* taken in May 1973, 10 years later. The old signalbox was still in use, but its new replacement can be seen peeping over the top of the cab. *I. J. Hodson*

about. It was particularly important for me to hear about any safety concerns. The local Regional people were quite happy for me to make my own arrangements about where I went and when, and provided me with the necessary inspectors (as well as fixing up overnight accommodation). I was careful never to make visits without telling them first. These trips were not inspections, and sometimes my Regional colleagues came along as well. They too liked an excuse to get out of the office and away from the demanding telephone.

After a night in a hotel I had a DMU cab trip with George McLellan from Glasgow to Stranraer and back, pausing at Ayr for a while. The weather was perfect – clear and sunny – and I felt almost like a tourist. After tea I spent the evening with George in Glasgow Central power signalbox. The RTC boffins were making the first very tentative steps towards automating the route setting and signalling of some of the more repetitive train movements, although it has to be said that the signalmen were not particularly impressed. They asked how a computer could replicate the human brain with all the thousands of individual decisions that the signalmen made each day. It may have seemed unlikely at the time, but in a very few years it was happening.

The following morning, 26 April, was also fine and sunny, so after kippers for breakfast I had another DMU cab trip, to Edinburgh via Shotts, not one of the more well-known routes between the two cities. A quick lunch was followed by the *pièce de résistance*, a cab trip in a 'Deltic' as far as York. By then fatigue had taken over, so I spent the rest of the journey to King's Cross in the train. Then after a snack in a pizzeria, it was off to the Staff Training College at The Grove in Watford for the night (after a refreshing beer with the students!).

Lectures and level crossings
One of my old colleagues from the Birmingham days was at The Grove, where I gave the usual safety lecture again.

These lectures were very good for the opportunity they provided for vital feedback from Area Managers from all over the country. I needed to know what concerns senior managers had about safety of operations, and we had some very fruitful discussions.

There being no rest for the wicked, I then hot-footed it to the Department of Transport for an afternoon meeting with the Railway Inspectorate about level crossings. Level crossings were then very much a current interest, because there were policy decisions to be taken about changes, and how the instructions regarding equipment and methods of operation were to be altered. This followed from a major review over the previous year or so, and the standards that were set following that review are still largely in being. After all that, I finally went home to Sutton Coldfield, where my wife met me at the station.

A new house at last
Domestic matters were also of some importance. On Saturday, Val and I went to Reading to have a look at the houses on our shortlist in that area, and after much mulling over during the next few days we settled on the one we liked, at Tilehurst, five minutes' walk from the station, which had a good HST morning service. It was £39,000, which was £8,000 more than we expected to get for our house at Sutton Coldfield. However, we felt that we could afford it with my salary increase. A railwayman in those days needed an understanding wife! Thank goodness I had one.

Signal Engineers and Inspecting Officers
The buying and selling process got pretty hectic towards the end, and it was a relief to be taken out to lunch by no less a person than the Chief S&T Engineer and Ken Hodgson, his No.2. Also there was Freddie Rose, properly known as Major Rose, one of the Railway Inspectorate's Inspecting Officers. In my job I was the chief contact in the Operating Department for the Signal Engineers, and a great deal of my time was taken up in meetings,

discussions, site visits, etc with them and Inspecting Officers. It was one of the most enjoyable parts of the job. The Inspecting Officers, all five of them, were all ex-Royal Engineers and were down-to-earth, practical men who never made unreasonable demands. Yes, it was still the 'grown-up railway'.

I revisit old haunts

I had to go back to Yorkshire for a family funeral, so naturally I went in the cab of the 14.45 from King's Cross to Leeds (Val having gone earlier). I had made prior arrangements to have a look at some signalboxes in the area, so I met two former colleagues who took me on a tour, starting with Leeds power signalbox, and then on to Keighley, where I had started work on the old LMSR in 1943, and finally on a nostalgic visit to Bingley manual signalbox, where I had spent so many hours as a young clerk anxious to learn all about signalling. It was 'All Our Yesterdays' writ large.

PART 4: INTERESTING PROSPECTS

A diet of level crossings

It was beginning to look as though level crossings were going to be quite a part of my life now. I spent a day in the York area with a colleague of many years' standing, Ken Appleby, who showed me a selection of the various types of level crossings in and around York. We had a very pleasant day together, complete with a lunch of smoked mackerel and salad in a country pub. Much better than being in London!

Junction signalling

This was another area of railway operations where changes were taking place. Now that the Civil Engineer was able to provide high-speed facing junctions, it was necessary to provide certain information to a driver to enable him to take full advantage of this. We had to bear in mind that the signals still needed to show the driver which way the points were set at a junction, so that he could reduce speed appropriately over the points leading to the diverging line if they were set that way. We still had to be able to show red, one yellow, two yellows and green in the normal way. And much depended on the difference in speeds at the points over the diverging line and over the main line. (There is more on this subject in Part 1 of the 1979 chapter.)

British railway signalling is based on the 'route signalling' principle, in which the signals indicate to the driver which way

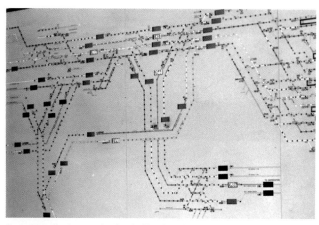

Part of the display panel at Leeds City signalbox, showing the train describer indicators that are controlled by the computer situated six floors below. *British Rail*

the junction is set. It is then up to him to pass through the junction at the laid-down speed. Continental signalling, which tends to be more complicated, is based on the 'speed signalling' principle, where the signal indications tell the driver the speed at which he should pass through the junction, provided the line ahead is clear.

The Eastern Region was proposing to introduce a new arrangement based on the use of flashing yellow aspects at Hitchin in the Down direction, so a site meeting was held there to discuss the detailed arrangements. A few days later we took the union reps (ASLEF and NUR) there to explain to them what was involved, and my notes indicate that it was a successful morning. This was followed some days later by a meeting at York Regional HQ with my opposite number, George Wood. He treated me to a lunch in a half-timbered café near the minster. George was very good to work with, as were all my opposite numbers in the Regions. It all helped to oil the wheels.

Level crossings again

The following day I attended a meeting at St Christopher's House in Southwark with the DoT people, including the Railway Inspectorate and various highway engineers, to discuss the proposed arrangements concerning highway level crossings. Much of the input into the new regulations came from the

The crossing at Nether Poppleton is situated to the north-west of York on the line towards Harrogate. *Author*

On 20 October 1979 a Newcastle-Middlesbrough DMU passes over the level crossing at Boldon. *Ian S. Carr*

On the suburban lines north from King's Cross, CCTV cameras and large mirrors are being erected to enable drivers of trains without guards to check that all is in order for the train to depart. *Author*

Department's Highway and Traffic Engineers because they were the experts so far as road traffic was concerned. Quite rightly, it was not left to the railway authorities to take decisions about road vehicle drivers and the precise wording of notices on the road approach to level crossings. I had lunch there with a lot of civil servants.

I met the DoT's Inspecting Officers again at the six-monthly meeting, held at the rather posh Great Western Royal Hotel at Paddington. This was a top-level affair, with the Board member for Operations present and several heads of Engineering Departments. I was just the office boy. I recorded that we had 'a very nice lunch, with wine and cigars etc', but I'm not sure what 'etc' included.

Interesting days out

My chairmanship of the West Midlands section of the Chartered Institute of Transport was not quite over, and our annual outing that year was to the car factory at Cowley in Oxford. My abiding memory of the visit was how bored and bolshie all the car workers looked, and the atmosphere was distinctly unfriendly.

We visited Blenheim Palace in the afternoon, but it rained all day, which literally put a dampener on the proceedings.

On the following Saturday I had another interesting day out. The railway authorities had declared that day to be a free day for all senior railcard holders, presumably to publicise railcards, so Val and I decided to take my mother to Colwyn Bay for the day. We travelled in a declassified first-class, air-conditioned coach all the way there and back. The entire railway system was heaving with people – I had never seen so many since wartime. Fortunately, it was sunny at Colwyn Bay, and my mother, then aged 78, loved it.

Off to the Manchester area

It was time to have a detailed look at the modern signalboxes in the Manchester area, and I visited Wilmslow, Piccadilly and Victoria East and West. I had lunch with Peter Rayner, the DOS, who was certainly a most congenial host. He was a laugh a minute, and very good company. Peter had a gift for getting on well with people and was very popular with the trade unions.

The Signalling Committee visits the North-West

We all met at Liverpool Lime Street station and had a tour of the new underground system, and in the afternoon we went on to Crewe for the meeting, which was held in the Royal Hotel where we spent the night. During the afternoon we had a look at a new design of the Temporary Speed Restriction (TSR) warning board, and later our hosts pushed the boat out and took us for a splendid dinner at a country pub. I had one of my favourites at the time, Tournedos Rossini, but we had to stay reasonably alert because we wanted to see the new TSR warning boards in the dark, which was well after 10pm, indeed, nearer 11pm.

London Transport Executive (LTE) involvement

At HQ level we had very little involvement with London Underground, except at the extremities of the semi-surface lines where LTE trains gain access to their terminal platforms. However, there was day-to-day contact on current operational matters, where close co-operation was normal practice.

One of their officers, Leo Armstrong, came to one of the regular monthly meetings of the Signalling Committee and afterwards invited me to accompany him on a visit to the LTE Control Rooms near Euston, which dealt with the Victoria and Northern lines. I was very impressed with the slickness of the working. Afterwards, we had lunch in a nearby pub to have a chat about railway affairs in general.

PART 5: LIFE GETS EXCITING

Moving day

On Monday 14 August at long last we were off to our new home at Tilehurst, after living in Sutton Coldfield for eight years. And we were leaving a garden full of produce. The furniture men arrived at 8.45am and were finished by 12.45pm. We walked round the rooms that were now empty yet were full of memories, but we were soon on our way south to Oxford, where we spent the night. Next morning we motored leisurely to Reading and

The signalbox at Manchester Piccadilly shown when new in 1960. Notice the integration in construction between the new box and the existing arches. *British Rail*

The scene at Liverpool Lime Street station on 3 July 1980 with Class 47 No.47404 departing with the 15.05 service for York. *David Flitcroft*

Class 508 EMU No.508043 is seen on a Garston to Kirkby working at Liverpool Central on 22 November 1982. *Mel Bryan*

During a UIC visit to East German Railways, a day trip was organised for the delegation up the narrow gauge steam railway to Oberwiesental, right on the Czech frontier. *Author*

A deviation via Prague on the way home. A celebrated view of Wenceslas Square. *Author*

A DB (West German railways) Class 111 electric locomotive rests between duties at Nuremberg. I took this photo when on a trip through Germany in 1976. *Author*

collected the key to our new home, 25 Elsley Road, Tilehurst. The previous occupants had left carpets almost everywhere, so settling in was reasonably easy, and I had a week off work to allow plenty of time to do so.

Back to work

I walked to the station (seven minutes) for the 07.47 train to Paddington, and was surprised to find that about 100 passengers joined it. I was in the office exactly an hour later, including the walk (or Tube) from Paddington. I spent the rest of the week in the office, dealing with the paperwork that had piled up. The following week I had an interesting little diversion with various level crossing people, having a look in the dark at some level crossing warning boards with various reflective surfaces on the Southminster branch near Wickford. As this was August we had to wait quite a while for darkness, but we all spent the night in a nearby hotel and didn't get to bed until 2am.

Another exciting UIC conference in prospect

On Sunday 3 September, I set off for East Germany and Czechoslovakia for another UIC committee meeting, crossing the channel from Dover to Calais on a calm sea in time-honoured style and arriving in Paris at about 7.30pm. The big trains of the SNCF seemed to run more smoothly than ours. I was not travelling alone this time, as both my wife and younger son had insisted on coming with me to share whatever goodies and delights there might be. We also intended to stay on for a few days after the conference in order to explore East Germany, and then return home via Prague, staying there for a few days. The next stage of the journey was on the Prague express, leaving

Paris at 23.20. We had couchettes, two in a compartment, but the train was very busy and young people were sleeping in the corridor. We rose next morning at about 7.30am, somewhere between Mainz and Frankfurt, and had a frugal breakfast of coffee and rolls in a rather bare buffet car which was not doing much business.

We changed at Nuremberg into a through train at 11.10 from Stuttgart to Görlitz, which took us through to Karl-Marx-Stadt (Chemnitz), our ultimate destination, in East Germany. We had reserved seats again, and at the border between West and East Germany there was the usual parade of border officials, but they were courteous as always to first-class passengers and seemed quite relaxed. There was no buffet car on this train and I had to nip out at Reichenbach station to see what refreshments I could find. This was my first taste of East German frugality, but I managed to find some milk and biscuits!

We arrived at Karl-Marx-Stadt at 17.21 and walked to our hotel, as there was quite a queue for taxis. The town, drab and grey, had been heavily bombed in the Second World War and rebuilt in utility form, but the Hotel Kongress, into which Dr Büsch had booked us, was a very modern, four-star, multi-storey hotel designed for western visitors. We were met by Dr Kühn, his secretary, and escorted to our rooms, which were of a modern international style. Later, we had a stroll round the town, but it seemed odd with no neon advertising signs, and the traffic was very light (so no problems crossing the road). This was our first experience of East Germany, and we found political slogans everywhere on banners in big red letters. We ventured into a bookshop, only to find that most of the books seemed either to be about Marx, Engels and Lenin or attacked fascists, capitalists and imperialists. Among the more notable features of the town were the open spaces with flowerbeds and fountains.

Tuesday 5 September

At breakfast with Dr Büsch and the Swiss representative there was an impressive array of cold meats and cheeses. Whilst Val, greatly daring, ventured out into the town, I went off to my meeting. There were delegates from East Germany, West Germany, Belgium, The Netherlands, Italy, Spain, Switzerland and Hungary. My son Tony went off to try to find Colditz (but did

not manage it). The series was probably on TV at the time. In the evening all the delegates, plus hangers-on, went to the splendid opera house – they were big on culture in East Germany. We were shown to the best seats in the dress circle (and yes, the audience were generally very well dressed too) and we saw a sparkling performance of *Boccaccio*. It was colourful and extremely well done and, of course, all in German, which I had some difficulty with, but the music was delightful. We did feel a bit of a fool when the audience laughed uproariously at a joke while we just sat there stony-faced or pretending to laugh.

Wednesday 6 September

This was 'excursion day' – there was always one during a UIC meeting – and a coach picked us all up and took us to a place called Hammer to see an old hammer worked by a waterwheel. Then there was a trip on a narrow-gauge steam railway right along the Czech frontier to Oberwiesenthal, followed by a cable-car trip to the Fichtelberg – a mere 3,985ft high. Here we had a splendid meal in the restaurant, with plenty of wine, followed by coffee and brandy. I made a little (carefully rehearsed) speech in German, thanking the chairman for his hospitality to Val, which went down very well. Tony had gone off on his own again and had got as far as Leipzig, managing not to get locked up. Fortunately, he could speak schoolboy German.

Thursday 7 September

The sub-committee worked in a desultory fashion for a couple of hours before we all broke up and went our respective ways. I cannot imagine that we achieved much, but no one seemed concerned. That was the end of railway affairs for us, and we went off to spend the next three nights in Dresden, which was extremely interesting and an experience. We came home via Prague (known as Praha by those who live there) and spent three nights there too. A feature of Prague is the River Vltava and the palace on the hill opposite. It was also a town full of bookshops, and people with sad, straight faces, and there was also a shortage of little cafés.

So after a very interesting visit to towns and cities behind the Iron Curtain we set off homewards, travelling on the 11.06 through train to Paris. There was, however, one more bit of

From Prague it was not very far to West Germany, the first station beyond the border being Schirnding, which was greeted with a sigh of relief. *Author*

excitement in store. When we reached the border with West Germany the train came to a stand in a sort of compound surrounded by barbed wire and full of machine-gun-toting guards. They searched every nook and cranny on the train, and underneath too, trying to find anyone foolhardy enough to try to escape to the West, but after a while they put the train together again and we set off for civilisation. We stopped at the first station in West Germany, just a halt really, so that our steam engine could be detached and sent back home, after which we relaxed and headed for the restaurant car. We had sleeper berths on this train too, all organised by the BR International Section, which had also supplied me with an interpreter for the stay in Karl-Marx-Stadt, East German Railways having made all the travel and hotel arrangements etc. Our stay behind the Iron Curtain had been quite an experience, and, notably, we had never felt unsafe.

Back to the grindstone again

After a couple of weeks away there was a considerable amount of work waiting, which occupied me for the next week or two, and I had to concoct some sort of story to describe what the UIC sub-committee had got up to. Dr Büsch would circulate a report in due course.

PART 6: A VARIED AGENDA

More lecturing

The monthly Signalling Committee meeting was held on the morning of Wednesday 4 October. This was the main BR Signalling Committee, on which the Signalling Officers from each Region were represented and where all questions of policy were discussed and any changes agreed. Any major policy changes that the committee proposed were submitted to the Board's main Operating Committee, but any such changes would have been discussed with the Regions previously to iron out any areas of dissent.

Following a buffet lunch I went off to the Staff Training College at Watford to give the usual lecture, highlighting lessons learnt and changes proposed. I always enjoyed these events because invariably there was a stimulating debate about the issues raised. Notably, Chris Green, the Chief Operating Manager of the Scottish Region, was the course leader. This was followed by drinks and dinner, and I was very late home.

More level crossings

With level crossings still being one of the main topics of the time, a number of changes were proposed in the various types of equipment and systems, resulting from in-depth studies and

discussions over many months. It was now necessary to compile the new standards in the form of the document entitled 'Railway Construction and Operation Requirements – Level Crossings', which was published by the DoT in 1981.

It has to be said that the gestation period of the new Requirements was a long one, but within the DoT itself several sections were involved, especially the Highway and Road Traffic Divisions. It always has to be remembered that railway level crossings were (and still are) of great interest to those Divisions also, and they provided considerable input. It was not for BR Safety Officers to concern themselves with highway engineering and road traffic matters, nor to consider how the drivers of road vehicles might behave in various circumstances or how much guidance should be given and how it should be conveyed. In that respect, the Railway Inspectorate took the initiative from those Divisions, but we often had meetings with them to thrash out the small print in the new Requirements, as they were referred to. In effect, the Requirements were legal documents, which was why they did not appear until 1981.

Below: On 2 June 1978 a four-car DMU set, comprising a Metro-Cammell two-car unit coupled to a two-car Derby unit, is pictured leaving Llandecwyn and crossing Traeth Bach. The train is the 08.22 from Dovey Junction to Pwllheli. *Brian Morrison*

Detailed and thorough consideration of matters such as these required protection from interference, and I quietly developed the practice of hopping on to an HST from Paddington to Weston-super-Mare and back, to be sure of having several hours of careful study fully immersed in the subject and interrupted only by the steward keeping the coffee cup filled up. Not many people have access to such a useful facility, and so far as my secretary was concerned, I was 'learning the road'.

'Genuine' road learning

I was anxious to learn more about peak-hour driving conditions in the London suburban area of the Southern Region. Following a modest lunch at Waterloo I met the Region's Chief Traction Inspector for a spell of cab-riding in the area. I found that such staff were always keen to help if you were genuinely interested and wanted to learn, so I spent a very interesting few hours, finishing at Charing Cross at 7pm. The Southern's suburban service, a very slick operation indeed, had been refined over many years, and I was impressed by the skills of the drivers in anticipating traffic conditions ahead and in driving on double yellows (preliminary caution). Station stops were a joy to watch. Remember, those were the days of slam-door stock. Drivers would enter stations at some speed, stop on a sixpence, passengers were already leaping out, and closing the doors after them, and

The 09.34 summer Saturdays service from Birmingham to Pwllheli, formed of a refurbished West Midlands PTE DMU, awaits departure from Machynlleth on 3 June 1978. *Dr E. W. Fellows*

then it was 'ding-ding' from the guard and away on full throttle. Brilliant! It couldn't be done today, with sliding-door stock and drivers terrified to put a foot wrong.

A week later, I had a cab ride from King's Cross to York and back to experience night-time conditions at 125mph and to familiarise myself as much as possible with the demands of the driver's job, especially in different parts of the country. It was quite exciting, hurtling along in the pitch darkness with only that little green light up ahead to help you (plus AWS, of course). The recognised limit for trains without cab signalling was to become 125mph. In any case, braking potential was at the limit at 125mph, based on the braking distance normally available from the signal spacing at that speed.

RETB again
As mentioned earlier, Radio Electronic Token Block had been developed in response to the need to devise a cheaper form of signalling to avoid the north Highland lines from being closed following many miles of severe damage to the overhead pole route as a result of a snowstorm and blizzard. Its success led to a further potential application on the Cambrian line from Shrewsbury to Aberystwyth and Pwllheli. A site visit was called for, and was held on 30 November and 1 December. Not the most auspicious time of the year for such a project, but it couldn't wait for several months, and it was just an exploratory meeting at this stage. We were a small group – a couple of S&T chaps, my opposite number from Crewe, and me.

Our main interest in level crossings (of which there were plenty on this route) was to enable us to judge whether this scheme was likely to be a potential winner. At each level crossing on a public road we had to decide whether it should have half-barriers and be converted to an AHB (Automatic Half Barrier) crossing (very expensive, and to be avoided if possible), or to one of the new AOCLs (Automatic Open Crossing Locally Monitored) as specified in the yet-to-be-authorised Requirements. AOCLs were looked upon with favour by the Inspectorate and ourselves, as enabling long, winding, single lines with lots of crossings to survive. They were fine in the traffic conditions of 30 years ago, but recent experience of misuse by road users has brought their suitability into question. The more difficult crossings were farm crossings (ie private crossings), some of which had telephones to a nearby signalbox so that users could phone up to see whether it was safe to cross, or they relied on a very good sight line of approaching trains.

There was snow on the hilltops and it was very picturesque but cold. We spent the night at the Wynnstay Hotel in Machynlleth, and dined on beef bourguignon washed down by a

bottle of Beaujolais as recompense for the rigours of the day. The next morning was also bitterly cold, but the sun was shining and we visited several crossings in the area (the LMR had provided a car for the four of us) before deciding that there was indeed an excellent case for proceeding with RETB and modernising the level crossings, which happened in due course. Now, things have come full circle, this line having again been selected as a guinea-pig, but for the more sophisticated and considerably more expensive ERTMS (European Rail Traffic Management System), which has recently been installed.

Living it up
Friday 8 December was the occasion of the six-monthly meeting between the five Railway Inspecting Officers from the Railway Inspectorate and the BRB chief officers, headed by Jim Urquhart, the Board member for Operations. I was the office boy. The meeting was held, as usual, in the Great Western Royal Hotel at Paddington followed, as one would expect on such an occasion, by a good meal, washed down with wine and finished off with brandy. It would have been out of the question to have treated the Inspectorate with anything else.

Nemesis strikes at Preston Park
A few days later, on 14 December, we had a serious accident on the Southern Region when one EMU ran into the back of another at Preston Park, near Brighton, killing four people. I had a quick trip to Waterloo in order to obtain full details so that I could inform the chief officers the next morning. The circumstances were as follows. The 21.50 EMU from Victoria to Brighton had come to an involuntary stand as a result of the power having been switched off. A 73-year-old woman, drunk, had alighted from a train and started to walk along the track, so the Electrical Control Office had switched off the live rail. Power was restored just as the second train, the 21.40 from Victoria to Littlehampton, came along and ran into the stationary 21.50 at almost full speed. Three passengers were killed, together with the driver of the 21.40. The signalling system had not yet been provided with AWS.

The signal protecting the stationary train should have been showing a red aspect. However, the light had failed, and the driver of the 21.40 failed to realise that there was something amiss. In modern signalling installations, the failure of a light in one signal will automatically switch to red the next signal in rear, but the scheme under which the signalling had been modernised many years previously did not provide such safeguards. The driver of the second train would have received a yellow signal some distance in rear of the 21.50, but he failed to reduce speed to be able to stop at the red signal ahead (which, in any event, was unlit – but he should have been aware of its approximate location from his familiarity with the route).

The Inspecting Officer who held the inquiry wrote in his report that it would never be known why the driver of the second train failed to reduce speed after passing the yellow signal. The report also contained an extensive examination of the reasons why the Southern Region had not yet installed the standard AWS on this important route. In simple terms, the Region had spent several fruitless years in trying to devise an AWS system more suited to its needs, but it was found to be three times more expensive than the standard system and ultimately had to be abandoned on cost grounds. There was then a lot of catching up to be done. But while the Southern was engaged in its quest for the holy grail it was completely unprotected, and suffered a few more accidents in the meantime. The Board should have stepped in earlier and laid down the law, but the Southern always regarded itself as distinct from other railways, rather like the Western. However, the signalling on the Brighton line was subsequently modernised, and AWS was provided.

1979

PART 1: I BECOME A FILM STAR

A new career beckons

THE Director had asked me how we were going to launch this new suite of level crossings and sell it to the public, the trade unions and the DoT (which would have to help with the funding). He suddenly had a brainwave and suggested that I should make a film to illustrate the way that the new level crossings operated and pointing out the benefits. We discussed this and concluded that I could demonstrate in the film how the crossings worked not only so far as the road user was concerned but also, and this was possibly more important, how they appeared to the train driver, as we needed them on our side.

BR still had a very good and highly regarded film unit, British Transport Films, but it was short of funding like everyone else and would welcome some work if it were paid for. I discussed the project with the unit and it jumped at the idea. So, on 12 January, the big adventure began. The plan was to find a couple of crossings of each type, and we visited several potential sites around Wimbledon, Egham and Maidenhead. At each crossing we did a film of the crossing being used with the gates/barriers open to the road and no train involved. The film unit people had a vehicle for all their equipment, and I had a car and a driver whose job it was to drive over the crossing just as normal with no train coming. Then there was a second take, with a train

Below: On 20 July 1978 two DMUs stand at Bourne End as commuters to London board. Until 4 May 1970 Bourne End was a through station with services heading northwards to High Wycombe as well as the branch to Marlow; although the latter remains, the former is now but a distant memory. *John Glover*

coming, which required quite a bit of co-operation with the signalman so that we could achieve a situation where the car approached the crossing just as the lights began to flash.

Acting came into it at miniature warning light crossings, where the road user has to open the gates, so again I took on the role of road user and went through all the procedures. I learnt later that the actors' union Equity had complained that the BTF film unit was using non-Equity members, but I cannot now recall if I became an honorary member. Anyway, we had a profitable day, finishing just before it snowed. But there was a lot more to

do yet. On 14 January, with a couple of inches of snow still on the ground, we did some more filming on the Marlow branch, which caused quite a stir among the local populace, and then it was back to the BTF film studio to see the 'rushes', which I think is what they call all the film runs that have been taken. Eventually, all the best bits have to be put together to make a continuous story.

ASLEF then held another one-day strike, so as it was impossible for me to get to Paddington, I went out by car and visited three crossings in the Guildford area to see if they were

On 13 October 1979 the 12.13 Maidenhead-Marlow DMU approaches the recently installed 'automatic open' level crossing at Furze Platt.
N. A. Hunt

suitable subjects. Val came too, to see what I was getting up to (she didn't really believe that I was actually filming). We had lunch in Debenhams and no doubt did a bit of shopping too. A couple of days later, ASLEF went on another one-day strike, but it was pointless as it had snowed very heavily and few trains could have run anyway.

The following Monday, 22 January, I spent in the BTF film unit studio, putting everything together and doing a practice commentary to accompany the film. No, we weren't going to hire a professional commentator – we couldn't afford it!

One way to escape the snow

There was no snow in Paris, which was where I was going for a routine UIC signalling committee meeting, but first I had to get there. I managed to get to London, but nearly all the trains on the Southern had been cancelled due to ice on the conductor rails. However, they managed to produce a train to Folkestone – three EMUs pulled by a diesel! I went straight on to the *Hengist*, a Sealink ship, and was away almost at once for a smooth crossing. The boat train was waiting at Calais, and I had a very smooth ride to Paris. I checked into my hotel and went for dinner at the nearby restaurant Le Fouquet, dining on pilau de rognons (kidneys) au Madère. *The Sunday Times* had been running an article about bijou but inexpensive restaurants in the Notre Dame area, so this was my first one, and it was good.

The committee meeting did not begin until after lunch, so I spent a very cold morning visiting the Arc de Triomphe and the Champs Élysées, and going halfway up the Eiffel Tower (the top half was closed). We all met in the afternoon, but it must have been a boring meeting as I can recall nothing other than that my interpreter, Mrs Cross, was very efficient. In the evening, I tried out another *Sunday Times* recommendation – Chez Fauré near the Tuileries – and this time I had sauté de lapin (rabbit) à la Ménagère.

There was an all-day meeting next day, after which I went to the Gare du Nord, bought four bottles of wine, had a meal and retired to my sleeper on the night ferry for another smooth crossing. I arrived home to be greeted by fog, frost, ice and snow. It was one of the worst winters for quite a few years.

Train fires

It was back to work on Monday, sliding all over the place on black ice. I received a phone call to say that the class on a course I was enrolled on had been cancelled that evening, as the caretaker was on strike. The following day I went to York for a meeting with my opposite number there about radio and got back home at 9pm. I was late home the following evening too, being delayed for an hour near Maidenhead by a fire on the preceding train. There are no details about it in the Railway Inspectorate's annual report, so it must have been a minor affair.

A couple of weeks later there was a much more serious fire on a train near Tilehurst, when the 18.41 HST from Paddington to Swansea hit two lengths of rail at 65mph just beyond Reading. There was no derailment, but the fuel tank underneath the leading power car was split and the contents caught fire. Before the train could be stopped the three leading coaches were enveloped in flames, although they rapidly died out. Several passengers leapt out from the leading offside door, needing no notices to tell them how to do so. It was a very frightening experience for the passengers in those front coaches, but the flames did not penetrate the interiors and no one was injured.

Junction signalling

Here was another holy grail – the attempt to find a foolproof signalling system that would enable a diverging route at a junction to be taken at the design speed of the track. It was not an issue for many years, when junctions were commonly negotiated at 15-20mph or occasionally slightly more, but as track technology enabled junctions to be taken at substantially higher speeds the problem arose of how to tell drivers that they were being routed on to the diverging line (which they were normally expecting in any case), leaving it to the driver to control the speed of his train so that the junction was taken at its design speed with minimum loss of speed. The critical and vital issue was how to ensure that the driver actually did reduce speed.

At that time, in the late 1970s, the only means of doing so was through the signalling system (the problem was confined to colour-light areas). For years, when a diverging route was set the junction signal was maintained at red until the train had reached a position at which it was calculated that its speed would have been safely reduced. The junction signal would then clear, and the row of white lights would appear, signifying the route for which the points were set.

Over quite a short period, junction speeds rose considerably, even up to 90-100mph in some cases. The driver then needed to be told some distance away which route had been set, and indeed that it had been set. At an approach speed of possibly 125mph, that information needs to be given at least two signal sections away, and a system of 'flashing yellows' was devised. The sequence of signals that a driver would see when the junction was set for the diverging route would then be as follows:

> Two signals from the junction – double yellow, flashing;
> One signal from the junction – single yellow, flashing;
> Junction signal – steady single yellow.

The junction signal would then clear to green (if the line ahead was clear) at a predetermined point at which it was assumed that the driver had braked to the junction speed.

If that all sounds complicated, it has to be said that the drivers took to it very quickly and with no problems. But there were other problems where bridges etc interfered with the driver's view of the junction signal. Didcot was a case in point, where trains for the Oxford direction were firstly diverted from the Down Main line on to the adjacent and parallel Down Relief line, and then diverted again on to the Oxford line. I travelled out with the driver to see this in action, and it worked beautifully, with no unnecessary loss of speed. The Regions were all enthusiastic, and submitted their proposals and locations. A programme was then drawn up and implemented in due course. But junction signalling will be a problem until we no longer have to rely on lineside signals, and that must await full implementation of ERTMS.

PART 2: IS HE NEVER IN?

A two-day outing back to Yorkshire

On Monday 26 March, I caught the 09.00 from King's Cross to York where I was met by my Regional opposite number, George Wood. After lunch we inspected a number of level crossings between York and Malton on the line to Scarborough, ending the day at Kirkham Abbey. I had not appreciated just how many level crossings there were on this line, especially if farm crossings were included, but it was one of the earliest lines to be built, when there was very little opposition to level crossings. Most were very suitable for conversion to AHBs or, for the quieter crossings, AOCLs (no barriers but with flashing red lights).

I spent the night locally and next morning took the train to Knottingley, where I met Traction Inspector Harry Jameson, who told me that he had worked at Skipton, Mirfield and Wakefield. I had a cab trip on an MGR coal train to Grimethorpe Colliery (home of the famous brass band), thence to Drax Power Station to observe unloading operations, and finally to Wakefield – a fascinating trip. I was spending the night at Bingley, and on the train from Leeds who should I come across but Fred Dalby and his wife. He had been Stationmaster at Blaydon when I was Yardmaster there back in 1959, and we were next door

This two-car DMU, the 14.46 from Carlisle to Barrow on 26 April 1987, has just left Seascale on its delightful, scenic run, with the Lake District giants on one side, and the Irish Sea on the other. *W. A. Sharman*

A Class 40 diesel, No.40138, takes a short train, the 15.37 Leeds to Carlisle, past Horton (in Ribblesdale) signalbox on 18 August 1982. The signalbox has long since disappeared, and the only permanent way left is the Up and Down main lines. The connections were the entry to the huge Horton quarry, which used to dispatch train loads of limestone, but it now all goes out by road and through the centre of Settle, much to the understandable chagrin of its inhabitants. *B. J. Beer*

neighbours. He moved from there to become SM at Shipley, and then retired but did not move away.

Next morning it was back to York, where I was met by Arthur Warner, a member of George Wood's 'team' (today's buzzword). Arthur really knew his stuff, and we had a very productive day visiting by car the remainder of the level crossings on the Scarborough line, some of which had already been modernised and unstaffed. The weather was absolutely awful for such an outing, with driving rain all day and the rivers very high. Scarborough looked at its worst, with a rough, grey sea lashing the promenade, and I was glad to be in the car and returning to York, off home on the 16.06 to King's Cross.

But there was to be no rest from level crossings. The next day I visited a crossing at North Camp, near Farnborough, with Tony Townsend-Rose, although I did not record the reason for the visit. The wet weather was not confined to Yorkshire – the Thames at Reading was just lapping the top of the riverbank.

A peaceful, sunny view of the signalbox and the junction at Settle Junction. *Unattributed*

Quite the opposite. Yet another pile up at Settle junction, with the Healey Mills 45-ton steam crane clearing the wreckage. Such mishaps were far from rare, and had their origins in the 14 miles downhill run, almost all at 1 in 100. *P. H. Dyson*

Another Parisian interlude

It might sound interesting and mysterious, but it was neither. It was another not very exciting UIC meeting. I had a smooth crossing from Folkestone to Calais on the *Vortigern*, but the boat was full of parties of school students making an early start for Easter. It was not like the good old days, when these boats had a bit of class and you lived in hope of being accosted by a mysterious and beautiful female spy. I was staying for three nights at the Hôtel de Londres, but had dinner at a nearby restaurant. Paris had no shortage of good, small, local restaurants.

I spent the following day in the meeting at the UIC offices with my cronies on the working party – Dr Büsch (DR) and Messrs Gerber (SBB), Treutler (DB) and Vasseur (SNCF). Lunch was in the UIC canteen, and in the evening my favourite little spots were full, so I settled for Le Fouquet, where I had chicken bourguignon. The meeting continued all next day, but the UIC provided lunch with plenty of red wine to stimulate the afternoon's proceedings. I managed to get into the Gourmet de l'Isle restaurant in the evening and had turbot with quenelles (like meatballs but made with fish) for the main course.

The meeting had concluded that day, but as it was too late go home I spent another night in Paris and returned in a leisurely fashion the following day, with another smooth, pleasant crossing. Again, I cannot recall what the meeting achieved, but I suspect not very much. The aim of the chairman seemed to be to ensure that there would be another meeting – not an unreasonable ambition if you lived in East Germany.

I become a night owl

In need of a bit more experience of cab-riding in the dark, I arranged an interesting excursion for myself (with a soupçon of nostalgia). I met Traction Inspector Charlie Golding for a cab ride on the 21.00 from St Pancras to Nottingham, which brought back

memories of the Nottingham Division ten years earlier. At Nottingham I met a Traction Inspector named Richards who accompanied me to Leeds on the 23.50 to Carlisle (the Glasgow sleeper?), where he was relieved by George Gordon. This was really the nostalgic part. Roaring through Bingley tunnel and the station at 55-60mph brought back childhood memories of lying awake in bed and hearing the night expresses rushing through and wondering what was on the front end.

Then it was on to Skipton and Carlisle over the Settle & Carlisle line, little dreaming of how I would become involved with the line and the area in the future. Dawn was just beginning to touch the tops of the fells, and I had no idea that within a few years – only five, as it turned out – I would be walking those self-same tops. We arrived at Carlisle at about 5am after what had been quite a night, and I felt I had absorbed quite a bit from the three Traction Inspectors involved. I am sorry that I kept them out of bed, but I think they enjoyed it too, meeting this big white chief from 'the Kremlin' as BRB HQ was known. I believed it was important then, and I still believe it today, to get out and about and experience the railway that we were supposed to be running. You couldn't do it all from a desk.

From Carlisle I took the first train, the 05.30, down the coast to Whitehaven, and then on to Lancaster with the 07.52, a very pleasant journey along the coast. I just had time for a belated snack there (having taken the precaution of bringing a flask and some sandwiches with me) before continuing to Euston and home.

Level crossings again!

We had a visit from a group of four Swedish railwaymen who wanted to have a look at our level crossings and how they operated. Fortunately, they all spoke good English, which made it much easier. In the afternoon I took them to the South Western

The new traction and coaching stock depot at Heaton in November 1977. The view shows the main depot area with, from left, the servicing, maintenance and bogie cleaning shops.
British Rail

The 09.24 Barrow-in-Furness to Lancaster DMU rolls into Grange-over-Sands station on 30 August 1978.
L. A. Nixon

Section of the Southern Region around Ascot because it had a good selection of the different types of crossing and was relatively close at hand.

Next morning we all met at King's Cross for the 09.00 to Peterborough and thence to Melton Mowbray where a minibus was waiting to take us to Nottingham. We booked in at the George Hotel and had lunch before setting off by road to visit crossings in the Colwick, Nottingham and Long Eaton areas, before finishing up at Trent power signalbox. Jack Reeks, an old friend and then Divisional Manager at Nottingham, joined us for dinner at the hotel, where a very convivial evening ensued.

Jack had organised a special DMU for us next morning and we travelled over the line to Newark, with its multitude of crossings, and then it was off to the Derby and Burton on Trent areas before returning for lunch at the George Hotel again. It was politic to look after foreign guests well, because you never knew when you might want a reciprocal visit. Actually, it came after I retired, as part of a Railway Study Association convention when the Swedish authorities wanted to show us their latest train control development, which the electrical firm Ericsson had produced. It was known as ATP – Automatic Train Protection. The BRB Director of Operations, Maurice Holmes (a first-class railwayman) was travelling with us, and the two of us went into the driving cab to witness the apparatus at work. We approached a yellow signal, and then the driver folded his arms and sat back in his seat. The alarm sounded and the brakes came on, and we stopped well before the red signal. It was a very impressive display and was one of the factors that led the BRB to decide to experiment with ATP on the Western Region main line to Bristol as well as on the Chiltern line.

Off out again

It was 10 May, and time to spend a couple of days in the North-East in the company of Ralph Lewis, the DOS, and his No.2, Les Binns, who hailed from Low Moor, Bradford. After lunch at the Station Hotel, courtesy of the DOS, we visited Newcastle and Tyne Yard power signalboxes, and then it was on to my old stamping ground at Heaton to have a tour of the new HST and carriage depot. By this time there was not much left of the old marshalling yard, but it was good to meet old colleagues who

were still 'out on the line' and have a chat about the various issues of the day. Two-way exchanges and feedback were always an important part of the job.

I spent the night in the Station Hotel, which I was sad to see had fallen on hard times. It had once been regarded as quite posh, but I have not been there since so have no idea of how it has fared under new ownership. BR was short of funds and there were so many demands on what was available. Trains had a higher priority than hotels.

Next morning, Les Binns called for me with a car and we set off northwards, visiting signalboxes and level crossings all the way to Berwick, with a stop for lunch at Warkworth. My mode of life had always included a hot lunch, and there were plenty of cafés around in those days that could provide just that. There were a lot of level crossings too, and still are. I came straight back to London from Berwick, travelling with the driver as far as Newcastle, and it was nearly midnight when I finally arrived home.

Next came a two-day trip to Grange-over-Sands, with an overnight stay at the Netherwood Hotel, a very imposing baronial pile. Val was tired of being left at home, so she came too, and said it was the best hotel she had ever stayed at. We met a couple of chaps from the HQ Staff & Welfare Department, who were concerned about complaints being made through trade union channels about the provision for relief crossing keepers generally. The purpose of the visit was to inspect newly built accommodation at a couple of crossings where the gates were worked by a resident crossing keeper, at Cart Lane and Wraysholme. The two chaps went home satisfied, and so did I.

PART 3: THERE'S NEVER A DULL MOMENT

A mishap at Milford

Milford, a wayside station three stops down the Portsmouth line from Guildford, had an automatic half-barrier crossing almost at the platform end and there was a signal there also, which worked automatically for nonstop trains but was switched to red for stopping trains. This was to avoid the road being closed for a longer period than normal. The driver of a stopping train had to

The signalbox at Grange-over-Sands recorded on 31 May 1979. The box here was a replacement built by British Railways (London Midland Region) in 1956. *John Scrace*

Milford signalbox pictured on 20 August 1969 before the level crossing was modernised by converting it to an automatic half-barrier crossing. *J. Scrace*

press a plunger when the train was ready to depart, which would initiate the barrier-closing sequence. When the lowering sequence was complete, the signal would change to 'proceed' (one yellow, two yellows or green, depending on the state of the line ahead). Unfortunately, the driver of a stopping train failed to stop in the platform and went across the road with the half-barriers raised, crashing into a car and killing the female driver. Members of the Railway Inspectorate dismissed it as a one-off and decided not to hold a public inquiry, and I do not recall any change being made. If the signal had been located further back down the platform it would not have helped, and it was quite likely that the platform would have had to be lengthened. There is a similar installation at Darsham, on the East Suffolk line.

I went out there with a signal engineering colleague to see what the effect would be if we allowed the signal to work normally, and we found that the additional road closure time was only about a minute (slam-door stock in those days), and the road was only a minor one. The danger scenario involved an impatient car driver waiting at the crossing, seeing the train stop in the station, and deciding to nip round by the barrier, only to be hit by a train coming the other way. I duly reported back to the Inspectorate, but cannot recall what was actually decided.

Into the fens

The line from March to Ely is full of crossings of various types, as is the whole of that area of flat fenland. It was a time for a visit, together with the Eastern Region, to see what could be achieved under the new Requirements when they were finally introduced. On 22 May, four of us rendezvoused at Peterborough where transport was awaiting, and we set off for March to begin our study of crossings on the way to Ely. We continued along as far as Manea, a full-barrier crossing, before knocking off for the day. We spent the

On 10 July 1976 one of the then relatively new Class 56 locomotives, No.56049, is seen passing through Oxford with a train of empty coal wagons heading north from Didcot Power station to the Midlands. *C. C. Cole*

Class 47 No.47011 arrives at March heading for Whitemoor Junction with a freight from Parkeston to Arpley. The box here closed following the closure of the ex-GN&GE Joint route to Spalding on 28 November 1982. *John Rudd*

The ex-Great Eastern Railway box at Whittlesea dates originally from 1887; it is seen here on 11 June 1986 as Class 31 No.31426 passes with the 13.30 service from Norwich to Birmingham. *D. M. May*

night there in a guesthouse after quite a tiring day. Next morning, after a leisurely breakfast, we continued our study of crossings, before completing what had been an interesting couple of days.

I venture further afield (and Val comes too)

The chairman of our UIC sub-committee had decided it was time for another meeting to report progress, and Swiss Railways had invited us to hold the meeting there, which was something to look forward to. I decided that we would cross the channel by BR hovercraft. The hoverport reception area was very luxurious, with glamorous purserettes, and was certainly a step up from the normal

boat crossing. We boarded the hovercraft *Princess Anne* for what we thought would be a pleasant 35-minute hop but turned out to be a very unpleasant 45 minutes of bump and bounce as the hovercraft ploughed its way through a rough sea. Both Val and I were very glad to be on terra firma at Boulogne. We then took a train to Paris, from where we had couchettes through to Berne, arriving there at 7.45am on 26 June. After booking in at our hotel, I went straight off to the first meeting of the sub-committee.

Dr Büsch (DR) was there as chairman again, together with Dr Kühn (DR), the secretary, and Messrs Gerber (SBB), our host for the meeting, Vasseur (SNCF) and Borgannio (?). I took an

The hovercraft *The Princess Anne* seen at Dover Hoverport; the SRN4 hovercraft was originally built by the British Hovercraft Corporation on the Isle of Wight and delivered in 1969. Christened *The Princess Anne* in 1971, the hovercraft was extended by 15m in 1977, increasing its capacity from 254 passengers and 30 cars to 418 and 60 respectively. *The Princess Anne* and sister craft *Princess Margaret* survived in service until withdrawn in 2000. *British Rail*

The exterior of the then new power signalbox at London Bridge recorded on 12 June 1975. *British Rail*

interpreter with me, from the BRB International Office, Mr Jenks. It was not all first names in those days. The meeting lasted all day, after which I met up with Val and we explored the city. Berne was one of the most attractive places I had ever seen – all cloisters and colonnades.

Next day was the obligatory 'excursion day' and we were taken on the Three Lakes Tour, starting with a steamer trip from Biel. Lunch was two platefuls of perch, washed down with the local white wine, but the evening was unbelievable. We had all been invited to supper at the Gerbers and travelled there by bus. The house was a large mansion set in quite big grounds with a very tall railway signal at the gate, appropriately in the 'Off' position, and we were greeted by Frau Gerber. Herr Gerber was my opposite number on Swiss Railways, but I guess his salary was about three times mine. He spoke quite good English but his wife had very little, so it was an opportunity for me to use my German, which improved by leaps and bounds as the evening progressed. After aperitifs in the summer house, we repaired to the house where a sumptuous cold buffet had been laid on for us on a truly gigantic table, with cheeses and meats of every description. We were waited upon by the Gerbers' twin daughters, beautiful girls of about 17, who performed their duties with efficiency and elegance. The whole evening lasted about four hours and grew more sublime as succeeding bottles were opened. I was glad that Val was there, as I would have found it difficult to describe it all to her, and fortunately I took many photographs to jog my memory. The *pièce de résistance* was in a cellar big enough to dance in – a huge gauge 'O' railway layout, all set up to work automatically to a pre-planned timetable. Unbelievable!

Next morning the chairman quickly wrapped up the meeting and Val and I set off home, breaking our journey for the night at Nierstein (more wine!).

Odds and ends

It was the fashion for representatives from different railways to meet each other, and on 8 July I had a visit from a Mr Heyman, who was Deputy General Manager of Israeli Railways. He wanted to learn about our safety methods (how much time did he have?), and then in the afternoon I took him to London Bridge signalbox, which was our showpiece.

A couple of days later, I spent a day at what had now been renamed the Ministry of Transport, going over every word, dot and comma in the new Requirements for level crossings with Tony Townsend-Rose. This would be a legal document, issued by the MoT, so it had to be spot on. A few days later, I was on the road again, this time to Newcastle, to look at level crossings on the Newcastle to Carlisle road. There were four of us, and we worked our way diligently westwards as far as Hexham, where we spent the night. Sadly, there was no sign of Addison Yard, at

The 16.10 DMU service from Newcastle to Hexham, with Metro-Cammell No.E56391 leading, pauses at Wylam station prior to crossing the level crossing on 23 April 1980. *Tom Heavyside*

Looking towards the west at Wylam in January 1980; the box was constructed by the North Eastern Railway towards the end of the 19th century and remained operational until c2000. Although disused, the box remains in situ at the time of writing. *Andrew Muckley*

The signalbox at Pooley Green, location for part of the recording of the author's film on level crossings. It is seen here on 12 September 1973. *J. Scrace*

Blaydon, where I had been the Yardmaster 20 years earlier – the entire site had been cleared and was now covered by trees and small factories. The next day we ploughed on and finished up at Carlisle, just in time for me to get home that night.

PART 4: MORE LEVEL CROSSINGS, AND A SPELL AT THE FRONT END

Level crossings and the film

The film needed an example of a particular type of open crossing, and the only one I could think of was on the Shrewsbury–Machynlleth line near Newtown, so I set off early with a couple of cameramen on the 06.50 from Reading to Birmingham, and thence to Shrewsbury and Newtown. At the latter we met the Assistant Area Manager who took us by car to the crossing so that I could do my little bit of play-acting and we could get the necessary film. I had chosen the weather well – it turned out to be a beautiful, sunny day. As we were a bit pushed for time we had sandwiches for lunch at the crossing and then reluctantly set off back. I was home by 7.15pm.

A couple of days later, we did some filming a little nearer home, at the unlikely-sounding crossings known as Whitmoor Bog near Ascot, and Pooley Green near Egham. I seem to recall that the former was a red/green miniature warning light crossing, and the latter an AHB crossing on a busy road with a bad record of misuse by impatient car drivers. Once more we were favoured with lovely weather, but we had no time to lose as the film had to be ready to be shown to the trade unions and the MoT as soon as the new Requirements were published. Moreover, I had to convince the trade unions, especially the footplatemen's union ASLEF, that what we were proposing was safe. I have to say that

the Railway Inspectorate was more gung-ho than we were. Caution ran through *our* bones like the lettering in a stick of Blackpool rock!

Back to the sharp end

It must sound like a jolly day out, riding around in the driving cab, but my ultimate aim was to know as much about train driving as I did about signalling, and that could not be achieved by sitting in an office. I was usually accompanied by one of the Regional Traction Inspectors because I could discuss things with them rather than distracting the driver. I was very keen to experience the morning rush hour into the London termini, especially on the Southern Region, so this being the 'dog days' of August (the 21st), I went to Basingstoke to travel into Waterloo on the 07.53 train, followed by a trip to Exeter to 'learn the route', with its mixture of double- and single-track sections and relatively high speed limit. I had always regarded the downgrading of the old LSWR route to Plymouth as the Western Region's revenge, determined that the route would never again challenge GWR supremacy. However, it might have been better during the rationalisation of the 1960s to have upgraded the LSWR route and closed the Berks & Hants route, which passes through mile after mile of fields and was built to get the GWR to Plymouth more quickly than the LSWR. Unfortunately, the LSWR route had been transferred to the Western Region in 1963, and the latter chose to downgrade it.

A few days later, on 30 August, I had a trip on the South Eastern Section of the Southern Region in company with Traction Inspector Terry Smith. The route was from Victoria to Sheerness, Ramsgate, Dover, Tonbridge and back to Charing Cross. My notes record that it was the hottest day in London for three years, so it was a good day to get out of the office.

Above and left: A trip to Penzance on 18 March 1979. The first photograph shows the hugely impressive Royal Albert Bridge just beyond Plymouth, and in the second one we have arrived at Penzance. *Author*

Not wanting to neglect the Western Region, I had a rather more comfortable ride to Swansea in an HST with Inspector Barrett. I used to think that racing along at 100mph on the old LNWR route from Euston to Rugby and Birmingham seemed pretty quick, but tearing along at 125mph required an even higher level of concentration from the driver, because things really did come at you pretty quickly. I came straight back, got out at Reading and had a trip to Oxford and back, just to round off the day.

A few weeks later I had a very interesting trip to Penzance with Inspector Harry Hill on a track-testing train, although I cannot recall all the details. The journey took all of six hours so it required an overnight stay at a B&B in Penzance. Next morning, I had a leisurely breakfast and eventually made my way

home. No, it was not a holiday – the weather in the West Country was dull and drizzly.

This was an awful period of local strikes, usually of 24 hours but sometimes longer. The staff at Paddington were on strike for some reason (no reason?), and it lasted several days, but it was possible to get to London by Southern Region EMUs from Reading – it just took longer. Incidentally, Val and I had both signed up for French and German night-school, which would be very useful to me for UIC business.

These chronicles might give the impression that I spent all my time swanning around the country, but my notes indicate that I was in the office every day that week, head down, working.

The Naas collision

My next trip was from Paddington to Newport, where I took a connection to Lydney because I wanted to have a close look at the nearby Naas crossing where there had been a serious collision on 13 March between an express and a rubbish lorry. This was a miniature warning light crossing, installed back in 1970 on a quiet country road and equipped with hydraulically operated lifting barriers. Road users were not only required to leave their vehicle to operate the barrier-raising apparatus, having first made sure that the warning light was green, but also had to recheck the warning light once they had rejoined their vehicle, an essential requirement that was easy to overlook.

The lorry was an eight-wheeled Scammell carrying a skip loaded with 10 tons of refuse – a fairly hefty obstruction – and the express, a 10-coach train headed by a diesel-electric locomotive, was travelling at about 60mph. In the collision, the cab of the locomotive was crushed and the two locomen were killed, whilst the lorry was largely wrecked and its driver killed. As a result of this accident it was decided that miniature warning light equipment was unsuitable for public roads, even quiet ones such as at Naas, and they were all converted to a higher level, often automatic open crossings. Significantly, after the accident the crossing equipment at Naas was upgraded to the new type of automatic open crossing (AOCR) without gates or barriers but with flashing warning lights and signs, as used at AHB crossings and as provided for in the new Requirements. However, this type of equipment was also found to be unsatisfactory and was involved in the serious accident at Lockington in 1986, when a DMU hit a light van on the crossing and was badly derailed, so it had to be upgraded. Throughout BR, 44 crossings had been converted to AOCRs, but all except one were converted to AHBs. As already mentioned, the Railway Inspectorate was keener on them than we were.

AWS becomes an issue

It was becoming clear to me as the installation of AWS was taking place all around the country that despite its undeniable virtues it had a serious hidden defect that the technical people did not really want to talk about. This concerned the scenario of a driver acknowledging an AWS warning, then forgetting he had done so and failing to apply the brake. It sounded highly unlikely, but it did happen, although the failure rate must have been one in millions. The issue really arose because the installation programme was proceeding at such a leisurely pace. Work had begun over 20 years earlier, in 1958, and at the present pace of progress it would be at least another ten years before the programme was complete. In the meantime, more modern systems were emerging and were being applied on the Continent.

The installation programme was based on obvious priorities – busy main lines and busy suburban routes were to be done first, before working down the routes of less importance and so on. It was never intended to equip all routes. We agreed an annual programme with the technical departments to fit in with their programmes for renewal and resignalling.

There was a particular problem with the Southern Region, based on its concern that for much of the time in busy suburban areas drivers were passing a succession of signals at double-yellow and yellow without necessarily needing to reduce speed. The Regional people feared that the routine acknowledgement of the AWS warning without a reduction in speed would in time become an automatic reaction, with obvious dangers. That was the flaw with AWS. The system had undoubtedly been of immense value in reducing the number of collisions, but it was an *advisory* system for the driver, and that was all that it had ever been intended to be. In the 1950s, when the design was finalised, there was really nothing better that was practical and affordable, and the benefits by far outweighed any hidden flaw. But the slow rate of installation had created a very difficult situation indeed.

The Southern Region alternative

As we have seen, the Southern had started work on a more advanced system that gave individual signal aspects in the driving cab and required the driver to acknowledge each indication by a separate and distinctive action, in order to overcome fears about repetitive cancellation. However, the project was beset with technical difficulties and by 1973 no proven system was available, while the cost was estimated to be nearly three times that of the standard BR system. By this time there was pressure from all sides for the Southern to install the standard AWS without further delay and development work on the Southern's own AWS finally came to a halt.

A conundrum for the Board

Twenty years of modernisation, and another ten needed for completion, put the Board in a quandary. More advanced, and safer, systems of train control were becoming available, so should the Board adopt one and stop the AWS programme? And if a safer system were to be adopted, it ought surely to be installed on the busiest routes, which were the routes already equipped with AWS. What, then, was to be done about the routes that were in the programme but had not yet been equipped with standard BR AWS? They could hardly be given priority over far busier routes. The stumbling block was the limited technical resources that the Board had available, and the Signalling Engineering Department was hostile to any proposal to adopt a new system, on the grounds that it did not have the resources to plan and install a new system at the same time as carrying out its existing programme of modernisation of signalling through the creation of new signalling centres. So we continued to install the outdated AWS for several more years before experimenting with a far more advanced system known as Automatic Train Protection (ATP). However, and quite fortuitously, since the turn of the century AWS has been rendered safer by the installation of the Train Protection & Warning System (TPWS), which plugs the loophole by checking that a driver has responded to an AWS warning and is actually reducing speed. That was the holy grail, and its success was plain for all to see.

PART 5: I BECOME A FILM PRODUCER

The preparations

The BTF film unit phoned me to say that the level crossing film was now ready, and to ask me who was going to do the voice-over for it. I thought that I should have a look at the finished product to be sure that it showed everything that I wanted included and looked accurate, so I went across to their studio and had a look at the film, which lasted about 30 minutes and looked very professional. Having already done the practice voice-over, it now looked as though I was in line to do the actual thing. So that was done, and the whole thing was ready for a showing.

The rehearsal

First in line for the showing were the Director of Operations and presumably Jim Urquhart. I have no doubt that they wanted to be briefed about it and, more importantly, wanted to be sure it was OK for showing. I cannot remember who the Director of Operations was at the time – I was at BRB HQ for five years and during that time there were five of them (one after the other, of course, not all at once). At one time a Director of Operations might expect to be in post for at least five years, to achieve continuity, but it had become a merry-go-round.

It transpired that the Minister of Transport himself, Norman Fowler, wanted to see it personally because he was going to do a press conference and obviously wanted to be fully briefed. It would also be shown to the railway trade unions, and it was essential to have them on board, but satisfying the unions was going to be much harder than convincing the Minister and the press. However, when we showed it to the unions they were good as gold, and I think they were quite impressed that we had gone to so much trouble. They knew about it, of course, and we had taken them along with us all of the way.

A private showing for the Minister
This was done at the MoT in its private cinema, and because I was the voice-over I had to field most of the questions afterwards, although I was supported in the discussions by colleagues from the S&T Department and, of course, by several of the Railway Inspectorate's Inspecting Officers. It was all quite exciting. There was no great shindig afterwards – I think we got a cup of tea and a biscuit, or something like that.

And just as an aside, this was the great period of strikes – ITV came back on air after being on strike for 11 weeks.

The big day
I had lunch in the mess that day as usual, and went to the MoT in the afternoon together with all the others for another showing of the film to the gentlemen of the press and presumably radio and television stations. This was the press conference at which the Minister announced that he had accepted all the recommendations of the Level Crossing Report, and so far as I recall it all went very smoothly. It was a successful end to a very long road that had begun two years earlier.

Anyway, it was back to the grindstone again, but I recall saying 'One crowded hour of glorious life is worth an age without a name'. This was written by Thomas Osbert Mordaunt

(1730–1809) during the Seven Years War (1756–63) according to my *Oxford Dictionary of Quotations*. We beat the French hands down and gained Canada, but the French got their own back by helping the Thirteen Colonies beat us in the American War of Independence.

Radio comes to the forefront

The National Radio Network (NRN)
BR had recognised the potential value of radio, but it had never been a burning issue. However, it became one in two ways. The NRN was first installed in about 1980 to provide radio communications between the Radio Control Office and men out on the line, in order to allow more efficient management of engineering possession of the line and also to enable electrification telephones on AC overhead electric lines to be removed. The system took a long time to reach its full potential due to the unreliability of the software and inadequate radio coverage, but additional base stations were eventually provided. It might also be added that BR was again being financially squeezed by the government of the day, which delayed the development of radio. The facilities allowed communication between radio sets, and between radio sets and the railway ETD telephone system.

Below: Class 47 No.47490 arrives at Banbury with the 08.49 Wolverhampton to Bournemouth service on 22 September 1979. *Les Bertram*

Radio on trains

The advantages of having radio communication with trains are obvious, but the high cost of cab-secure radio (see below) and the technical difficulties of installing it nationwide meant that thoughts turned to the possibility of using or adapting the NRN for this purpose, which was done, enabling driving cabs to be equipped. The driver now had access to the radio telephone network and could make an emergency call by pressing a red button, which connected him immediately with a Railway Control Office. On receiving an emergency call, the Control Office could broadcast a message to all trains within a particular base station radio coverage area, which would be heard over the loudspeaker in driving cabs. The NRN was not a secure radio system, since there was no correlation between a train's radio call number and the train description number. The signalman was not normally aware of the radio call number of a particular train, and the radio traffic was normally initiated by drivers.

Cab-secure radio

This was designed in the late 1970s for installation in those trains that were to be operated without guards. The provision of this type of radio system was one of the safety requirements agreed between the BRB and the Railway Inspectorate for the operation of suburban passenger trains without guards. The other main requirements were that the line must be equipped with continuous track circuiting and multiple-aspect colour-light signalling worked from a signalbox with modern train describer equipment.

In operation, it was necessary for the train's reporting number – eg 2E34 – to be correlated with the train's radio equipment number because the train reporting number was used by the signalman to call the driver. The correlation was achieved when the train entered service for the day and was done by the driver sending a data message to the controlling signalbox stating the number of the signal at which the train was standing. Radio messages could not be overheard by other drivers.

I become involved in on-train radio

On 16 November, I was given a demonstration of the workings of the system at King's Cross powerbox. It was immediately obvious that it was streets ahead of the National Radio Network, but was also far more expensive. The cost was likely to limit its widespread application to areas of driver-only operation (DOO), and then only to DOO trains in those areas. DOO was quite simply an economy measure, first and last, but it often required very expensive CCTV on station platforms to enable the driver to see that all was safe with the train for him to depart. Personally I was not in favour of passenger trains without guards, in what were even then becoming lawless times in suburban areas and with stations becoming unstaffed. I felt that passengers wanted to

see someone in authority on a suburban train. Naturally, the NUR was bitterly opposed, but only on the ground of loss of jobs. However, I had no objection to the removal of guards from fully fitted freight trains. Neither did the drivers, in general! No brotherly love there, and different unions.

Revision of the General Appendix

It sounds a bit medical, but to give the book its full name, the LMS called it the General Appendix to the Working Time Tables, whist the GWR called it (more accurately) the General Appendix to the Rule Book. BR adopted both and called it the General Appendix to Working Timetables and Books of Rules and Regulations. The original BR book was dated 1 October 1960 and, being full of subsequent amendments and deletions, was reprinted in 1972 with 12 additional pages. I felt that it was time to update it and, more importantly, to simplify it. By way of explanation, the Rule Book is an instruction manual, whilst the Appendix describes equipment and situations, eg the air brake, train heating systems, accident procedures, bad weather, etc.

Eddie, a very reliable and trustworthy old Great Western man, worked in my office and was responsible for the contents of the Rule Book and for ensuring that any alterations were OK. It so happened that about this time BR was having its perennial trouble with the unions, with the usual one-day strikes etc. When there was a strike I could get to Reading by bus, and Eddie, who lived on the other side of the town, could do the same. The Divisional Operating Manager at Reading agreed to put a room at our disposal on strike days, and Eddie and I met there to do our work, although during the first one-day strike we met and worked in my dining room.

I had two objectives. The first was to scrutinise every item in the Appendix to see if there was still any justification for it being there, in view of all the changes over the previous 20 years in traction, signalling, freight traffic, railway organisation and so on. That thinned it out quite a bit. The second objective was to create a logical separation of items into chapters, with major items such as train braking systems having their own chapters. We had already decided that it should be in loose-leaf form in a ring binder.

The first hurdle was to clear the finished product – the new book – with the Signalling Committee and, through them, the Regions. That being accomplished with a bit of effort, we had next to clear it through the Engineering Departments to the extent to which they were concerned. Then Eddie could go ahead and have the book printed. It came into operation on 6 June 1981 and, I have to say, I was very pleased with the result of our efforts. The first six sections covered general matters, traction, working of passenger and other trains, accidents, fires, and bad weather. They were followed by single-issue sections covering level crossings, AWS, buckeye couplings, the vacuum brake, the air brake, DMUs, and EMUs.

The empty stock to form the 15.42 Longbridge to Lichfield City passes Halesowen Junction heading for Longbridge station on 23 February 1979.
Chris Perkins

1980

PART 1: A NEW YEAR DAWNS

A typical week in January

Monday – A day in the office getting ready for a busy week.

Tuesday – It was time to have a good look at the Liverpool Street Division, where I knew the DOS, Geoff Dent. One of the new Integrated Electronic Control Centres was being planned there, and I was keen to learn all about it and have Geoff's views on the project. He was one of the old hands-on school of operators, and I knew that he would already have thought it through. We had a good tour around, visiting the signalboxes at Bethnal Green and Ilford, and the carriage sidings, and then it was on to Shenfield and Colchester. Lunch was taken in a fish and chip shop at Ilford. It was a long day, but worthwhile.

Wednesday – The monthly meeting of the Signalling Committee took place, with all the Regional Signalling and Accident Officers. This was the forum for discussing any matter of general interest, together with any proposed amendments to the Rule Book, the Train Signalling Regulations, and other books of signalling and operating instructions. No changes were allowed until they had been approved by this committee. In the case of major changes, our proposals were submitted to the Board's Main Operating Committee for confirmation.

In the evening I went to the Staff Training College at Watford to have dinner and a chat with the management trainees on the Rules and Regulations course. I always enjoyed a visit to

The signalbox at Bethnal Green pictured when virtually new in 1949; the box was to survive until 1997 when it was replaced by the IECC at Liverpool Street. *British Rail*

The Grove. I was there again a couple of weeks later to give the usual talk on safety to a course of Area Managers, and although I enjoyed giving these lectures to various groups, it could be hard work and tiring. It was about the real nitty-gritty of railway work.

Thursday – I wanted to have a look at the evening peak workings from Waterloo, so I had a ride out to Basingstoke and back with the Regional Chief Inspector, Terry Smith. Like all these Locomotive Inspectors, he was a good chap, with a lifetime's experience, and it was important to let them know that their

advice was valued. On a one-to-one basis on their home ground – ie the driving cab – they would speak out freely.

Friday – A relatively easy day, taking an HST from Reading to Swansea with a chap from the Signal Engineer's Department and Major Kit Holden, a Railway Inspecting Officer, to have a look at some level crossings in the area. The Regional people met us there with transport and took us to a pub for lunch. We came back 'on the cushions' from Llanelli so that we could have a round-up on the visits. In the following week, I had a cab trip

The power signalbox at Colchester dated originally to 1962 when this photograph was taken. The box remains operational at the time of writing but is scheduled to close in 2017 when its duties are taken over by the Romford Rail Operating Centre. *British Rail*

Below: On 10 July 1980, Class 312 EMU No.312204 departs from Walsall with the 16.25 service to Birmingham New Street. *Les Bertram*

The 07.52 service from Newcastle to Poole, headed by Class 47 No.47407 passes through King's Sutton station on 15 May 1980. *John Acton*

Class 25 No.25305 heads north from Walsall with a Freightliner service on 10 July 1980.
Les Bertram

A Class 122 diesel railcar departs from the new station at Stourbridge Town on 4 August 1980.
The short branch linking the Town and Junction stations was reduced slightly when the original station at Stourbridge Town was closed and a new station constructed 70 yards closer to the junction in 1979.
John Glover

On 5 July 1980, a Derby three-car DMU departs the rural station at Alvechurch with the 11.52 service from Four Oaks to Redditch. *C. Morrison*

from King's Cross to Doncaster and back with Inspector Clem Britton on the 15.55 Down and 18.13 Up. This was good experience, picking out signals in the dark at 125mph. That is when you are grateful for AWS, and you begin to appreciate the strain that generations of footplatemen must have felt on steam engines in the days before AWS, particularly when fog was more prevalent than now.

And so ended a busy week (or two) in late January.

The social side

My section at BRB HQ consisted mainly of a small group of people who were experts in their own particular field of signalling and accidents, and from time to time we all met with our wives and had an evening meal in one of the multitude of good restaurants around the West London area. This time it was the Manor Hotel at Datchet. We usually had one or two guests as well, and it was a bit of a reward for our wives. I have to say that I was fortunate to inherit such a very friendly group of people.

The AWS Principles Group

The design of AWS equipment was quite complicated and involved several departments – the Signal Engineers, the Mechanical Engineers, the Civil Engineers and the Operators. The Research people were also part of the Principles Group. For many years the AWS system was solely employed in connection with signals, but following a derailment caused by excessive speed over a speed-restricted section of line at Morpeth

it was decided to employ AWS equipment to warn drivers that they were approaching a permanent speed restriction.

There were thousands of permanent speed restrictions on the BR network, but it would have been technically difficult, and also highly confusing to drivers, to put a permanent magnet on the tracks at all of them, so it was necessary to establish parameters. The Railway Inspectorate thought that they should be installed on those lines where trains were allowed to travel at 75mph or more and wherever a speed restriction demanded a reduction in speed of one third or more. The Signal Engineers were not happy about using equipment associated with signals – ie AWS – for a non-signalling purpose, and I could see their point of view. In fact, I agreed with them in principle, but something had to be done about the problem of excessive speed over curves, and AWS seemed the obvious answer.

It was decided that the magnet should be placed on the track 200 yards before the lineside warning sign for the restriction, with variations if there was already an AWS magnet for a signal in the vicinity. It sounds relatively simple, but the actual signalling principle ran to several fairly complicated pages. Unfortunately, I cannot recall what was discussed at the actual meeting, which was held in an office at Birmingham International station.

Some years later it was decided, after another serious derailment, that portable magnets should be used at certain temporary speed restrictions, which was very popular with drivers.

A dramatic picture of the almost total derailment at about 100mph of the 20.25 express from Euston to Manchester at Bushey on 16 February 1980. The cause was a broken weld in the rail. As can be seen, several of the derailed coaches fell over on to their sides and slid along the adjacent DC electric line. There were no fatalities.
© *The Daily Telegraph*

One of the ill-fated APT units pictured on test in Scotland. *British Rail*

High-speed derailment at Bushey

On the evening of Saturday 16 February, the 20.25 express from Euston to Manchester, travelling at about 100mph, was almost completely derailed at Bushey on the West Coast main line. Several of the coaches fell over on to their sides on the adjacent DC electric line, but thanks to the structural integrity of the Mk 3 coaches, the bodywork remained intact and there were no fatalities.

The cause was a broken weld in the rail. The track along the Down fast line had been relaid in 1965, but in October 1979 the cess side rail was found to be worn and two 720ft lengths of CWR were welded in. One of the welds between the old and new rails was not up to the standard required and failed. Unfortunately, there was little supervision of this work, the welding supervisor being almost fully occupied in the office doing administrative and clerical work and rarely able to get out to exercise supervision. He needed a clerk, but this post had been withdrawn during one of the economy drives. Perhaps it would be oversimplifying the matter to point out that the cost of the Bushey accident would have paid for an army of clerks for several years in order to allow supervisors to supervise. But economy was all, and there were targets to be attained if you wanted to keep your job.

Farewell to the management trainees

It was a leap year and the end of the course fell on Friday 29 February. It was customary for me to say goodbye to the trainees and wish them good fortune. Having spoken to them several times, I had got to know them quite well, so I went to have a last lunch and a chat with them at The Grove. I was very impressed by the high standard of trainees that year, many of whom came straight from university, and I was happy that the future of the industry was in good hands. They will all be in their mid-50s now, possibly in senior positions, but I fear that I cannot remember any of their names.

The trip of a lifetime

The Advanced Passenger Train (APT) Group wanted to get people's reactions to riding in the train, so they arranged an 'invited trip' from Euston to Stafford and back for volunteers from the Board and the Region. I was invited, but all I recorded afterwards was that it was a very good journey with smooth tilts. And so the saga rolled on. Fortunately, BR's Mechanical Engineers had introduced their alternative – the HST – several years earlier and it was proving to be a great success. It is still generally regarded as one of the best trains that BR has ever produced.

I meet an old colleague

I was on a power signalbox and level crossing visit, beginning with Peterborough power signalbox, built on the site of the old LMS Spital locomotive shed. Twenty years had passed since I was Yardmaster at Peterborough, and the yards had been considerably run down. The passenger station had also been rebuilt – proposed originally in the LNER's 1946 glossy brochure of its plans – and the track layout had been altered to allow nonstop expresses to pass through Peterborough at high speed. It was adequate at the time, but there has been considerable growth since then in both passenger numbers and train services, and major improvements are now taking place, including a new island platform and additional running lines.

I then went forward to Doncaster to visit the power signalbox there and was very surprised to bump into an old colleague from our relief clerk days back in 1950 in the Leeds District. I think he was now the DOS. Naturally we chatted about the good old days and what we had both been doing since then. He seemed to have spent most of his time in the West Riding, whilst I had been roaming far and wide.

I spent the night at Doncaster and next day did a marathon level crossing spotting trip with George Wood, the Regional Signalling Officer. It started with the 08.57 to Hull, followed by the 10.35 to Scarborough and then the 12.35 to York. We were grateful for the excellent forward visibility from a DMU, and we probably saw over 100 boxes. The trip raised quite a few queries for George to follow up.

The interior of the then new power signalbox at Peterborough. This was one of three boxes scheduled to control the southern end of the East Coast main line by 1978; the other two were situated at Doncaster and King's Cross. *British Rail*

Heslerton box, on the York-Scarborough line, pictured on 9 August 1980 as Class 31 No.31246 passes at the head of the 11.10 Scarborough-Sheffield train. *Keith Smith*

Seamer West box recorded on 11 August 1983 as Class 47 No.47455 accelerates away with the 17.00 service from Scarborough to Liverpool. The box was constructed for the North Eastern Railway in 1906 and remained operational until 2000; although out of use, the structure remains at the time of writing. *W. A. Sharman*

PART 2: SOME INTERESTING DEVELOPMENTS

Arranging the September 'do'

Every year, one of the countries in the UIC sub-committee hosted one of the meetings instead of it being held in Paris, and this year it was Britain's turn. Dates had already been allotted and invitations sent out so that the BR International Section could make appropriate arrangements. Foremost amongst these were the venue and the programme of meetings, visits and excursions. The delegates had already expressed an interest in visiting the Railway Technical Centre at Derby, so it seemed appropriate to hold our meetings in Derby too. The Midland Hotel outside the station was a high-class establishment that would make a suitable place both for accommodation for the delegates and their wives and for the meetings to be held.

On 9 April, Roy Jenks of BR's International Section accompanied me to Derby to discuss arrangements with the hotel and the RTC. It was all straightforward, but every detail had to be considered and we had to work out a programme and timetable with the Technical Centre people for the day's visit. However, they were getting used to such visits by now, because the RTC was gaining a reputation in the technical world, so no problems were envisaged.

The provisional programme for the week was as follows:
Sunday 7 September – All arrive and assemble for dinner.
Monday 8 September – All-day working meeting in the hotel.
Tuesday 9 September – A visit to the Severn Valley Railway.
Wednesday 10 September – An all-day visit to the RTC.
Thursday 11 September – The final meeting in the morning, and then disperse after lunch.

Roy Jenks said he would make all the arrangements for the hotel, the meetings, the outings and the hospitality. That was very helpful indeed, but the International Section did this for various departments several times a year and were expert at it. In view of the importance of Derby in the railway sphere and the number of continental delegates, it seemed appropriate to ask the Mayor

A beautiful picture of the remarkable Forth Bridge. I travelled over it in the driving cab of the 09.10 from Edinburgh to Aberdeen on 24 April 1980, and I also went over the Tay Bridge that morning. I was favoured with a beautiful, sunny day as I made my way to Inverness. *W. A. Sharman*

to hold an official reception on the Monday evening, which he readily agreed to. There was also to be an official dinner on the Wednesday for guests from the RTC, the Region and the BRB. No expense would be spared!

I lose no time in visiting the Severn Valley Railway

What could be nicer on a pleasant spring morning than to be setting out for Shropshire? I caught the train to Birmingham and was met there by John Hubble from the Divisional Office. He took me by car to Bridgnorth and then on to Bewdley so that I could discuss with the Severn Valley people the arrangements for the UIC visit. That included the timings of a special train from Bridgnorth to Bewdley and back, the provision of a first-class open coach, a hot meal and drinks on the train, and the choice of locomotive – preferably a nice big green one, but that would depend on what was available at the time. Oh, and an estimate of the cost. The Severn Valley people were, of course, only too happy to oblige. More about this later.

Another lecture

I was getting plenty of experience in delivering lectures, not knowing that I would be doing it for the next 30-plus years. This one was at Crewe to the Locomotive & Carriage Institution, a venerable society, and was mostly for traction inspectors, senior drivers and supervisors. In other words, they were all experts and down-to-earth. My talk was entitled 'Protection of the Line'. I already knew quite a lot of people there, especially those from my Birmingham days, and it was a very enjoyable evening. I stayed the night at the Royal Hotel and after a good breakfast I went off to Manchester to spend the day with the Divisional people there, visiting signalboxes in the Bolton and Rochdale areas. The signalbox at Bolton West Junction was becoming quite famous, being one of the first electro-pneumatic systems in Britain, dating from before the First World War. Several pre-Grouping companies had developed power-signalling schemes.

A Scottish interlude

In April I had a few visits to make in Scotland, and I knew that my opposite number there would be delighted to escort me round. I went north on the 13.45 from Euston and joined the driver in the cab at Preston for the run to Glasgow. Electric locomotives are very comfortable and quiet and we had a good run. Next morning, buttressed by a bowl of genuine Scottish

A driver's eye view of the Forth Bridge; a view taken in 1965, sees two DMUs passing under the awe-inspiring girders of the bridge. *Chris Burton*

porridge, I made my way to Scottish Region HQ at Buchanan House for a discussion on methods of working single lines. After lunch in the canteen I had a cab trip to Dundee and back to see the signalling at Longforgan, the site of a bad smash in October the previous year. It was a perfect day for such a trip, being clear and sunny. Then it was back to the hotel.

The next day was a marathon. I went to Edinburgh on the 09.19, which was followed by a very interesting cab trip to Aberdeen over the Forth and Tay bridges. Again, I was favoured with a beautiful sunny day as I made my way to Inverness. There I had dinner – a casserole of venison – in a restaurant overlooking the river before joining my sleeper berth in the 'Royal Highlander'. Inverness in those days was a quiet and rather proper Highland town. After arrival at Euston at 07.45, I had breakfast at the Marylebone station buffet and spent the day in the office, catching up with the correspondence.

Off again

A few days later, I went to South Wales with a chap from the BRB Industrial Relations people to visit some level crossings at Brynmenyn and Llangeinor. The NUR had requested this visit and came with us, so we had a very friendly journey and all had a buffet lunch in the BRSA club at Port Talbot. Away from formal meetings you could have a sensible discussion, but I cannot recall what the particular problem was on this occasion. I was very impressed with the HST service from Paddington to South Wales and back.

The Signal Engineers' annual convention

I was an associate member of the IRSE and decided that I would like to join them on their annual convention, which was held in May at Stuttgart. Val also came along – these were international affairs with a large attendance and most wives seemed to come

The southern approaches to the Tay Bridge on 31 May 1977 as a rake of seven DMU vehicles, with Gloucester Class 131 No.Sc55015 leading, forms the 19.22 local service from Dundee to Edinburgh. The train is approaching Tay Bridge South box; this was built for the North British Railway in 1887 and remains in use at the time of writing. *Brian Morrison*

The old order at Inverness: on 23 January 1980 Class 26 No.26035 awaits departure with the 11.10 service for Wick and Thurso.
Brian Morrison

A view of the mainline terminal station at Stuttgart from the operating floor of the modern signalbox. *Author*

A DB Class 110 electric locomotive is just entering Stuttgart station at the head of its train. *Author*

A DB suburban train is just running into the suburban side of Stuttgart station on an S-Bahn service, which then goes underground. *Author*

Below: Railway stations are not a natural environment for young ladies, so these three wives took the opportunity to escape to the more attractive surroundings of Munich. We all went there the following day. *Author*

along too. It was much better than being left at home whilst their husbands went off making whoopee.

Tuesday – The convention begins

The convention was to begin on 20 May, and we set off the previous Sunday evening via Harwich and the Hook of Holland, with a twin-berth cabin on the overnight sailing, the *Koningin Juliana*, which connected with a through service to Stuttgart. We arrived there at 15.45 on the Monday, and our hotel was only a few minutes away from the station. Next morning, we all assembled at the railway HQ offices, with the ladies then detaching themselves for the day on the basis that they would not want to sit and listen to lectures on points and interlockings. The 140 delegates, all men, were split into five groups (there were no female signalling engineers – that was for the future). After lunch at the station restaurant, with plenty of wine, we visited the very modern signalbox, which was elevated and had a splendid view over the whole station area, which was huge, as most continental stations are. The mainline part of the station was a terminus, but there was also a through S-Bahn underground system. It was all very impressive.

The evening began with a champagne reception followed by a superb meal of smoked trout soup, pork schnitzel and unlimited wine, all provided by a firm of signal engineering contractors, SEL. Good for business. And so ended an excellent first day, accompanied by warm, sunny weather.

Wednesday – A trip to Munich

We had an early start, setting off at 7.20am on a special train to Munich, where we continued by a special U-Bahn train to Kieferngarten maintenance depot. It was all shiny and new, as we had come to expect. Then it was back into Munich for lunch at the railway HQ offices, followed by a visit to the Regional Control Centre. We met up with the ladies at 4.30pm at the Marienplatz, in the centre of Munich, for a coffee and a stroll along the pedestrianised area before enjoying another splendid champagne reception and dinner. Our host this time was the signal engineering branch of Siemens. We then returned to Stuttgart on a special train at 21.56, courtesy of DB. I think we all just tumbled into bed, it had been such a long day.

A splendid and striking memorial to the Austrian emperor Franz Joseph. *Author*

A very attractive-looking electric locomotive of Italian State Railways (FS — *Azienda Autonoma delle Ferrovie dello Stato),* standing in Domodossola station, just over the border from Switzerland. *Author*

Thursday – A visit to SEL

On the last day of the convention we visited the SEL factory in the suburbs of Stuttgart to see telecommunications equipment being made, followed by lunch in the canteen. The afternoon was free, so we met up with our wives and had a stroll around the very pleasant city of Stuttgart – modern, clean and well laid out – presumably all rebuilt from the ashes of the Second World War. In the evening we entertained our hosts at the official IRSE dinner, with plenty of speeches, and wine. It had been an excellent and very enjoyable convention, and the signal engineering contractors had pushed the boat out.

Val and I came back via Vienna, Budapest, Siofok (in Hungary, on Lake Balaton), Zagreb, Trieste, Milan, Stresa, Brig, Vallorcine, Chamonix and Paris, with a mixture of sleepers and B&Bs. It took us exactly a week and was quite a marathon, travelling through Austria, Hungary, Italy, Switzerland and France. Fortunately, I have quite a few slides of the trip, so at least I can recapture parts of it quite easily, and Val kept a detailed record of the whole trip.

PART 3: A VARIETY OF ISSUES

A hullabaloo about child trespassers

I was called to Marsham Street (the home of the Ministry of Transport) to discuss the deaths of child trespassers with the Railway Inspectorate. Apparently some Liverpool councillors were up in arms about children getting on to the railway and being knocked down by trains, and the first question to be asked was whether this was a national issue or a burning issue only in Liverpool. A glance at the statistical results for the whole of BR for the previous year, 1979, showed that 115 trespassers had been killed by trains on the railway that year, only five of whom were children. On the other hand, six children had been electrocuted by contact with the third rail and two killed by contact with overhead live wires, which was the average for the previous ten years. In fact, these results had been remarkably consistent for many years.

The discussion continued over lunch in a nearby pub (not the sort of thing that would happen today), and it was decided that we should jointly meet the Liverpool councillors to find out what had caused their concern and to discuss the size of the problem in their area and what might be done about it in an attempt to douse the flames. There was no point in blaming bad parenting, although we quickly discovered that the councillors regarded this as a major issue, about which 'something must be done'. They had also contacted councils in other areas.

Considering the changed conditions on the railways in the previous 20 years, you might have expected the figures to have worsened, but that had not been the case, despite a number of factors:

    modern trains approached more quickly and more quietly;
    many small stations had closed but buildings remained to tempt adventurous children;
    the change from manual maintenance of the track, with gangs located every mile or two, to centrally operated mechanised maintenance with no permanent lineside staff, although many lineside buildings previously used by

trackworkers still remained in some places – an obvious attraction;
many lineside signalboxes had closed, resulting in less supervision of the track.

The maintenance of the lineside fencing had always been a problem. Children often damaged it, and adults sometimes made a way through it as a short cut. Nonetheless, BR was responsible for maintaining fencing, despite the problems. The one area where something positive could be done was the removal of redundant lineside buildings, and we said that we would bring the attention of the Civil Engineer to this matter. But to put the matter in perspective, one child is killed by a train for every 20 adults who are killed.

However, the matter was not going to go away, and Liverpool City Council enlisted the aid of the Association of Metropolitan Authorities (AMA). A meeting of the AMA was subsequently arranged, and I again found myself on a train to Liverpool. I was relieved to find that it was not a burning issue for most authorities, and I took the opportunity to ask the AMA for help with it. Where municipal-owned land bordered the railway I asked that the authority should consider erecting its own childproof fencing in addition to the railway fence, where the land was used by children as a play area. Throwing caution to the winds, and with the bit between my teeth, I pointed out that the railway's obligation to fence the line did not include a requirement that it should be childproof, except where there was an electrified third rail.

The law regarding trespass on the railway is set out in a very early piece of legislation, the Railway Clauses Consolidation Act of 1845, which states:

'The [railway] company shall make … the following works for the accommodation of the owners and the occupiers of lands adjoining the railway … sufficient posts, rails, hedges, ditches, mounds or other fences for separating the land taken for the use of the railway from the adjoining lands not taken, and protecting such lands from trespass, or the cattle of the owners or occupiers thereof from straying thereout, by reason of the railway …'

The duty imposed by the Act upon the railway undertakings is for the benefit of the owners and occupiers of the adjacent land and is not for the benefit of the general public. The object of the fencing is to protect the owner of the land from the consequence of his cattle straying on to the railway, and from members of the public (or railway workers) trespassing on his land.

Trespass on the railway has always been an offence against the railway by-laws, but for some years the courts had been taking a more lenient view when young child trespassers were involved, especially when they had gained access through faulty fencing and been injured. The Act had not changed, but the courts were placing their own interpretation on it. . This was influenced by the emerging duty on the BRB under the Health and Safety at Work etc. Act 1974 to conduct its undertaking in such a way that members of the public, even trespassers, were not exposed to risk so far as it was possible to prevent it. Soon after Railtrack was formed it took action to prevent trespass by erecting metal palisade fencing along many hundreds of miles at both sides of the main lines.

Another visit to the RTC

After a quick turnround at home, I was off again next morning to the Railway Technical Centre at Derby, where I spent a busy day on the Radio Signalling project. The RTC was *the* centre of technological expertise and development, populated by highly intelligent people with a hive of ideas. You could feel the buzz when you were there, and it was a great tragedy when it was all destroyed in a supreme act of vandalism during privatisation. Railtrack did not want it, since it was concerned only to make money out of its property, and everything else was franchised out or sold off. Parts of the RTC, especially those concerned with signalling, were rescued by signalling firms, but even that did not last forever. It was one of the saddest episodes in British railway history.

I arrived home an hour late due to a points failure at Coventry. The following day I went to a retirement presentation for an old colleague at Sheffield and came back on the train to St Pancras with Dick Hardy, who has a background in managing motive power depots and had worked at several during the steam era. He subsequently went on to write many railway books following retirement and is one of the nicest men you could ever wish to meet. Again, I got home an hour late due to a points failure at Trent and a signal failure at Twyford. We weren't doing very well, were we?

The listed signalbox at Garden Street, Grimsby, recorded on 12 September 1970. The box has been provided with thick blast walls; these were added in 1940 as a wartime measure during the Second World War. The box was decommissioned in 1993 but remains in situ at the time of writing. *S. C. Dent*

The signalbox and Level crossing at Hensall pictured on 25 February 1987 as Class 141 unit Nos.55539/55319 picks up a solitary passenger with a service from Goole to Leeds. The box is a Lancashire & Yorkshire Railway design dating from 1875. *Tom Heavyside*

Built in 1934, the PS *Wingfield Castle* was one of three paddlesteamers constructed for the LNER to provide a link across the Humber estuary between Hull and New Holland before the completion of the suspension bridge. *Wingfield Castle* was eventually withdrawn in 1974 and preserved; it is at the time of writing on display at Hartlepool where the ferry was originally built. The remaining two ferries remained active until the suspension bridge was opened in 1981. *A. Eaton*

Back to level crossings

On Thursday 31 July, I caught the 09.35 from King's Cross to Doncaster with a signal engineering colleague, Tom Craig, for a couple of days of level crossing visits in Lincolnshire. Arthur Warner, the Regional representative, met us at Doncaster with a car and took us to Grimsby, visiting several of the many crossings en route. This was followed by a DMU trip to Cleethorpes, with time for a walk along the prom enjoying the hot and sunny weather. We had our evening meal in a Berni Inn, still popular at the time, but a brand that had gone out of fashion by the end of the decade.

Next morning, after a hearty breakfast, we caught a DMU to New Holland and then went across on the ferry to Hull, which had plenty of level crossings for our attention. Then it was off by car to Doncaster, with several more level crossings en route. My records note that for lunch we had pie and mushy peas in a pub at Barnby Dun before continuing to Doncaster for the train back to King's Cross. No delays that day, and we hadn't been living it up.

A thorny issue – single-manning of trains

As already mentioned, I was against the single-manning of trains in principle, because I firmly believed that passengers wanted to see a railway presence both on a local station and on the train. However, considerable staff savings could be made by removing staff from small stations and cutting out guards, but my official concern was limited to any operational safety issues that might arise. The NUR was solidly against the concept, and there were strikes for years afterwards whenever there were proposals to introduce it somewhere. But it was the Board's response to incessant demands from the Government that we reduce our costs, and the Government did not care how we did it.

One of the main technicalities concerned the ability of the driver to look back to see if it was safe to depart from a station,

Although the 25kV catenary has been installed, the old order continues to reign on the Bedford-St Pancras line as a four-car DMU is pictured at Hendon heading south with a service for St Pancras on 14 May 1983. *John Rickard*

that all doors were closed and that no one was trapped between them. There was no great problem at a straight platform, or one with a favourable curve, but on a platform that curved out of the driver's line of sight it was proposed to install a television system, with cameras at suitable intervals and a TV screen opposite the point at which a driver should stop. I cannot recall drivers raising any objection to this (drivers are practical people), but they pointed out that they would, of course, expect suitable remuneration for the increased responsibility. The battle was one

The Class 317 EMUs were constructed for operation over the St Pancras-Bedford route. Until agreement was reached for their operation, they remained idle, standing in the sidings as illustrated by No.317335 at Bedford on 26 October 1982. *David Brown*

GWR 'Manor' class 4-6-0 No.7819 *Hinton Manor* pictured at Bridgnorth on 9 September 1978 with a service to Bewdley; this was the locomotive used to haul the UIC special on the Severn Valley Railway on 9 September 1980. *Charles P. Friel*

between the Personnel Department at BRB HQ and the HQ of the NUR, with ASLEF sitting in. I had to attend these meetings at BRB HQ to deal with any safety issues that might arise (and the NUR dreamt up as many as it could), but the proceedings were mind-bendingly boring.

Eventually the Railway Inspectorate became involved, and between us we drew up a formula for changes that would need to be made to the Rule Book and other operational publications. The proposals were known as Requirements for One-Man Operation of Suburban Passenger Trains on British Railways, and there were other sets of Requirements for Passenger Trains on Non-Suburban Lightly Used Lines, and Fully Fitted Non-Passenger-Carrying Trains (these included empty coaching stock trains and freight trains). Signalmen also became involved, and, not to be outdone by the drivers, they too wanted payment for the extra responsibilities. The initials DOO (driver-only operation) and OMO (one-man operation) became household terms. Although OMO rolled off the tongue more easily, it was also the name of a washing powder, so I believe that DOO won the day. I still have copies of the Requirements dated July 1982, and must have had a premonition that they would come in handy 30 years later.

The arguments over single-manning went on for years. Pay trains helped to some extent, because there was still a guard on the train who collected the fares, and it did become possible to unstaff some small stations. Sliding doors under the control of the guard also eased his responsibilities, although he still had to check that no one was trapped between the doors.

Finally, I had a trip from St Pancras to Bedford on the Midland line to look at CCTV proposals. We had a ploughman's lunch in a pub at Bedford – even HQ staff seemed to be economising. But I thought that we had not heard the last of this subject.

PART 4: ON MY TRAVELS AGAIN

Britain's UIC meeting takes place

It was now our turn to host a meeting of the UIC sub-committee, and it was important that our hospitality was at least equal to that which we received on the Continent. This was work, and not a holiday, or at least that was our excuse for pushing the boat out. It was a matter of national pride, no less.

On Sunday 7 September, my wife and I arrived at the Midland Hotel in Derby at about 4pm and we were shown to our bedroom – the suite that Queen Victoria was said to have used. It had a big bedroom, a big bathroom (Val remarked that the bath was big enough for two, but we didn't put it to the test) and a big lounge, which the two chaps from the International Section had thoughtfully well stocked with drinks. We had dinner with the Gerbers (from Berne), whom we had met previously, after which we invited them to have drinks in our room, together with Dr Büsch and Dr Kühn, both from East German Railways. Dr Büsch was very expansive, and was not averse to telling us about conditions in East Germany. He must have trusted his secretary Dr Kühn not to betray him!

On the Monday the men spent all day in a meeting room working hard on the matter in hand – I had an excellent interpreter, Major Tebbs, at my elbow – whilst Val excelled herself as a hostess by taking the ladies (five of them) by taxi to the centre of Derby for some shopping. I hope they were suitably impressed. In the evening a coach took all of us to the Mayor's Parlour for a reception, where we were treated very well, given sherry and shown the mayoral regalia. That certainly was impressive.

The following day was the obligatory 'day off', with an outing for the whole party. Each host country did its best to outdo the others, and we had selected a trip by private train on the Severn Valley Railway with the most sumptuous lunch (six courses) that the SVR could conjure up. They did not disappoint. Our engine was No.7819 *Hinton Manor*, beautifully cleaned up, and Val, greatly daring, had a ride on the engine – a first for her. On the way there, by coach, we called at the Ironbridge Gorge Museum so that we could show off a bit. It was a memorable day, and all the arrangements by the International Section people worked out very well.

It was back to work on the Wednesday, the sub-committee members spending the whole day as guests of the RTC, which was the main reason for basing the convention at Derby. Val, assisted by a chap from the International Section who also acted as interpreter, had a minibus trip to Rowsley, not to visit the engine shed (17D) but to have lunch at the historic Peacock Hotel followed by a visit to Chatsworth House. The official dinner was held that evening. The guests came to our suite beforehand, including the Director of Operations and his wife, the Deputy Mayor and Mayoress, and the Director of the Technical Centre and his wife. Then came the dinner, which should have been heralded with a fanfare of trumpets – turtle soup, sole and veal cordon bleu, with the appropriate wines. After that, everyone came back to our suite for more drinks and stayed until 1am. And

An unidentified BRCW Type 2 Class 26 diesel runs into Golspie station with the morning train from Inverness to Wick and Thurso. Golspie is about halfway along the route — 84 miles from Inverness and 70 miles to Thurso. A fascinating journey. We spent the night there, and were treated with real Scottish hospitality. *Author*

so ended a very memorable day. Val performed her hostess duties admirably and quite enjoyed it (when it was over).

Friday morning was an anticlimax. There was a meeting to wrap everything up, followed by a modest lunch and then the goodbyes on the platform at Derby where we saw everyone off. It had been enormously successful, everything had gone according to plan, and it hadn't cost me a penny!

The Signalling Committee meets in Glasgow

From time to time the Signalling Committee met away from London, and this September it was the turn of Scotland to act as hosts. I travelled north on the engine from Preston to Carlisle, accompanied by Inspector Davie Tweedie. We all met at Glasgow Central and stayed for a couple of nights at the Ewington Hotel (the Scottish Region couldn't afford the Grand Central Hotel!). The meeting included a visit to Edinburgh power signalbox, after which everyone dispersed, while I remained there to meet Val off the 'Flying Scotsman' at 2.40pm.

Off to the far north

Val and I caught the 15.25 to Inverness, and I travelled on the loco from Perth to Aviemore. We spent the night at the Haughdale Hotel in Inverness, and the next morning, with the sun shining brightly, we walked to the station to meet Sid Atkinson, Manager of the Highland District as well as of the station. I had followed in his footsteps 20 years earlier when I took over from him as Yardmaster at New England and he went off to be the SM at Inverness. He had stayed there and prospered. I also met Inspector Ronnie Munro, who took us in his car to some of the more important stations on the line to Thurso, such as Ardgay and Lairg. We lunched at Invershin Falls and finished up at Golspie, where overnight accommodation had been arranged for us. I don't know how we had been described to the lovely couple who ran this guesthouse (some important people from London?) but we were treated right royally. A big dinner was followed at quite a short interval by tea, cakes and Scotch pancakes.

Next morning, we were up early and with the sun shining on the magnificent statue of the 1st Duke of Sutherland, we set off to Thurso on the 08.52 train (I was on leave now). Once there, we just had time to see the sea before returning south on the 11.48 to Inverness, before finally completing the trip in first-class sleepers on the 'Royal Highlander', the 20.35 to London. Countess Mountbatten was in the next compartment and further along were

Duty done, I was now on leave, but we took the opportunity to continue northwards to Thurso. Val enjoyed the afternoon sun there. *Author*

the Duke and Duchess of Marlborough and Lord Brabourne. Such company! Unfortunately, we were two hours late into Euston. Long-distance punctuality was not brilliant in those days. The Office of Rail Regulation and Passenger Focus would have had a fit. And yet, for quite a while I had been regularly visiting my mother in hospital at Keighley, and 19 out of 20 HST journeys between King's Cross and Leeds had been spot on.

An intriguing excursion

I had heard and read of a remarkable radio controlled signalling system on the narrow-gauge Ravenglass & Eskdale Railway and wondered rather idly whether there might possibly be something in it for us. BR's Chief Signal Engineer was keen to have a look at it, so on 6 October off we went on the 12.00 from Euston with Major Peter Olver, one of the Railway Inspecting Officers. We missed the connection at Preston (poor punctuality on the LM Region!) so had to go via Carlisle. A minibus had been provided to take us to a hotel in Eskdale, and we were relieved to get there. There was a gale blowing and it was pouring with rain, but a noggin soon revived us. Next morning, we went back to Ravenglass to see the radio system in operation and were very impressed by its potential for BR, especially on the line from Inverness to Wick and Thurso. It was time well spent.

It was then back home for a quick turnround and then off to the RTC at Derby for an all-day discussion on radio and signalling control, which ultimately resulted in RETB. All trains on the line would be controlled by radio from a central point, and instead of the driver obtaining a physical token from a local signalman he would obtain an electronic one from the centre. The concept was so beautifully simple and brought considerable economies in the signalling grade. The boffins quickly got to work, but I had to be careful not to tread on the toes of the BR Signal Engineering Department. One sensed a slight undercurrent of tension between the two departments, which had to be handled with kid gloves as I did not want anything to interfere with the development. I could see the potential for it on several rural routes that might otherwise close.

PART 5: HERE, THERE AND EVERYWHERE

A visit to the LT&S

Reading through these pages, you might get the impression that my life consisted entirely of roaming the rails and never being in the office. In reality, the reverse was the case, long days being spent on paperwork or at internal meetings and in discussions and debates. There were lengthy papers to be studied, but in most cases these activities would not make exciting reading – hence the emphasis on outdoor visits.

I had not yet paid an official visit to the LT&S (the erstwhile London, Tilbury & Southend Railway) that runs from London Fenchurch Street station to Southend and on to Shoeburyness, with a loop via Tilbury. It had been electrified about 20 years earlier. Geoff Dent, the local Superintendent, invited me to take a trip with him, so I willingly responded and we spent the day together, including a modest lunch at Southend, which is not a very exciting place in the middle of November. The LT&S was (and still is) primarily a commuter line, and high standards of punctuality were required. The line had been prone to fogs in the past, resulting in accidents, and the LMS had planned in 1935 to install a system of automatic train control known as the Hudd System. However, development was slow, and it had not been installed when war broke out in 1939. The line was later equipped with standard BR AWS.

Management trainees must learn the Rules

A good working knowledge of the Rules was essential for a management trainee, otherwise many avenues of promotion would be closed to him (or to her – more and more young

An unusual visit to search for new ideas — at the Ravenglass & Eskdale Railway. The weather was fierce when we arrived, but it had calmed down by next morning, enabling us to have a good look at the Ravenglass Railway's revolutionary new ideas for controlling the movement of trains. Just what we wanted. Here is a view of one of the 'River' class engines at Ravenglass during the tourist season. *Author*

Class 302 EMUs Nos.287 and 228 seen at Leigh-on-Sea with the 15.45 service from Shoeburyness to Fenchurch Street on 28 September 1980. *Les Bertram*

The interior of the power signalbox at Euston. *British Rail*

The operating floor of the power signalbox at West Hampstead seen on 23 July 1980; the box controlled all the signals and points between Moorgate, St Pancras and Irchester (north of Bedford) when introduced — this was a distance of some 70 route miles. *British Rail*

women were coming forward at the time as trainees, some of whom showed considerable promise). The term 'Rules' included a mass of information and instructions in all conceivable aspects of railway operation, but the railway was becoming a much simpler place to be compared to 20-30 years earlier when it did everything and carried everything. And it must be admitted that it was a more interesting place back then.

The training course for management trainees occupied 18 months, and each annual course followed the same programme. Some of the trainees came straight from university and could be a bit cocky at first, but it was soon knocked out of them. They all spent a month at the Staff Training College in Watford, where I was overseeing the planning and running of the course. A small number of Operating Inspectors were seconded each year to run the course, and the purpose of my visit was to run through with them the syllabus and check on the preparations.

I generally visited the course once a week to check on progress, and possibly stay the night to chat to the trainees in a more relaxed atmosphere. It was an intensive course, and you were expected to pass out successfully at the end of it. Failure was not allowed, but it did occur sometimes, and the trainee was expected to catch up and submit himself for re-examination. Further failure would mean an interview with the original selection board, which could then result in rejection from the whole course. It was rather like being reduced to the ranks in HM Forces.

Visits to power signalboxes

I knew the DOS at Euston very well, and he arranged for me to visit Euston and West Hampstead powerboxes, as they were called

in everyday parlance, accompanied by Signalman's Inspector Les Bowler (a very appropriate surname for such a job) on 20 November. A bowler was a badge of office, especially when accompanied by the long black mac (I think it was something like Prussian Blue).

I had not been in either of these boxes previously. The track layout between Euston station and Camden (at the top of the bank) had, I believe, been rationalised in pre-Grouping days by the LNWR and included a couple of 'diveunders' to enable empty stock to be taken from the station to the carriage sidings without blocking the lines to incoming trains. West Hampstead box was on the Midland line. In order to save time, Les and I had lunch in a café – inspectors usually knew where the best ones were.

More level crossing visits

On 24 November, a visit to some level crossings in the Cambridge area was arranged for Peter Olver, together with a Regional representative, Arthur Warner. Arthur was an expert, but asked me to come along for moral support. Major Olver was a bit of a stickler, and on this occasion he was particularly interested in a crossing near a mental institution whose inmates occasionally caused problems. Arthur also provided the car to take us from one crossing to another. The Cambridge area was well supplied with level crossings of many types, a number of which could be classified as 'problem crossings'. Peter Olver was particularly interested in these, and how we might deal with the difficulties that would arise if they were modernised.

One of the particular problems related to the road approaches, and the level crossings concerned could be ranked by the number

Histon was situated on the freight-only branch from Cambridge to St Ives; on 31 March 1979 a charter train from Cambridge to Swavesey is pictured approaching the closed station. Although there was a strenuous campaign to see the St Ives branch reopened for passenger services, ultimately the track was lifted and the formation used to construct a dedicated busway. *Iain Scotchman*

of times that the gates had been run into by road vehicles and damaged. Actually, it was a very interesting day, deciding what type of equipment would be most appropriate for a particular crossing, and I came back to Liverpool Street from Audley End. However, I do not know why Peter Olver was involved with level crossings that day, as they were usually the domain of Tony Townsend-Rose. There being only five Railway Inspecting Officers, there was a degree of specialisation.

I go to sea

These were the days when BR still had a fleet of cross-channel steamships, and as the chairman of the Board's Operating Committee had come from the Southern Region, he decided that the December meeting should be held on board one. It sounded like a good 'wheeze', so we all trotted off to Dover and up the gangplank. As luck would have it, the ship was a French one, the *Saint Eloi*, so perhaps we got a better lunch, which was the first item on the agenda. A certain amount of work was done on the voyage to Dunkerque and on the return journey (we did not disembark), but the sea became quite rough and our papers kept sliding off the table. (Let them go – save the drinks!) In fact, the ship rode very well and no one was seasick. We even had a visit to the bridge, clinging on to the handrails for dear life. It was a journey I had made many times, and was to make many more. I always loved to lean over the taffrail and watch the white cliffs of Dover gradually disappear.

A visit with the IRSE

A visit to the newly opened Victoria power signalbox had been arranged on Saturday 6 December. Situated at Clapham Junction, it signalled all the lines in and out of Victoria station and was one of the largest installations I had seen, with many desks from which the signalmen controlled all train movements. It was also one of the last of that generation of signalboxes known as NX push-button. When a signalman wanted to set a route he pressed a button at the beginning of the chosen route (N) and then pressed another button at the end of that portion of route (X). If the route was available it would be set automatically and a row of white lights would appear all along the route; these would change to red when the train entered that portion of the route. But the future belonged to video display units and automatic route

setting, with tracker ball control. We were just beginning to visualise it, and now the very large control and indications panels are going.

Signalling has changed very little since 1980, but major changes are in the pipeline, albeit some way off yet. Colour-light signals are likely to be with us for quite a few more years yet, until the European Train Control System (ETCS) is installed, just on the main trunk routes, and it could take many years before it is installed nationwide. So don't hold your breath.

Christmas comes early

On the morning of 11 December, the Signalling Committee visited the London Transport Control Rooms at Cobourg Street in Euston to see how it all worked. Because LT interfaced with BR at several locations on the perimeter of London, where LT trains ran over BR metals, the LT Signalling Representative sometimes joined the BR Committee if the agenda had an issue of common interest.

After the visit, it was time to relax. Later in the afternoon Malcolm Southgate, the Director of Operations, held his Christmas cocktail party to which wives were invited. All his senior staff were there, and the presence of our wives helped to keep us in check.

Still work to do

I needed to have talks about radio signalling with Chris Green, who was in charge in Scotland, to see how his plans were going. He was always positive and forward looking, and was a pleasure to work with. After lunch I came home via Edinburgh, in order to have a cab trip on the 15.15 to King's Cross as far as York. Inspector Liddle (sounds like a good Scottish name) accompanied me, and I remember it as a lovely journey down the coast for the first hour or so. I was home at 9.30pm, just in time to catch the last half of *Great Railway Journeys*.

Christmas 1980 was now only three more working days away, but I don't think any more work was done. It was one long round of drinks and lunches, regaled by the '222' choir's annual carol concert. I thought to myself, 'This is how it is at HQ. Out in the sticks, they are all working hard to cope with the extra Christmas traffic.' But I didn't feel guilty at all because I had done my share of it for the last 30 years before coming to the Board.

An Eastern Region DMU crosses the level crossing at Cherry Hinton on 21 October 1972 with a working from Newmarket to Cambridge. *P. R. Foster*

1981

PART 1: ANOTHER YEAR BEGINS

A day with the Signalling Standards Working Party

THIS was quite a small working party, with about three of us from the Operating Department and three from the Signal Engineering Department. Our remit was to produce national standards in signalling and associated matters from a host of different standards that had developed over many years. The work had been ongoing for some considerable years now and looked set to continue as new standards emerged.

The standards were many and varied, and dealt with a host of issues, such as:

subsidiary signals, ground shunting signals, colour-light signals, junction signals, outer and inner home signals; and replacement switches for automatic signals, route indicators (almost a section on its own), location of signal post telephones, overlaps beyond signals and route setting panels (a major subject on its own, likely to have taken many meetings).

Many of these topics had already been dealt with, but there were others still to come, and it was a very big issue and very time-consuming, to be done as time permitted.

An IRSE meeting at Savoy Place

These meetings were held in the evenings at Savoy Place, London, and were very well attended. The meeting on 7 January concerned developments in German railway signalling, and in particular the developments in Automatic Train Control. BR was still slowly extending AWS after 25 years of gradual progress, although the main lines had by now been equipped. Papers of these lectures, known as proceedings, were produced, and bound in an annual format.

This year's course for management trainees

The Rules and Regulations course began on Monday 12 January, and as usual I went along to The Grove at Watford to open the course and to wish the trainees all success. They now had several tough weeks ahead of them. On 30 January, I had another look to see how they were going on and gave them my customary pep talk entitled 'The Management of Safety'. I had lunch there as usual, which gave me a chance to chat with the trainees and relax a little before the afternoon (and probably the evening) sessions.

Continued on page 196

Full house at Birmingham Moor Street on 4 April 1981. Four sets of Derby Class 116 DMUs stand in the station whilst, on the extreme right, nature has taken over the through route to Snow Hill. *Brian Morrison*

Class 47 No.47583, recently named *County of Hertfordshire*, pauses briefly at Brundall with the 19.30 service from Liverpool Street to Yarmouth on 15 July 1981. *C. F. Burton*

On 12 September 1981, the 11.50 from Wolverhampton to Chester awaits departure from Wellington formed of a two-car refurbished Metro-Cammell DMU on the rear of a Swindon Class 120. *Brian Morrison*

On the same evening, I went along to the Royal Commonwealth Hall in London to hear Sir Peter Parker deliver his address to the Chartered Institute of Transport. He was, of course, very good.

A few days later, I delivered the final lecture to the trainees, more of a fatherly talk really, explaining to the trainees what would be required of them when they finally took charge, and indeed how to conduct themselves.

A visit to Hornsey EMU depot
I needed to have a meeting with the DOS and Depot Manager at Hornsey about radio and CCTV, which was becoming a major issue. The radio system was quite complex, and included both the drivers and the signalmen, but applied only to the electric multiple-units. However, it was far superior to the National Radio Network. One of my chaps came with me, and we reviewed CCTV proposals between Finsbury Park and Welwyn Garden City.

A couple of days later, I travelled from St Pancras to Luton to check on CCTV requirements on the Midland line, and then finally to Paddington to see a new-style tail lamp. There was plenty to be going on with. But that was not all. Next day I visited Bounds Green HST depot to look at brake continuity test arrangements.

More meetings on radio signalling
The Railway Inspectorate was very interested in this development, and we had an all-day meeting attended by Inspecting Officers Lt-Col Ian McNaughton and Major Peter Olver. Ian McNaughton had joined the Inspectorate in 1962, and became Chief Inspecting Officer in 1973. The scheme was progressing rapidly, with the help of the RTC people at Derby.

I later went to Derby to discuss radio signalling with a couple of the RTC boffins, Mike Birkin and David Cree, and to see what progress they were making. Matters seemed to be hotting up. On the same evening, I went to a Chartered Institute of Transport meeting to hear John Palmer, Under Secretary of State for Railways, give a very interesting talk on the topic of railways. I had met him before, and he seemed a decent sort of chap.

I was soon off again, this time from St Pancras to Derby to spend the whole day at the RTC, dealing yet again with radio signalling. I must say, I seemed to be spending a lot of time on this issue, but we did have a very nice buffet lunch. The staff at the Technical Centre did themselves well.

Another level crossing
I caught the 09.50 DMU from Leeds to Manchester, where I met Eric Crosby (from the Signalling and Operations Section, Crewe) and Tom Craig (Signal Engineer). Fortunately, we had sunny weather for our visit, which was to Dinting Crossing. But it was a long way to go to visit a level crossing that was proposed for automation.

A welcome spell of cab-riding
It seemed like a long time since I had enjoyed a spell of cab-riding, so it was time to put matters right. I had a trip from Paddington with Inspector Watson, on the 12.55 to Worcester and Ledbury via Reading, Oxford and Evesham, and then it was back to base. Slightly off the beaten track, but a very interesting journey nevertheless.

By way of a slight change, I travelled in the cab from Paddington to Reading on the 17.03 for a couple of nights.

On 21 April 1977 Class 313 EMU No.313033, on an afternoon service from Moorgate to Hertford North, passes the then new HST depot at Bounds Green. On the horizon can be see Alexandra Palace.
M. P. Higginson

On Saturday 2 May 1981 Class 47 No.47560 heads the 10.50 Paddington to Worcester service towards Honeybourne. The line heading left links the Oxford-Worcester main line to the Stratford-Cheltenham line; when the latter was closed, the line was retained to maintain access to Long Marston. *Paul Harris*

Class 50 No.50049 *Defiance* stands at Evesham station on 25 May 1981 with the 14.25 service from Worcester Shrub Hill to Paddington. *Les Bertram*

A three-day excursion to France with the IRSE

It began after work on Thursday 19 February with a meal at the Grosvenor Hotel before catching the 21.00 from Victoria to Dover and crossing the Channel to Dunkerque, with a berth for 50p. I had about three hours' sleep before joining the train to Paris, sleeping most of the way there. The weather was cold and bright, and I dined somewhat frugally on coffee and croissants near the Gare du Nord.

I had a few hours to spare before meeting the rest of party, so I visited the Louvre for a bit of culture with the Mona Lisa and the Venus de Milo. Actually, I found the visit very interesting. We all met at the Gare de Lyon at 13.30 and had a splendid trip on one of the super new TGV (Train à Grande Vitesse) 160mph trains, although the new line was not yet open. This was followed by the technical address at Chalon-sur-Saône, and then it was off by coach to our respective hotels. About 25 of us were staying at the Ibis, a nice modern hotel – £12 for a double room with bath. We had a rather good dinner in a nearby restaurant, but I should stress that we were paying for the hotel and meals ourselves.

Next morning there was the customary continental breakfast before the coaches collected us and took us to see installations on the new high-speed line. Then we were ready for lunch, provided free of charge by the signalling contractors, and with unlimited wine. Well, this was France, after all. After we all dispersed at 3.30pm, I caught a train to Dijon and looked round the town, buying wine and mustard, as one does. Next stop, an evening meal, and then a train to Aix-les-Bains in order to get a couchette. I slept quite well, not waking until arrival at Paris Austerlitz at 6.30am. Then I took the Métro to the Gare du Nord, with time for the inevitable coffee and croissants. It was snowing in Paris as I left, but I managed to catch the *Earl Siward* in time for lunch and endured a choppy crossing of a grey sea. I finally got back to Reading at 4pm, where Val kindly met me with the car.

Another interesting interlude

Val and I went to the House of Commons to hear David Owen give an address to a TSSA Group (the Transport Salaried Staffs'

Paris Gare de Lyon on 11 February 1981 sees two TGV rakes coupled together to form the 12.10 'Lyonaisse' service for Lyon. *C. R. Davis*

Above: The exterior of Paris Gare du Nord station. The façade was constructed between May 1861 and December 1865 and was designed by the French architect Jacques Ignace Hottorff. Internally, the main support pillars of the station roof were supplied by the Glasgow company of Alston & Gourley. *SNCF*

Association). It was a bit noisy, understandably so, as the delegates felt that Dr Owen had betrayed them. It was the beginning of the Social Democrat spring and an interesting time.

PART 2: OUT AND ABOUT AS USUAL

A memorable cab ride

On Thursday 5 March, after a day in the office, I went across to Liverpool Street on my way to meet Inspector Clem Britton at Stratford. We then went to Temple Mills to join the 19.54 freightliner to Dundee, but our departure was delayed by 90 minutes owing to a derailment in the yard. However, we were finally away at 9.30pm for a very interesting journey as far as Newcastle, where we arrived at 3.50am, just in time for a cup of tea before going on to Edinburgh 'on the cushions'. I was fortunate to have a compartment to myself, so managed a couple of hours' sleep before grabbing a quick breakfast and catching the 07.17 to Carlisle. There was snow on the tops. After more cups of tea etc, what should have been a delightful trip over the Settle & Carlisle line was somewhat dampened by rain in England, with grey skies and low cloud. There was time for a fish and chip dinner in Keighley – renowned for the quality of its offerings – and a bit of nostalgia from my days as a junior clerk there in 1943/44, and then it was on to Leeds and back home to Reading, sleeping most of the way. Sadly, the years had not been kind to Keighley station – it was a pale shadow of its former glory.

Involving the unions in train radio developments

I went to King's Cross to do an 'on-train radio' demonstration of the cab-secure radio system to both ASLEF and NUR headquarters people. In this advanced version of train radio the signalman could be sure of which driver he was speaking to and which particular train it was. I was not entirely sure if the union reps really understood what it was all about, but they seemed quite impressed. They were more concerned to know that there were no jobs at stake and, as expected, they then raised the issue of the extra responsibilities that would fall on both the drivers and the signalmen, and the extra pay they would be entitled to. Fortunately, that was not within my area of responsibility and I handed the question over to the industrial relations people.

Out with Peter Olver again

Major Olver asked me to accompany him on a visit to two cement depots in the Southampton area where there were concerns about the safety of working. This would normally have been left to the Regional people, who met us at Southampton, to deal with, but as I had been specifically asked to accompany him, it was politic for me to do so. We always made a special effort to maintain a high level of co-operation with the Inspectorate. And it paid dividends. Unfortunately, it was an awful, wet, squally day, and not the sort of weather in which to be walking round cement depots.

Yet more power signalbox visits

Sheffield power signalbox had so far escaped my attention, but it was time to rectify matters and have a day out on my ancestral line. I went straight from home to Sheffield via Birmingham and spent the afternoon in the signalbox. I knew the Superintendent there, although on the Eastern Region they had started to call them Managers. How quaint. Any Tom, Dick or Harry could be a manager – and many were – but Superintendent was one of the oldest titles on the railway system, dating back to the mid-19th century, and was a title that had always commanded respect.

I stayed that night because I wanted to do some cab-riding in the Leeds area the following day. I met Inspector Nunn – another honourable title that always commanded respect but seems now to have disappeared from view – at Leeds and we began with the 09.12 to Hull, followed by the 10.53 back to

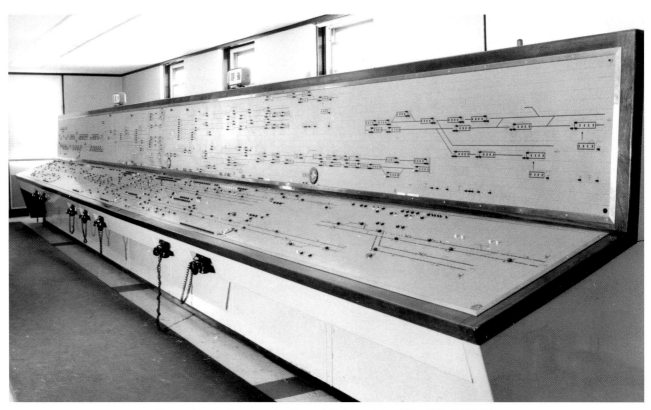

The panel serving the power signalbox at Bristol recorded on 5 May 1971. *British Rail*

Leeds, then the 12.21 to Manchester via Stalybridge, and then back to Leeds via Rochdale. No time is ever wasted when cab-riding – you are picking up information all the time, especially in conversations with the inspector, and with the driver if his attention permits (eg when standing in stations). It was a two-way process. Then it was back to London on the 15.45 HST from Leeds.

A few days later, I caught up with Bristol powerbox. The Western Region always liked to be different, and even the panels and controls had the distinctive GWR stamp. Standardisation was a long time coming, but it was preferable to have one national system, particularly from the signalling contractors' point of view. I managed to get back just in time – there was a 24-hour strike at Paddington the next day. Not that there was anything unusual in that, as strikes seemed to be a way of life at that time. Fortunately, from Reading there was the alternative route into London, over the Southern to Waterloo.

A few weeks later, I decided to revisit some of my old haunts on the Birmingham Division. I went directly from Reading to Coventry via Banbury and Leamington, where I met the Divisional Operating Officer, Chris Blackman, who took me into Coventry power signalbox. This was followed by a visit to Saltley power signalbox and then it was back home for the weekend.

A marathon operation to deal with trains without guards

On Friday 1 May, I spent the day in the office getting things straight. The following Monday was the May Day holiday, and on the Tuesday I went to The Grove (another of my ancestral homes) to spend three days with the entire Signalling Committee on a revision to the Rule Book etc, to provide for the operation of trains without guards. This was a new venture, and each rule concerned had to be carefully scrutinised to ensure that we had got it right. It was probably the biggest revision of the Rule Book for many years.

Freight trains were fairly straightforward. Almost all such trains were now fully fitted, with automatic brake, and guards were largely superfluous. Parcels and empty coaching stock trains would, in many cases, still need a guard. However, passenger trains were a

different kettle of fish. A good case could be made for retaining guards on express passenger trains, but there was less need for them on local services. The situation was becoming more complicated by the introduction of pay trains and the unstaffing of local stations, but the Signalling Committee was solely concerned with operational safety and whether we could allow passenger trains to be run without a member of staff being present in addition to the driver. It became obvious that we would have to consult other departments and we had made good progress, but we would in due course also have to consult the trade unions about the proposed changes, and we might well have a fight on our hands.

A few days later, Major Freddie Rose wanted to visit St Pancras and Kentish Town in connection with driver-only operation. Eric Crosby, from the Crewe office, also attended. There were a lot of questions still to be answered, but not necessarily within my remit, which was passenger safety, not security – a fine distinction.

A visit from South African Railways

From time to time we were hosts to overseas railway administrations, and now it was the turn of South Africa. I do not know how long they spent with us, but I had a full day with them, discussing all the latest developments in signalling and accident prevention. We did have a break for lunch, when the delegation took us to 'Maxims' no less. I cannot recall how long the lunch lasted (I can remember having Tournedos) or whether we ever returned to the Board or continued our discussions over coffee and liqueurs. So often the best, most productive, debates emerged in such comfortable and relaxed surroundings.

Level crossing maintenance gets up to speed

The semi-rural line from Ipswich to Lowestoft had been selected for a complete makeover in order to avoid its ultimate closure, and a group of us assembled at Liverpool Street on 23 June to travel to Beccles, which was the starting point of the exercise. The party consisted of Tony Townsend-Rose (Railway Inspectorate), Tom Craig (Signal Engineer), Arthur Warner

(Operations, Eastern Region), Gordon Clarke (Divisional Manager, Norwich), who was to escort us round, and me. The plan was to visit every level crossing of every type all the way from Beccles to Ipswich, which was a distance just short of 40 miles and full of crossings. It was to be a fascinating two days.

The aim was to unstaff as many crossings as possible and replace them with a range of alternatives, such as AHBs (as few as possible, because they were expensive), AOCLs, and open crossings. Farm crossings were included. Fortunately, I took my camera with me and still have a complete set of photographs. We steadily proceeded along the line – by car – visiting each crossing and deciding what was the best way to deal with it. It might appear to have been a pleasant rural outing, but in fact it was quite hard, tiring work. We were favoured with fine weather and made good progress, calling a halt for the day at Halesworth. Gordon Clarke had arranged for us to spend the night at the Crown Hotel in Southwold, an excellent place in which to relax and have a stroll on the prom before dinner.

Next morning we awoke to louring grey skies, rain and drizzle, and a large drop in temperature. However, fortified by a good breakfast, we ploughed along with the project, stopping for lunch in a pub in Melton (to dry out a little). We eventually reached Ipswich, having completed our task. The question of train control was left to another day. It was intended to single the line and provide a number of crossing loops.

PART 3: NO LACK OF VARIETY

Development of the radio signalling system

The lines which it was planned to equip with this system stretched for many miles through rural country, and even with a sparse train service it was necessary to have some means of allowing trains approaching each other from opposite directions to do so safely by the provision of a loop (ie a short stretch of double track with points at each end). It was not intended to have

staff at these loops, so the design of the points had to ensure that trains approaching the loop always took the route to the left (with an illuminated points indicator).

The technical people had designed a hydraulically operated point which achieved this automatically. So far, so good. However, a train leaving the loop would have to force its way through the points, which would face the opposite direction. This could damage the points and possibly cause a derailment. The points were therefore spring-loaded to ensure that they would always lie towards the left-hand route but could be run through in the other direction without damaging them. A demonstration of a set of such points was arranged to be held at Willesden, and I went along to see how it all worked. I came away very satisfied. I was there again a few days later, when I took Major Freddie Rose along.

The advent of the flashing tail lamp

Technology provides new opportunities and it was therefore always necessary to keep up to date with emerging technical developments. The simple tail lamp at the rear of a train had been standard practice almost since the birth of the railways but was on its way out. I was prompted to do something about it by an experience at New Street station when I was Superintendent at Birmingham. During darkness (and it was always gloomy at New Street, whether day and night) an EMU driver running into a platform saw a red light ahead and mistakenly took it for a signal at the end of the platform. Unfortunately, it was the taillight of another EMU and he ran into it, albeit at slow speed.

We discussed this at a monthly Signalling Committee meeting and noted that some new multiple-units had just been delivered that had twin rear lights. Should we take the plunge and go for twin rear lights as standard on all new builds to avoid the possibility of such confusion? The unanimous decision was that we should, so we did. That was perhaps the easy bit.

The oil lamp was still standard practice on freight trains and on loco-hauled coaches. It would not have been practical to require two taillights on freight trains because freight vehicles had only one lamp bracket. I cannot recall which member of the

A two-car Cravens DMU on the 07.02 from Ipswich to Lowestoft on the East Suffolk line approaches Brampton station on 20 September 1983. This line was a test-bed for conversion to the Radio Electronic Token Block system in order to avoid possible closure. It came into operation shortly afterwards, controlled from Saxmundham. *Peter Doel*

Two designs of portable battery-operated tail lamps: the one with the rounded case won. *Author's collection*

A Swiss Railways (SBB) coach displaying its built-in twin tail lamps. BR was adopting this as a policy. *Author*

committee it was who said, 'Eureka, let's make the lamp flash every second.' That spelt the end of the oil tail lamp, because with the best will in the world it would have been difficult to have made a flashing oil lamp. Battery-operated hand lamps had become standard practice, so why not a battery-operated tail lamp? Nothing could be easier.

I contacted a firm I had recently had some dealings with, and with the prospect of an order for several thousand lamps it was naturally very keen on the idea. It quickly produced a mock-up, and I felt that we should try this out in darkness before we went any further, so on the evening of 1 July 1981 I arranged for the firm to meet me at about 11pm at Reading station with the prototype, the local staff having provided me with a standard oil lamp for comparison purposes. The firm had come in a van, so we all piled in and went a mile or so along the riverbank until we found a suitable spot with virtually no ambient light where we could carry out our test. A member of the firm stayed there with the two lamps lit while we moved about a quarter of a mile further along the bank. The oil lamp could clearly be seen, but the battery-operated one scored because the flashing light was more arresting.

When I reported back at the next monthly meeting, the committee agreed that we should go ahead. The Stores Department procured a trial batch, which the Regions used so that they could carry out actual tests on trains. The results were satisfactory, and flashing tail lamps became part of standard equipment, with the Regions doing all the work, ordering lamps through the Stores Department and arranging distribution and tests etc.

So far, so good. Multiple-unit trains would have two built-in steady-light tail lamps, and freight trains would have portable battery-operated flashing tail lamps. We found that many coaches already had built-in electric tail lamps, and these lamps could be fitted to other coaches that were not already so equipped. In the meantime, we would have to soldier on with oil lamps. It felt like a major breakthrough – a leap into the 20th century.

A meeting at the DoT

As the Operating Department representative, I attended a meeting of the Railway Industry Advisory Committee Working Group on the Safety of Staff Working on the Track. Try saying that in a hurry! It was an all-day meeting, mainly between the Railway Inspectorate and the BR Civil Engineering Department. A buffet lunch was provided. The Department of Transport (as the Ministry of Transport had been renamed) was not in the habit of providing a hot lunch for this sort of meeting, despite there being a decent dining room for the staff and visitors. However, to have stopped for a leisurely lunch would have delayed the meeting, and there was a long agenda.

The usual form of protection for day-to-day work on the track by a small group of men was the use of one or more lookoutmen armed with flags and horns. It had worked from time immemorial but was by no means foolproof, as the records of fatalities showed. It was not fail-safe, and railway operations were based on the fail-safe principle. The instructions to engineering staff were contained in the Rule Book, and my concern at this meeting was to ensure that any alterations to the Rules were designed to increase safety, and be clearly expressed. The responsibility for the content belonged to the Civil Engineer, who was reluctant to make any changes that might increase his costs. I had come across this attitude before, so it was not a surprise to me, but I was expecting the Railway Inspectorate to require improvements to be made. The arguments went back and forth, with the Civil Engineer taking the firm view that it was up to the workmen to obey the warning horn and get out of the way when a train came along, as they had always done. I do not have the details of any alterations that were made to the Rules as a result of the discussions, but I expect that there would have been some minor concessions. In 1981, ten staff were killed, under the heading 'Struck by trains etc when working on or about the track'. The following year it was seven, including two handsignalmen. The figures fluctuated from year to year.

However, the meeting of the Railway Industry Advisory Committee did not appear to have much effect. On 2 October 1983, near Salfords station on the Brighton line, a group of men was repairing a timber footpath crossing on the line when they were struck by a train. The lookoutman, normally employed as a plumber, had failed to give a warning. Two men, father and son, were killed and the lookoutman himself had a leg severed. On 7 September 1984, near Carpenders Park, a lookoutman was killed standing with his back to oncoming traffic for which he had given a warning to his colleagues. Three months later, another lookoutman was killed at Macclesfield. He was protecting a man carrying tools and walking along the track in daylight. However, there was a much more serious occurrence at Severn Tunnel Junction on 11 February 1985, when shortly after midnight four men of a gang of six on snow clearance duties at points were run down and killed. It transpired that they had had a break, during which some of the men had gone to a nearby pub and had 'three rounds'. There were no proper lookout arrangements at all and the working was very lax.

Significantly, the instructions for ensuring the safety of men working on the line had been strengthened following a double fatality at Hellifield in February 1979, when two men clearing snow from points were struck and killed by a Down express. I was involved in this, and the Signalling Committee arranged for the Rule Book to be amended to read:

'If the running of trains has already been stopped, the man in charge of the work must obtain an assurance from the signalman that trains will not re-commence running without his authority. If trains are still running, the man in charge must agree with the signalman a suitable time for the running of trains to be stopped.'

Railway jargon can sometimes become convoluted. In the Hellifield case, the two men were of the same grade, and the Rules provided for this by allocating responsibility to the man who was senior (in years in the grade, from memory).

All these occurrences took place some 30 years ago, and a much stricter regime is now in place. Now they would all have been thoroughly investigated by the RAIB, and a full report would have been prepared. The Office of Rail Regulation (ORR) would have investigated separately, with a view to possible prosecution under the Health and Safety at Work etc Act 1974. These arrangements resulted from the recommendations following the inquiry by Lord Cullen into the Ladbroke Grove accident of 5 October 1999 in which 31 people were killed.

A relaxing cab ride

It was time for some fresh air, so I had a day cab-riding on the Central Section of the Southern Region with Inspector George Holloway. The feedback from these outings could be considerable and valuable, and I would usually go back to the office next day with a pocketful of notes. Our route covered the Victoria to Brighton line, then along the coast to Portsmouth, before returning to Victoria via Horsham. As a sign of the times, my wife met me at Reading station and took me straight to a meeting of the newly formed West Reading local group of the Social Democratic Party. Reading had thriving groups, as David Owen was a local man and often came to the meetings. Val and I were almost the first members.

Having had a taste for cab-riding, I had another day out in the cab, this time on the LM Region, with Inspector Harry Phillipson on the 08.50 Euston to Manchester Piccadilly, and thence on the CLC section to Liverpool before returning to Euston.

The following day I went to a meeting at the RTC in Derby. I cannot remember what the subject under discussion was, but they put on a very nice buffet lunch as usual. Visits to the RTC were always instructive, and they enjoyed showing you their latest offerings and were always very hospitable too. I went again soon after for yet another meeting about radio signalling, the details of which I did not record.

Something out of the ordinary

I have no idea how many detonators were supplied to BR annually, but I seem to recall that Clayton's at Penistone provided many of them. However, supplies were becoming difficult to obtain, so I had a trip to the Royal Ordnance Factory at Glascoed in Monmouthshire, between Usk and Pontypool Road, to discuss with them the possibility of their producing detonators for BR. I cannot remember much about the visit, although I recall that they provided transport to and from Newport station. Any commercial negotiations that might have followed would have been the province of the BR Stores Department.

PART 4: MORE OF THE SAME

Scottish Region concerns about arrangements for working single lines

Andy McCaig, the Regional Signalling Officer in Scotland, phoned to see if I could meet him for a discussion about single lines, and we settled on Newcastle, which we could both do in a day and would save me an overnight stop. Andy, a true Scot, was a genius on Scottish signalling and very helpful. I knew that he would have something interesting up his sleeve, and he did. More about that later.

Radio signalling again!

Yes, the issue of radio signalling was now coming to the boil and it was time to present it to the trade unions, who, by their very nature, were sceptical about anything new coming from management that did not involve job losses. The RTC people were fully prepared to mount the presentation and explain how it would all work, and as there were four unions involved it was decided that it would be preferable to have two separate meetings on different days, with the NUR and ASLEF on the first day, and the TSSA and BTOG on the second. (BTOG, the British Transport Officers Guild, was not normally invited to such meetings, as officially it did not have any formal recognition.)

For the first meeting I travelled to Derby the previous evening and spent the night at the Clarendon Hotel, having had dinner on the train with half a bottle of Malmaison red. Just to digress for a moment, all the wines for use on BR, both in British Transport Hotels and in restaurant cars, were supplied by BTH from its stores in the cellars at the old St Pancras Hotel and were highly regarded. Senior railway managers could obtain supplies for their own personal use at favourable rates – a nice little perk. Malmaison was the wine's brand name. No doubt I slept well.

Next morning, after a leisurely breakfast, I walked across to the Railway Technical Centre to prepare the demonstration for the NUR and ASLEF, who came in force, not wanting to miss a day out and a good lunch. The RTC people did a splendid job, and we confined ourselves to the technicalities; any staff issues could be dealt with later. The unions had agreed to this approach, which resulted in a reasonably convivial meeting. A few days later we hosted the TSSA and BTOG, and had another very productive meeting. If only it were always so. Next day I was off to Derby again for a meeting at the RTC with the NUR to discuss technical issues for the working of Class 317 EMUs without a guard, and another RTC lunch followed.

The following week I went to the Staff Training College at Crewe to open the Rules and Signalling course. There are no arguments about the Rules, but they can be quite complex, hence a week's course was needed to iron them all out.

A social interlude

Val and I were invited to a dinner dance to celebrate the 50th anniversary of the local branch of the Institution of Mechanical Engineers. It was quite a posh black tie affair, with the ladies in long dresses. Val recorded that we danced until midnight, so I must have had plenty of energy in those days. Such social affairs were always welcome.

The IRSE was a very progressive technical body, and held regular meetings both in London and in the provinces. As an Associate of the Institution, I attended an evening meeting at Savoy Place, just off the Embankment, on 7 October. These meetings attracted audiences of a hundred or more, including all the top brass. The subject on this occasion was – yes, you've guessed – 'Radio Signalling'.

Back to the grindstone

The following morning I had a meeting at '222' (BRB HQ), the former Great Central Hotel, opposite Marylebone station. It was not well situated to be a hotel, and consequently had not flourished. During the Second World War it was requisitioned by the military, and it had been vacated afterwards in time for it to be refurbished as the headquarters of the British Transport Commission (BTC). The BTC itself was abolished in the early 1960s and the building became the headquarters of the British Railways Board under the redoubtable and much-maligned Dr Richard Beeching.

Nowadays the BTC would have built for itself a shiny new office block, but in 1947 the country was in the midst of an austerity crisis and the BTC had to make do with what was available. '222' was a rabbit warren of narrow passages and bedrooms, as you might expect. However, parts of it had been

adapted to form meeting and committee rooms, and I used one of these for a meeting with the NUR to discuss the working of trains without guards, which was likely to be a bit explosive. My records indicate that we made about half an inch of progress.

Seeking more convivial company, I went off to Crewe on the 19.00 from Euston to spend the night at Rail House, preparatory to a meeting the following day. I casually mentioned the subject of the earlier meeting with the NUR to the driver. He almost exploded with indignation. (I knew he would.) 'Why do we need guards on freight trains and parcels trains anyway?' he expostulated. 'They never do anything except sit in the back cab.' It was a common response, and I had to chuckle to myself. Life does have its moments.

PART 5: GOING FOR A SAIL

An excursion to France

Occasionally the members of the Operating Committee would get together and have a day out to relax. In those days Sealink and SNCF ran the cross–channel service jointly, and the Southern Region people in particular had very good contacts with SNCF. So, on 14 October, we all assembled at Charing Cross to travel on the 08.20 to Folkestone, joining the *Hengist* there for the short sea crossing to Boulogne. This fortuitously coincided with

Above: The Sealink ferry *Hengist*: the ferry and its sister ship *Horsa* were both built at the French naval dockyard at Brest. Ordered in 1970, the two ferries entered service two years later. The *Hengist* was to survive on cross-Channel services until 1992 when both ferries were sold to new Greek owners. At the time of writing, the now-renamed ferry continues to ply its trade in Greek waters. *Ian Allan Library*

lunchtime, which was enjoyed with plenty of French bread and wine and Gallic hospitality. This was followed by a short hop to Calais, to join the *Horsa* back to Folkestone and sleep off our lunches, assisted by a 'slight sea' as the captain told us. On such occasions wives were not allowed, so it was customary to take back a little present. Being in France, I took a bottle of Chanel No 5, which was well received.

Western Region hospitality
The following day I had a meeting at Paddington, followed by lunch in the Western Region officers' mess. In those days officers'

Below: The station of Calais Maritime was once one of the most important for travellers on cross-Channel ferry services. The ferry seen alongside the quay is the French-owned *Compiegne,* which entered service in 1958 and remained operational until 1980 being used in place of either *Hengist* or *Horsa* in later years. With the construction and opening of the Channel Tunnel, Calais Maritime station became less significant and was closed in 1994. *Ian Allan Library*

messes were full of lieutenant-colonels, so the designation seemed quite appropriate. It was said that in Great Western days, senior railway officers never worked beyond lunch but were always careful to claim their lunch expenses. They would have felt enormously slighted to be called 'managers'. In the whole of my 40-year railway career I was never once called a manager. I moved up from clerk to stationmaster, then to superintendent, and finally to officer. 'What's in a name?' you might ask. 'Plenty,' I would say. 'What does it signify to people, and are they quietly impressed? Is the owner quietly proud of his calling?'

Back to the RTC
The Railway Technical Centre at Derby was rapidly becoming my second home, and I was musing about that as I travelled down to Derby at the front end in the company of Traction Inspector Bob Armitage. As usual, we had a very valuable (to both of us) two-way interchange of views, bringing in the driver whenever practicable.

I was always welcome at the RTC, because the boffins were anxious to have a good workload and looked to the various railway departments to provide it for them. Anything to do with radio was meat and drink to them, so the development of RETB, track-to-train radio systems, etc provided them with a lot of work. We had a busy day and hardly found time for a buffet lunch. Boffins by their very nature had lively minds, so you had to be on your toes.

Back to the office (but not for long)

The next day a couple of representatives from Crompton Parkinson called in to discuss the design of the new battery-operated tail lamp. There were a couple of points they wanted to clear up. Then it was lunchtime, which consisted of chicken curry at Marylebone station refreshment room, followed by a quick dash to Marsham Street (the DoT offices) for an afternoon meeting with the Railway Inspectorate about one-man operation (OMO). It was top-level stuff as Malcolm Southgate, the Director of Operations, was there together with a couple of his sidekicks. (I never found out what the latter actually did.) As previously mentioned, the term 'OMO' was fairly quickly changed to driver-only operation (DOO), as it was more accurate.

The Inspectorate had drawn up its Requirements, setting out the procedures that it would wish to be dealt with for the different categories of trains to be worked without guards. Radio was one of the Requirements for such suburban passenger trains, but there were other ancillary considerations. Should there be platform staff at the stations en route? Such staff would have safety responsibilities. What about fare evasion? How was revenue to be protected? The following morning there was a meeting with NUR and ASLEF reps at Cricklewood to enable the union reps

to examine the new electric multiple-units to be introduced on the St Pancras to Bedford service. It was a very busy period.

The driver-only operation saga dragged on. A couple of days later there was yet another meeting with the unions regarding the operation of trains without guards. They were supporting their members and requiring firm answers from management on every possible danger scenario they could think of. But that was their job. My job was to deal with their concerns. It was an exhausting day, but at the end of it I felt that we had moved forward another half an inch. As far as possible, you had to remain calm and attempt to answer their concerns with the utmost patience. Now I knew how Job felt.

But that was not the end of it. Only a week later, the NUR wished to meet us again for further discussions about the driver-only operation of trains. The NUR was carrying out its proper responsibilities of protecting the guards' jobs, as far as it could, and had more questions for discussion, to which answers were required. That was perfectly reasonable, but there is a saying that the biggest fool can ask questions that even the wisest man cannot answer.

Off to the provinces

The following Monday I went to York on the 09.00 HST from King's Cross, forsaking the pleasures of the driving cab for a trip 'on the cushions'. I met George Wood, my opposite number at Eastern Region HQ, housed in the palatial former North Eastern Railway headquarters offices, which have now taken on an even more upmarket role as a very posh hotel. There were a number of issues that he wished to discuss, particularly the development of the driver-only operation of suburban trains from King's Cross, and, at the other end of the spectrum, the plans for the East

The regional headquarters at York; the buildings were originally the headquarters of the North Eastern Railway and were designed by the railway's own architect, William Bell, along with the London-based Horace Field. As with a number of ex-railway office buildings, the Queen Anne-style building has been converted into a luxury hotel — the Cedar Court Grand Hotel and Spa. *British Railways*

Class 47 No.47016 approaches East Suffolk Junction, Ipswich, with the 10.30 service from Lowestoft to Liverpool Street on 25 August 1979. *Les Bertram*

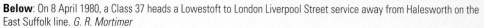

Below: On 8 April 1980, a Class 37 heads a Lowestoft to London Liverpool Street service away from Halesworth on the East Suffolk line. *G. R. Mortimer*

Saxmundham station with its level crossings viewed on 7 August 1976. The ex-Great Eastern Railway box visible in the distance dates to 1881; at the time of writing it is still in use although it received replacement equipment internally for RETB a decade after this photograph was taken. *J. Scrace*

Suffolk line. Level crossing developments were another lively topic – much of the Eastern Region being flat and rural and thronged with level crossings of various types.

A couple of days later I revisited the East Suffolk line with Arthur Warner, who was George Wood's level crossing expert, to discuss the proposals. I liked Arthur – he knew his stuff. It must have been a flask and sandwiches day.

On the Saturday I went on a Railway Study Association (RSA) excursion for a bit of light relief. Wives could come along too, and Val wasn't going to be left out. The party assembled at Liverpool Street for a trip to Norwich over the East Suffolk line. RSA members alighted at Ipswich whilst the ladies went forward to Norwich for a tour of the city and a visit to the cathedral, and doubtless a look at the shops, now known as 'retail therapy' I believe. The Divisional Manager at Norwich had provided a special DMU for the members to travel over the line, stopping en route to examine stations and level crossings as required. After a buffet lunch at Norwich a number of papers were presented, including mine on the modernisation of level crossings on the line and the proposals for radio signalling. It was more congenial than a meeting with the NUR!

Time for a bit more cab-riding

After the rigours of my seemingly endless meetings with the trade unions, I felt in need of a bit of relaxation on the real railway, so I organised a day of cab-riding for myself with a companionable Western Region inspector. The day began with the 08.31 from Reading to New Street with a Class 47 diesel, and then it was 'on the cushions' to Crewe, where there was time for a cup of tea (where would we be without cups of tea to cheer us?) before experiencing a fascinating trip to Newport over the old North & West of happy memory. The route took us to Shrewsbury,

which was pure ex-LNWR, except for the last few chains that marked the beginning of the Joint Line with the Great Western as far as Hereford.

On a fine day, this is a beautiful stretch of line, with the Malvern Hills on one side and the Long Mynd on the other, and passing though (or calling at) stations with names which smacked of romance – Church Stretton, Craven Arms (where the purely LNWR line branched off to Swansea), Ludlow, with its castle, Leominster (with long-gone GWR branches at each side) – before finally arriving at Hereford, served not only by the LNWR and the GWR but also, surprisingly, by the Midland. It was an important route for the Midland, the prize being the goods traffic to and from Swansea, achieved with running powers over the lines of the Neath & Brecon Joint line, then the Brecon & Merthyr line, followed by a few miles of the Cambrian from Talyllyn Junction to Three Cocks Junction, and finally over the Midland itself to Hereford, arriving at the passenger station for the last half mile over the North & West. The story of the Midland route from Hereford to Swansea is worth a chapter on its own. What a pity we can no longer travel over it.

From now on we fairly galloped along, past Pontrilas, Pandy and Llanvihangel, alongside the A465 main road to Abergavenny, where the LNWR branched off to the Heads of the Valleys and into several of the Valleys. That would also be worth another chapter on its own. Then it was on past the marshalling yards and erstwhile engine shed at Pontypool Road before the last few miles into Newport. Many years ago I saw a 'Royal Scot' there, probably having worked through over the North & West from Crewe or even Manchester London Road. After another cup of tea, and probably a sandwich, it was time for the final leg on an HST back home to Reading. What a day it had been. I felt refreshed and ready for the fray.

Heading south at Church Stretton, BRCW Type 3, Class 33, No.33082 is seen at Marshbrook on 23 October 1982 with the 12.25 service from Crewe to Cardiff. *W. A. Sharman*

It's 3 June 1981 and Longsight-based Class 25 No.25150 is seen approaching Ludlow on the 07.50 service from Cardiff to Crewe. *G. B. Gartside*

Signalling for safe turn-outs

Stanley Hall *describes the evolution of methods of controlling trains approaching junctions and explains how approach control using modern signalling maintains safety without imposing unnecessary time penalties on today's high-speed trains.*

THE FUNCTION of signals is to tell the driver of a train whether or not the line ahead is clear, and secondly to tell him which way the points are set at a facing junction. Where one leg of a facing junction has to be taken at a much lower speed than the other leg, the driver has to be told by the signals in good time which way he is going so that he can reduce speed to the required level, if such a reduction is necessary. Speed limits through junctions are part of a driver's route knowledge so it is not necessary for the signals to tell him what speed he should run at, but merely which way the points are set, leaving him to adjust his speed accordingly.

This history of junction signalling is an interesting one, and the transition from semaphore signals under the absolute block system, to multiple-aspect colour light signals under the track circuit block system has not been entirely without problems. But let us start at the beginning.

Early distant signals were duplicates of the home signals to which they applied, and drivers were expected to be ready to stop at a distant signal when 'on'. Indeed, distants were regarded as danger signals, were painted red, and showed a red light, the only identifying feature being a notch cut in the end of the arm. As train speeds rose it became more and more impracticable to expect drivers to be able to stop at distant signals, and eventually the rule was changed, but the red light and arm lingered on until the 1920s. Distant signals for

junctions took the same form and arrangement as the home signals to which they applied, and that is how the junction distant signal with two arms, known as the 'splitting distant', evolved, with a separate signal for each route. This became the standard arrangement on most pre-grouping railways, the arms being worked according to the route set at the junction. It was then left entirely to the driver to adjust his speed to the required level.

Splitting distants continued in use until recent years, indeed occasional examples can still be found where they have been retained for specific purposes, but where there was a considerable difference in speed between the low speed and high speed routes at a junction it became the practice to erect only one distant signal, which was cleared only for the high speed route. When the single distant was cleared the driver was given an unambiguous

Right:
Signal 300 on the up East Coast main line near Doncaster. With a position 1 route indicator on signal 300 showing single yellow, preceded by flashing double and single yellows, up East Coast trains are routed to the up slow platform through the 70mph turnout immediately beyond the signal, or with the position 1 route indicator and normal approach control from red to single yellow through the alternative 40mph turnout nearer the station, which is also the normal route for up Leeds trains to reach the up slow platform. With a theatre type route indicator the signals govern moves to other lines with a 25mph speed limit, and with a position light shunting signal low-speed shunting moves at 5-10mph. Special entrance control buttons are provided on the panel at certain locations to allow the establishment of a route for a shunting move into an occupied section for attaching or detaching vehicles. *BR*

Below:
The aftermath of Bourne End, 30 September 1945. Recovering LMSR 'Royal Scot' locomotive No 6157 *The Royal Artilleryman* from the field in which it came to rest after the derailment. *C. R. L. Coles*

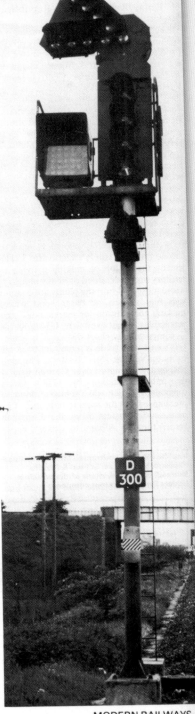

D 300

MODERN RAILWAYS

The first page from the author's first published article in *Modern Railways* in February 1985. This led to Ian Allan Ltd commissioning the author to publish his first book — *Danger Signals* — in 1987.

More socialising

Every year the Regional Train Planning Office at Paddington organised a trip to Torquay, which included a dinner dance and an overnight stay. It was held at the Livermead Hotel. Val and I were invited because I knew the organisers, and we had a very enjoyable time. Malcolm Southgate came along too. He was a splendid chap, laid back and very easy to get on with, and had been the SM at King's Cross on his way up. In many respects the railway in those days was like one big family.

An interesting digression

The Social Democratic Party (SDP) was firing ahead and attracting enormous support from disaffected Labour Party members who were fed up with the antics of those in power. There was a by-election in the Crosby constituency and Shirley Williams got in with a majority of 5,000, overturning a previous Conservative majority of 19,000. As David Owen lived locally to us we met him several times during that period, and there was a particularly strong following in the Reading area.

The cover for the author's first commissioned railway title. This was followed by a number of further volumes — such as Danger on the Line, Hidden Dangers and Beyond Hidden Dangers — that largely focused on issues of railway accidents and safety and resulted in the author becoming a regular commentator in the media on the subject and an expert witness in court.

PART 6: HEADING FOR A COLD WINTER

My *Modern Railways* article leads to greater things

An occurrence of little significance at the time, but which was to have a major impact on my life years later, was the completion of an article on junction signalling which I had prepared for the magazine *Modern Railways*. I wrote the article at work to point out a number of errors I had noticed in an article in the magazine on the subject which I felt ought to be corrected.

In those days you did not go public just if you felt like it. First, you had to get the agreement of any other sections in BR HQ that might be affected, especially the Signal Engineers (not easy, because they felt that the less the public at large knew about railway signalling, the better). Having cleared that hurdle, you had to deal with the Press Office (another hurdle because they were afraid that you were stepping on their lawn). However, it was finally cleared, and I sent it off to *Modern Railways* on 29 November. That was the last I heard of it, and I forgot all about it.

Several years later, and long after I had retired to grow tomatoes, or whatever it was that you were supposed to do when retired, I had a letter from James Abbott, the editor of *Modern Railways*, who had just discovered the article and asked if I would like to have it published in the magazine. Having checked that it was still OK, I gave him the go-ahead and the article duly appeared.

It must have made an impact because some years later, on 7 June 1985, I received another letter from *Modern Railways* asking if I would like to expand the article into a book, covering both signalling and accidents. I signed the

contract in October that year, and it was a turning point. Since then, getting on for 30 years ago, I have never stopped writing books for Ian Allan Publishing, until recently, when I ran out of material.

However, there was still one book to be written – about the railway as I had experienced it from 1930, as a tiny tot, until 1970 and the end of steam, but Ian Allan Publishing said that it didn't do autobiographies. Fortunately, I was able to persuade them to let me do one freelance, with its assistance (and at my expense), and that became *A Railwayman's Odyssey*, published in 2012.

The front end of Class 317 No.317305 stabled in a non-electrified siding at Cricklewood depot on 18 April 1982 prior to entering service on the St Pancras/Moorgate to Bedford electrification scheme. *R. G. Bradford*

An APT on the mainline: Class 370 No.370001 forming a test train slows for Trent Valley Junction at Rugby on 24 July 1980. The APT was launched in full public service on 7 December 1981. *P. Grand*

Back to the real world

On 30 November 1981 it was back to business as usual. I went to Cricklewood EMU depot with quite a large party, including all five DoT Railway Inspecting Officers, to have a look at one of the new trains. That was followed by a buffet lunch, although a stronger substance might have been more appropriate as the afternoon was spent in a meeting at Rail House of the Loco Division of the Railway Staff Joint Council (RSJC), the top body for discussions between the BRB and union HQ (both ASLEF and the NUR). We did not get very far on the vexed question of working trains without guards.

The following day it was the turn of the Traffic Division of the RSJC, with the NUR. I recorded that we made 'infinitesimal progress'. And not to be outdone, the TSSA also had to be consulted. They represented the salaried staff and were generally more pliable – but not on this occasion. My notes record that we 'didn't get very far'. We just had to go laboriously through the motions.

Just for the record, the Advanced Passenger Train entered service on Monday 7 December. It ran three times a week, from Glasgow to London and back. It was not a good time to be introducing such a service – the following day it snowed heavily –

212

Gerrards Cross signalbox, where the tragic events of 11 December 1981 began, and which resulted in a collision between two DMUs and the deaths of four people. *Author's collection*

The Seer Green accident

The winter of 1981/82 was exceptionally severe in the south of England, with heavy falls of snow and hard frosts. On 11 December, there was a problem on the Marylebone–High Wycombe route with tree branches being brought down across the line by the sheer weight of snow on them. An empty DMU going north was approaching Gerrards Cross signalbox when the signalman received a report of the previous train having struck a tree. Accordingly, he kept his home signal at danger and showed a red flag to the driver, telling him that the driver of the previous train through the section had reported striking a tree and that he was to proceed at extreme caution, to examine the track, and to report any obstruction. So far, so good.

The DMU set off slowly into the driving snow, but when the driver reached a cutting he saw the top few feet of a tree lying across the track and went to a nearby telephone to notify the signalman at High Wycombe. Having said that he would be able to move the tree within about five minutes, the driver went to the guard's compartment to get a saw and an axe from the emergency toolbox – clearly a resourceful chap.

Meanwhile, back at Gerrards Cross the signalman had accepted the following train, the 07.31 DMU from Marylebone to Banbury. When the train arrived, he repeated the previous procedure, informed the driver of the circumstances and told him to proceed cautiously. Between Seer Green and the next signalbox the signalling arrangements were a little unusual. That section contained both a semi-automatic section and an intermediate block section, and the signalman was unable to clear his starting signal because the previous DMU was still at a stand in the section.

At that point, the signalman, who was relatively inexperienced, instructed the driver to pass the starting signal at danger. He said that he had a track circuit failure (in fact, it was the previous DMU still standing there) and that he should proceed at extreme caution, suggesting a speed of between 10 and 20mph. The train set off, and it was then that the signalman realised what he had just done: he had sent a train into a section where there was already another train, and stationary too. However, he had told the driver to proceed at caution and hoped that he was going sufficiently slowly to stop before hitting the stationary DMU, or that, better still, the first DMU had now set off.

but there was tremendous pressure to demonstrate some real progress, especially to the Government.

I later went to the BR Training College at Watford to discuss with my inspectors the preparations for the management trainees' Rules and Regulations course. The inspectors, who enjoyed running the course and were very good at it, were seconded to me for the duration of the course. I had lunch with them and we chatted over a glass of beer. This was a bit more like the real world.

He did not have long to wait. Within a few minutes the telephone rang and he answered it, to be told that the second train had crashed into the first one, which was still at a stand. The second train must have been travelling quite fast, as the leading coach partly telescoped under the last coach of the standing train, killing the driver, two schoolboys and a young man of 17. Was there some misunderstanding between the driver of the second DMU and the signalman? We shall never know. And the relatively inexperienced signalman had found a situation that had taxed him beyond his limits.

A more relaxing day with the management trainees

The end of their course had arrived, so I went off again to The Grove at Watford to wind up the session and give them the usual pep talk, setting out what would be required of them when they took up their first supervisory post. But I had no worries – I was very impressed by the high standard of the trainees. My inspectors had done a good job and the future of the railway looked to be in good hands. Then we all had a jolly lunch together. That was one of the nicer parts of the job.

Pictured arriving at Wellington station in Shropshire on 12 September 1981, A Swindon DMU, with No.M50674 leading, forms the 10.40 service from Wolverhampton to Shrewsbury.
Brian Morrison

On 18 May 1981, single railcar No.55004 arrives at Stourbridge Junction with the 16.29 service from Stourbridge Town.
Les Bertram

1982

PART 1: A TROUBLED NEW YEAR

A signalling day to start off the New Year in style

I had some power signalbox visits – to Salisbury and Eastleigh – and then went straight through to London to a very interesting meeting of the IRSE about junction signalling and speed signalling. Junction signalling was very much a topic of the moment, and speed signalling concerned continental practice whereby the signalling indicates to drivers the speed which applies at a junction, usually by variations in the arrangement of coloured lights. In other words, a continental driver does not need to know the laid-down speed through a junction as drivers in Britain do – he just obeys the signals.

Industrial relations problems

Commuting to work in the winter of 1981/82 was somewhat fraught. It was generally considered to have been the most severe winter for several years, resulting in train delays and cancellations amid all the normal problems of maintaining a punctual and reliable train service. The railways were always well prepared for normal winter conditions, but the conditions that prevailed at that period were abnormal. However, there were other clouds on the horizon.

ASLEF was compounding the difficulties by being troublesome over what was called variable rostering. It dated back to 1919, when the railway companies were still under

Right: The then new signalling control panel at Salisbury pictured on 18 August 1981. *British Rail*

Below: Tilehurst station on the snowy morning of 12 December 1981. A westbound HST approaches at high speed amid a flurry of snow, causing the photographer to dive for cover. *Author*

Government control, and was part of a complex series of agreements between the companies and their employees that, among other things, established a machinery of negotiation for resolving disputes between the two sides. It continued in existence when the railways were nationalised in 1948, and the railway unions regarded it as sacrosanct.

The BRB wished to introduce a variable day of between six and ten hours, which would have been more economical, and also proposed a 3% rise. ASLEF was vehemently opposed to any change from the eight-hour day and responded by holding a series of two-day strikes for several weeks, starting on 12 January. In the event, it was a question of taking work home, and it was a good opportunity to deal with matters that had got put on one side. There was even an astonishing *Panorama* programme on 8 February, with the BR Chairman, Sir Peter Parker, the ASLEF General Secretary, Ray Buckton, and the NUR General Secretary, Sid Weighell, sitting round a table. It was a risky venture that could so easily have swayed public opinion in favour of ASLEF, but it had no effect and ASLEF went on strike again the following day. Ray Buckton was not given to making a hullabaloo – in fact, quite the reverse – but he could be very firm when the position demanded it. Some would have called it obstinate, but he had to act in his members' interests. Next day I had a very pleasant day out with my boss Malcolm Southgate (the Director of Operations) and Bill Whitehouse (the Chief S&T Engineer). You couldn't get higher than that. We all met at Reading and went in Bill's car to the Westinghouse Signal Works at Chippenham, where we were treated right royally.

Peter Parker's efforts at negotiation appeared not to have been successful, and there was another one-day strike on 16 February. As usual, I took work home and was hard at it all day without any interruptions (except for Val bringing cups of tea). The Government had set up a Court of Inquiry, which reported on that day, mainly supporting ASLEF and saying that BR should pay the 3% and get back to the negotiating table. The BRB, still working out what to do, met at the Advisory, Conciliation and Arbitration Service (ACAS) the following day. (The whole nation knew about ACAS by then.) ASLEF was also there. The day after that, news came that the Board and ASLEF had come to some sort of agreement, and the 3% was paid. It must have been one of the longest-running disputes in railway history. Was this my last 'work at home' day? No, it was not – the guards at Paddington were now on strike over flexible rostering.

Another trip to the far north

Now it was time to get down to business again, but not until after having a little trip to Scotland. Tony Townsend-Rose wanted to travel over the Far North line between Inverness and Wick/Thurso to survey the line in order to assess its suitability for electronic token radio signalling (RETB). Our wives were not to be left out. Val enjoyed coming on these trips, and Tony brought his wife Brenda too. They got on well right from the start, so it was a very enjoyable outing.

On 24 February, we went north from London by first-class sleeper and were met at Inverness by Chris Green, the Scottish Region's Chief Operating Manager, Andy McCaig, the Regional

The Radio Electronic Token Block (RETB) instrument in the driving cab. The driver is concentrating on pressing a button to send the electronic token. *Author's collection*

The inspection saloon has now reached Forsinard station in the Railway Inspectorate's survey of the line to assess its suitability for the installation of the RETB system. A lonely outpost at any time of the year, especially on 25 February 1982 when this picture was taken. *Author*

Next day, the Inspectorate turned its attention to the Kyle line. We are standing in Garve station. *Author*

Signalling Officer, and Robin Nelson, the Regional S&T Engineer. A very illustrious group indeed, with whom I have kept in touch ever since. After breakfast we set off in the inspection saloon, surveying the line and its level crossings and penetrating as far north as that bleak and lonely outpost, Forsinard. The weather could not have been better – fine, clear and quite mild. Then it was back to Inverness nonstop for dinner in the station hotel (beef stroganoff and Malmaison burgundy).

However, that was not the end of our excursion. The following day we were off to the Kyle of Lochalsh to survey that line too. At Inverness the weather was fine, but it was raining long rods at the Kyle as usual. But the job had to be done, long rods or not, so we put on our waterproofs and got on with it.

People who are used to the vagaries of Scottish weather know to come prepared. There was, however, one sad note on our trip. At one of the public road level crossings the crossing keeper lived happily in the crossing house, and there we were breaking the news to him that his dream was nearly over. I think he was a PhD or something and he had swapped it for this. There were times when you felt a bit uncomfortable, that you were playing with people's lives, but it was all part of the job. We were back in Inverness by 4pm, the job done, satisfied that RETB was a 'goer'. All four of us dined together before joining our sleeper to London.

As mentioned earlier, this close relationship with the officers of the Railway Inspectorate has since been criticised in some

Along the line is the lonely outpost of Balnacra level crossing, with the adjacent cottage for the crossing keeper. *Author*

quarters by people who have no idea what they are talking about. We would never have dreamed of taking liberties, and we respected the Inspectorate because of their expertise. Of course, it all changed later, very much for the worse, but fortunately I had retired by then.

A trip along the North Wales coast

One of the Traction Inspectors at Crewe had asked me if I would give a talk to the Locomotive & Carriage Institution one evening on the subject of temporary speed restrictions. I never refused such an offer to spread the gospel, but first I had a cab trip from Crewe to Holyhead with one of the Crewe inspectors. I had been over the line many times as a passenger but had never seen it from

the front end. I firmly believed that getting out and about, and being seen and open to discussion, was an important part of the job.

A bombshell!

The Government felt that BR had too many senior managers (which was true) and told the Board bluntly to get rid of some. This was to apply to anyone over the age of 55, all of whom were asked if they wished to be considered for early retirement, irrespective of whether their job could be dispensed with or not. So, on 24 March, at the age of 56, I received a letter asking me if I wished to be considered for early retirement. I decided that I did, surprisingly quickly, having discussed it previously with Val. The considerations were simple: I could stay on until I was 60 and then retire with my superannuation in the normal way, or I could take early retirement on very favourable financial terms with my superannuation intact. I already had 39 years' membership, but I did not realise then that I would be involved with the railways in one way or another for the next 30 years. The railways had been my life, and in many ways would continue to be.

I celebrated with a cab trip from Edinburgh to Aberdeen and back, and then the sleeper to King's Cross. This was not just a joy-ride. The Scottish Region had wished to run HSTs over the Edinburgh–Aberdeen route at higher than the line speed in view of their superior riding characteristics and had erected 'HST Line Speed' notices along the route. I wanted to experience the higher speeds from the cab, and get the drivers' reaction to it. They were generally in favour.

Ray Buckton in a new guise

The Chartered Institute of Transport was holding one of its periodic meetings in the Commonwealth Hall in London. Ray Buckton was the speaker, on the subject of Government subsidies for passenger transport, and there was quite a good attendance. Ray put his views across effectively and his talk went down well too, which helped to improve his image. But then, I always liked him.

PART 2: CONTINENTAL EXCURSIONS

The RSA annual convention in Vienna

The members of the Railway Study Association were mainly of middle management and above, with quite a number of more senior managers. Formed in 1909 to provide a forum for informal discussion of issues facing the railways of the day, the RSA was quite independent of railway management and was closely associated with the London School of Economics. Most of the meetings were held in London, and I had joined it some years earlier. It was a thriving organisation, with its own governance, and indeed is still going strong at the present time.

Each year the RSA organised a convention, normally in Europe, and this year Vienna had been chosen. The Austrian railway authorities, Österreichische Bundesbahnen (ÖBB), had organised an extensive programme for us, and we were clearly welcome guests and going to be very busy. Wives were also invited – indeed, they were welcome because it made the convention much more of a social affair – and a separate programme of activities and sightseeing (and time for shopping) was organised for them.

We had rather a rough channel crossing from Dover to Ostend on the *Prinses Paola*, an SNCB ferry, and the next leg of the journey was in a very comfortable two-berth sleeper in a big DSG (Deutsche Schlafwagen Gesellschaft) sleeping car on the 'Tauern' express, the 21.10 to Salzburg. Arriving in Salzburg at

Holyhead station in 1979; a Class 47 awaits departure whilst the Sealink ferry *St Columba* loads in the background prior to its crossing of the Irish Sea. *J. C. Hillmer*

The SNCB ferry *Prinses Paola* (on the left) with her older sister ship *Koning Albert* pictured at Dover in 1971. Built by Boelwerf Cockerill of Hoboken in Belgium, the *Prinses Paola* operated cross-Channel services until 1988. The *Koning Albert* was built in the same yard and launched in 1947. By the date of the photograph the earlier ferry was coming towards the end of its life; laid up in 1973, the *Koning Albert* was scrapped five years later. *British Rail*

A Viennese tramcar. The Union Jack on the side of the tramcar leads me to believe that the authorities had provided this tramcar specially for the Convention. The date is 30 April 1982. *Author*

11am, we had lunch in the station restaurant before leaving for Vienna on the 14.40 train, arriving at our final destination at 5.55pm. Then it was straight to our hotel for dinner and eventually off to bed, but not until we had sampled the trams.

Monday 26 April

After breakfast, coaches took us to ÖBB HQ for the formal opening of the convention, after which the ladies went off on a coach tour of the city whilst we had a presentation by ÖBB. We all lunched together in a huge bierkeller on noodle soup, boiled beef and sauté potatoes, and in the afternoon we visited the Vienna City Transport offices for another presentation, followed by a visit to the U-Bahn and its Control Centre.

After tea in a café, with toasted cheese and apple strudel (no one else can make apple strudel like the Viennese) we went to the Volksoper opera house to see the comic operetta *White Horse Inn* (in German, of course). It was a splendid performance, and we all laughed when the audience did. Afterwards, we had another apple strudel, but *mit schlag* (with a big dollop of cream) this time – no wonder the Viennese looked so happy. It's known as *Gemütlichkeit* (ie just relax and enjoy it).

Tuesday 27 April

We went off by train to Linz (near where Adolf Hitler spent much of his childhood) for a trip up to the mountains, and had been warned to take warm clothes. Buses met us at the station to take us to a 'mountain-tram' and up to the snow line. We didn't linger there for long. After lunch the ladies went to a monastery and heard an organ recital of Bruckner's music, while the men paid a visit to the Plasser & Theurer works, which manufactured track maintenance equipment. BR was a good customer.

Wednesday 28 April

There was a morning visit to the Simmering-Graz-Pauker works, which built coaches, wagons and trams. Lunch in the canteen was followed by a visit to the well-known Vienna Arsenal Testing Station, where the running characteristics of vehicles were tested. I gathered that the arsenal served most European railway systems, including Britain's. The ladies had a trip to the Vienna Woods. In the evening we all travelled out to the village of Grinzing up in the wooded hills in bone-shattering old trams (as a special treat!). We had a very nice meal there, washed down with plenty of the very palatable local new wine (the *heurige*). I seem to recall, through the mists of time, that it was followed by a lot of singing and possibly dancing, and I certainly did not notice any bones being shattered on the return journey.

Thursday 29 April

It was a tradition that every convention of every railway organisation should have a free day in the middle of the week to allow the members to unwind. Actually, conventions were not as onerous as all that, but it was nice to have a spare day for a bit of sightseeing or whatever a member (and his wife) wished to do. Most chose to follow the programme.

The day's programme included a trip by train to the town of Gmünd, about a two-hour ride on the line from Vienna. It was in the Waldviertel, a wooded, hilly area right on the Czech border. We were met by the town band at Langschlag, our ultimate destination, where a lovely meal was provided for us and the wine flowed freely as ever. Then it was back to Vienna for an early night, but not until I had had my usual nightcap in our favourite little café in the heart of the city opposite the Volksoper, so romantic! 'Wien, Wien, nur du allein.'

Friday 30 April

In the morning we went on our last working visit by special underground train to a maintenance and servicing depot to see how they dealt with trains. After that we could relax, with lunch first and then off by tram to the Prater amusement park and a ride on the big Ferris wheel made famous in the 1949 film *The Third Man*. Most people will remember Anton Karas's rendition of the haunting theme, and many can probably still recite the names of most of the well-known members of the cast.

Then it was another tram ride, to the Belvedere, Prinz Eugen's splendid palace, but unfortunately there was no time for the beautiful Schönbrunn Palace; that would have to wait for another visit. Finally we returned to our hotel by tram to prepare for the formal dinner – a splendid four-course meal with lots of Austrian wine.

Saturday 1 May

We were up at 6am for a quick breakfast, and after saying our goodbyes it was off to the Südbahnhof by taxi at what seemed like 90mph for the 07.55 train to Villach. This was a roundabout but very scenic route through the Semmering Pass and Klagenfurt. Lunch was taken in the excellent station restaurant at Villach before we travelled up through the mountains again on the 'Tauern' express to Salzburg. The final leg of our continental journey was by sleeper to Ostend, and we arrived just in time for the 10.5am sailing to Dover.

It had been a very enjoyable and interesting convention. The RSA people were (and still are) a very sociable crowd, and I should emphasise that we paid our own way – BR was in no way involved, apart from assisting in the arrangements with ÖBB. The host country provided practically everything else and had really pushed the boat out. Val loved it.

A retirement lunch, and a trip to South Wales

Bill Walton, one of my 'boys', retired and on 11 May I took him and his wife to the Great Western Royal Hotel at Paddington for lunch. Val came too, to keep Bill's wife Margaret company. Bill had worked in the Signalling Section for many years and was an expert – and quite unflappable. I would miss his fund of knowledge.

However, more serious business called. It was necessary to have a trial ride on an iron-ore train in South Wales with a couple of men from the NUR to test the suitability (and indeed the practicality and safety) of working such a train without a guard. For the NUR it was a very sensitive issue, and in order to strike up a working relationship with the two NUR men I travelled in the driving cab with one of them from Paddington to Swansea, whilst two other BRB people looked after the other NUR man. We spent the night at the Grand Hotel in Swansea and had dinner all together. The following morning dawned fine and sunny, and after breakfast we set off for Port Talbot steelworks, before travelling to Llanwern with a train of iron ore. The trial run went well, and whilst the NUR men were non-committal, they seemed satisfied. The hard bargaining would come later.

The annual convention of the IRSE

That year's convention was held in Italy, and we were the guests of the Italian State Railways – FS (Ferrovie dello Stato). My wife Val was coming as well, of course, and it looked like being a very sociable affair, but would it be my last one? Only time would tell, but retired members of the IRSE could also join the conventions.

So, Val and I set off on Saturday 15 May for Folkestone, where we spent the night in a B&B. Next morning we woke to clear, blue skies and had a stroll along the prom before catching the 12 noon sailing for Calais. We had a very smooth crossing on the *Horsa*, full of noisy French schoolchildren, and thence to Paris.

On 1 March 1979, a down HST, the 11.20 from Paddington, passes the site of the troughs at Goring. *Brian Stephenson*

Two Class 56 Diesels, Nos.56104 and 56105, stand at Llanwern on 12 May 1982, having hauled a train of iron-ore from Port Talbot during an exercise to demonstrate to the railway trade unions that the journey could be done safely without having a guard. *Author*

Class 56s Nos.56041 and 56035 cross the River Usk at Newport with a Port Talbot to Llanwern iron ore train on 22 May 1981. *Les Bertram*

The concourse of Milan Central (Milano Centrale) station recorded on 8 September 1990. The station was completely rebuilt between 1925 and 1931. *Colin Boocock*

The Gare du Nord seemed such a civilised place in those days – you could get a decent meal at the restaurant upstairs – but it is now far busier and a madhouse most of the time.

We had couchettes booked on the 10pm train Gare de Lyon to Milan, having already met several members of the party, including our friends Brenda and Tony Townsend-Rose. Arrival at Milan was at 8.15am, where we all assembled at the palatial station. The members were then taken to visit the new and impressive power signalbox, which was not yet complete, and from the balcony we had a splendid view of all the platforms. I cannot recall how many, but the station was huge. Whilst we were thus engaged, the ladies were enjoying themselves on a coach trip around the city and a conducted tour of La Scala opera house.

A special train was provided for us by FS, a four-car intercity EMU, on which both lunch and dinner were served. We had a two-hour break at Modena, where the men visited the signalbox and the ladies had a coach tour of the town, and then it was on to Rome, an opulent dinner being served en route. After seemingly unlimited quantities of wine, we were ready for bed when we arrived at 10pm.

Tuesday 18 May

The day was spent with signalling contractors Intermetro, a company that had installed the signalling on the Rome underground system. After lunch, provided by the company, it was back to work whilst the ladies enjoyed themselves on a coach tour of Rome, including visits to St Peter's Basilica and the Vatican. In the evening, coaches took us to the 'Fantasie di Trastevere' restaurant for a marvellous meal, again provided by Intermetro. Just a glance at the menu would have had you drooling. We were serenaded by a very good choir, and with a rather charming touch (literally), the tenors in the choir provided all the ladies with roses. This was truly wine, women and song, and really put package holidays to shame!

Wednesday 19 May

We were up early to board a special train to Naples at 07.50, where we became the guests of the Circumvesuviana Railway on

Yet another Convention. This time for the Institution of Railway Signal Engineers, when we were the guests of the Italian State Railways. On the 'Excursion' day, we went to Sorrento by special train as far as Naples, then by another special train on the Circumvesuviana Railway. We had a lovely meal in a stupendous hotel. The Italians don't do things by half, or so it seemed. Pictured with our wives are Lt-Col Tony Townsend Rose (an Inspecting Officer), myself and Jack Reeks, Divisional Manager, BR, Nottingham. *Author*

another lovely sunny day. First stop was Pompeii for an hour's tour of the ruins, and then it was on to Sorrento for a lovely meal in a stupendous hotel. After returning to our hotel in Rome, we visited a trattoria for another excellent meal and, fortified by coffee and wine, went for a walk around the city's lively streets with Tony and Brenda, visiting the Trevi Fountain on the way. We were certainly filling every minute. ('If you can fill the unforgiving minute with sixty seconds' worth of distance run, you'll be very tired' – apologies to Rudyard Kipling.)

Menton — Val's most favourite place in the whole of France. I quite liked it too. *Author*

A DB Class 103 electric locomotive stands at the head of the Munich train at Zurich on 2 June 1982. *Author*

Thursday 20 May

It was another lovely day and we were up with the lark and into the coaches for a trip to Orvieto by special railcar over the new 'Direttissima' high-speed line. The Italians were building these lines over 30 years ago, yet we are still only talking about it. Shame on us! At Orvieto we had refreshments and a talk, and then it was up into the old town perched high on a hill for the usual slap-up meal with the ladies. We returned to Rome by coach to see the 'Direttissima' control room, and finally got back to our hotel after an 11-hour day. It was now time for the ladies to put on all their finery, ready to go to the formal dinner in the Brancaccio Palace, a super place (a real palace), and an equally splendid meal of umpteen courses and copious supplies of excellent wine. It was a very enjoyable evening, and the Italians' hospitality was beyond praise.

And that was the end of the convention. It had been one of the most enjoyable, and FS really had pulled out all the stops. Val and I spent the next day visiting all the sights of Rome, staying the night at a slightly more modest hotel before returning home via Florence, where we spent three nights, and Menton (one of my wife's favourite resorts on the French Riviera), where we stayed for another couple of nights. Couchettes from Marseille rounded everything off nicely.

PART 3: TIME TO START RUNNING DOWN?

Not finished gallivanting yet

No sooner had I got back to my desk when Malcolm Southgate, our very capable Director of Operations, called me and said, 'I want you to come with me tomorrow for two or three days in Switzerland and Germany to look at a new form of automatic train control which the railways there are developing. It'll be a small party, with Bill Whitehouse and his No 2, Ken Hodgson. Just the four of us.' This sounded very exciting, and I phoned Val to tell her that we would be leaving Heathrow on the 8.30am flight to Zurich, and spending three days there and in Germany. That was on 2 June.

Our flight from Heathrow in a DC-9 took one and a half hours, and we were met at Zurich by Swiss rail staff who took us to the very impressive new signalbox. Next we had a cab ride to see the new signalling, followed by a discussion in the SBB offices. Then it was off to our hotel, after which our hosts took us to a lovely lakeside restaurant for dinner. I mused to myself that this glamorous style of living would soon be over for me, so I might as well make the most of it. I had enjoyed it several times in the previous few years, both on and off duty, and knew my opposite number on Swiss Railways, Herr Gerber (and his charming wife), quite well.

Next morning we went on a visit to the Oerlikon works of Integra, makers of signalling equipment, after which our hosts took us to the end of the lake by train, returning by steamer, with time for lunch in the restaurant and no doubt a technical discussion about signalling equipment with Bill Whitehouse. Back in Zurich we joined the 16.19 DB express to Munich, part of the journey being spent in the driving cab to see the train protection system at work – the main reason for the visit. After arrival in Munich at about 9.15pm we booked in at a hotel, and as it was still daylight and very warm, we had a meal at a pavement café. A fitting end to a long but fascinating day.

Someone from DB picked us up at 7.45am the following day, and we spent the morning in the Regional Office and the Traffic Control Centre, followed by lunch in their private dining room. Then came the *pièce de résistance* – I travelled in the spacious driving cab of the 13.43 express to Stuttgart to see DB's new train control system, a form of ATP that eventually became the

LZB, in operation. (LZB stands for *Linienzugbeeinflussen* – very loosely translated as track-to-train signalling.) I was hugely impressed. This was just what BR needed, but we did not have such generous funding as DB and had to be content with TPWS, which, it has to be said, has given us almost the same standard of safety for a fraction of the price.

After arrival at Stuttgart we were shown the new signalbox and control room, just to make us even more envious, and then it was off by car to the airport and farewell to our splendid hosts. We came home in a BA-111, leaving at 19.05, an hour late, but were rewarded with unlimited drinks. I got home tired but very impressed with what I had seen, and I slept like a log. The next day was a Saturday, so I could linger in bed for a little while and reflect on a crowded three days. Would there be any more such outings, or was that it?

Life at the Board was never boring. I entertained a man from Sri Lankan Railways (not in DB and SBB style, though – BR couldn't afford that!). And I indicated to the Staff Department that I would be ready to finish in six months, and would accept early retirement and the associated financial benefits. Then I went to The Grove at Watford to give the usual pep talk to the Area Managers. Would this be the last time? But nothing changes – there was a threat of another rail strike in three weeks' time.

Retirement looms ever nearer

On 17 June, I received the official letter from the Board notifying me that I would retire on Thursday 2 December with redundancy benefits. The latter was the sweetener – very few of us would have retired without it. When I got home and showed Val the letter we celebrated with a glass or two of something. We would both be sad to leave our present home, especially Val, as she had made so many good friends in the last five years. We had not yet decided where we would go, but the county of broad acres was the leading candidate, and we still had friends and relatives there. In my railway career we had moved home nine times, but where would the tenth take us to? Ee, by gum, lad!

More strikes and threats

One benefit of retirement would be living in a strike-free environment. At least, as long as the dustmen, the firemen, the busmen and other associated groups didn't join the free for all. In the meantime, the Underground was on strike, so I had to walk between Paddington and the office. That evening, having walked in the reverse direction, I arrived at Paddington to find that the Old Oak Common drivers were being difficult. It was anarchy – and the NUR intended to strike the following Monday. But this time the Board had had enough and threatened to sack anyone who went on strike. It was also being said that all staff would be suspended if the strike lasted more than a week. The Board had taken its courage in both hands and had to win this time. The public were fed up too.

Monday 28 June was the first day of the strike. The NUR had voted at its emergency conference to suspend the strike, but in the meantime I had prepared for a siege. I set off for work by car, leaving home at 5.30am. Traffic was OK until near London, but I still arrived at the office at 6.50am and found somewhere to park near the office. The Underground was still on strike, and even some of the buses. I slept in the office on an airbed and set off for home next day at 3.30pm, but it took well over two hours. Imagine doing that every day! On the ten o'clock news there was an announcement that ASLEF were going to strike from the following Sunday. Talk about Fred Karno's Army! But in any case, I had already booked a week's leave for next week. I was going to the Lake District and camping in the car so that I could climb the hills. The unions could do what they liked! I had originally intended to go climbing in the Scottish hills, using the car-sleeper to Inverness, but the Lake District was a very acceptable alternative.

ASLEF went on strike on Monday 12 July. I went to work by coach and bus, a couple of hours each way, although a few DMUs were running to Paddington. It was like that all week. On Friday, the Board announced that all ASLEF strikers would be sacked the following Wednesday and that the railway would be closed down. Fighting talk indeed! But it worked. ASLEF caved in on the Saturday and called off the strike. The TUC was not supporting them. On the following Monday everything was back to normal.

During the ASLEF strike BR operated a number of services between Bristol and Birmingham using HSTs. Here a Birmingham to Bristol service passes through Droitwich Spa on 5 July 1982.
Peter J. Green

A Class 47 diesel, No.47538, takes the 16.05 Leeds to Carlisle over the impressive Smardale viaduct on the Settle to Carlisle line on 1 July 1982. *J. Checkley*

PART 4: MORE INTERESTING EXPEDITIONS

An interlude in the Crown Court

A case was heard in the Shire Hall at Nottingham concerning a fatality at a private (user-worked) level crossing near Bingham on the Nottingham–Grantham line. At such crossings, users were expected to check for themselves that no train was approaching before crossing the line. The court sat for three days, laboriously sifting through the evidence, and on the second day I gave my evidence, explaining the responsibility of crossing users for their

own safety, and the responsibility of BR. I pointed out that the crossing user should obey the instruction 'Stop Look Listen', which meant: 1. Stop clear of the crossing; 2. Look both ways to see if any train is approaching; 3. Listen, but very carefully; trains may approach very quietly. After nightfall different circumstances might arise in respect of Instruction 2, where the crossing user needed to look out for the headlights of an approaching train, bearing in mind that the frontal illumination of a DMU is greater than that given by a steam engine with one or two oil headlamps.

The issue finally centred on the extent of the lighting at the front of the train, and whether it was adequate. The judge did not indicate whether he had visited the crossing to see the situation for himself, but BR shot itself in the foot by presenting no scientific evidence from the Research Department regarding the luminosity of the train and, in the event, the judge decided that BR was negligent for not providing better lighting at the front of the train. He awarded £40,000 and costs, which seemed to me to be an astonishingly high figure and almost unprecedented. He was 30 years in advance of his time. However, it had been good to see my old colleagues in the Nottingham Division again, and to discuss matters over lunch in the George Hotel. Val had joined us as well.

Another crossing fatality

Somewhere in these annals I recall a similar case in which I was involved – a fatality at a footpath crossing in the dark. The train was a DMU, and the frontal lighting became an issue. Fortunately, I was prepared for this because I had asked the motive power people to explain to me the lighting arrangements at the front and carefully explained this to the court. They seemed impressed and we won the case, the judge returning a verdict of misadventure. Justice is a lottery

For more than a century, pedestrians using footpath level crossings were expected to use their own vigilance, but it must be remembered that in those days steam trains were generally more visible and noisy, and approached at lower speeds. DMUs can approach almost silently, and it could be argued that the

railways have intensified the perils at footpath and similar crossings and should therefore improve the standard of safety, with 'Sound horn' boards and miniature warning lights. The only safe way is to separate pedestrians from trains altogether by means of footbridges, but this can be very expensive and brings its own problems. It was not really a problem in 1982.

By coincidence, a couple of days later I attended a meeting of the Railways Joint Safety Committee (jointly with the trade unions). Ray Buckton from ASLEF was there, together with Russell Tuck of the NUR. For whatever reason, they were subdued and amenable. I do not recall level crossings being an issue, and the judge in the Bingham case was years before his time. Other judges perhaps remembered that public money was involved and that it would be the travelling public who would foot the bill.

A visit to the seaside

That is assuming that Immingham qualifies as 'seaside'. The BRB had decided to move forward a little further in the never-ending dispute with the trade unions over the vexed question of single-manning. Trainloads of iron-ore from the docks at Immingham to the steelworks at Frodingham seemed a reasonable target, so the Traction Officer, Tom Greaves, asked me to accompany him on a trial trip attended by the NUR reps. The latter enjoyed these jamborees and, in a way, so did we. Tom lived near Malton, so he invited me to spend the night at his home and have dinner with him and his wife. I travelled north on the 17.30 from King's Cross to York, where I got a connection to Malton. Tom lived in state at Rillington in a modern bungalow, which was complete, inevitably, with a model railway layout. I can recommend the lodgings and the hospitality.

Next morning, 2 September, we travelled from Tom's home by car over the Wolds and the Humber Bridge to Immingham, which was the quickest possible route. It was a beautiful sunny morning and a very pleasant drive. We met the NUR reps at Immingham and had an incident-free trip to the Appleby Frodingham steelworks less than 30 miles away. Afterwards I

Yet another trip with the trade unions to demonstrate that freight trains such as these can safely be worked without a guard. Two Class 37s, Nos.37221 and 37211, are the motive power for this trial trip, with a trainload of iron-ore from the docks at Immingham to the Appleby-Frodingham steelworks. As usual, everything turned out well. The train is pictured at Wrawby Junction on 2 September 1982. *Author*

travelled with the NUR men in a minibus to Doncaster, where I left them and joined the 16.12 to King's Cross.

Back in the office next morning I found my desk to have several interesting brown manila envelopes waiting for me, containing lots of literature regarding my forthcoming retirement, mainly from a financial adviser at a prestigious firm in the city who was being paid by the Board to advise me on what was best to do with all the pots of money that were to come my way. This was very generous of the Board, and the adviser gave me excellent advice, saying that I would be in possession of substantial capital. I imagine that I broke into a smile at that stage. I still have the file of papers. When I got home I declared to Val that when I was retired I was going to get up every morning at 7am and not waste my retirement in bed, and I have stuck to that ever since.

Yet another DOO expedition

However, there was still work to be done. The BRB Personnel Department had arranged with the LM Region for NUR reps to travel on a freightliner train from Willesden to Garston. I had a sandwich at Euston before meeting the two NUR men – Brian Arundel and Bill Fordham. They were reasonable people, as was usually the case with small groups away from the office, the melodramatics being reserved for the big set-piece meetings. The meeting was also attended by a couple of folks from the Personnel Department. There was a three-hour layover at Crewe, so we all went to the Crewe Arms Hotel for a very pleasant meal (paid for by the staff folks) before completing the trip and arriving at Garston around midnight. Finally we got transport into Liverpool and spent the night at the Adelphi Hotel (which I believe was still owned by BR in those days).

Next morning I had a trip to Southport and back on the electric line before returning home via Birkenhead, Chester and Crewe. It had been quite an interesting couple of days. I thought, 'I shall miss these days out when I retire and become a nobody.'

The world beats a path to our door

I had long been accustomed to playing host to a variety of overseas visitors from the less well developed nations, and now it was the turn of the Chinese, who wanted to learn all about rules and regulations and safety. I had an English-style Chinese lunch with them, which probably left them a little confused (the world is a very different place now).

After the Chinese had departed I had a trip over the GN main line in the suburban area during the rush hour to see how the flashing yellow junction signalling was working. It was working well, and when I chatted to the driver he told me that he was in favour of the system because it gave him advance information about the state of the line ahead.

Preparations for my retirement begin in earnest

I had a yearning to revisit the haunts of my early days on the railway, but before setting off north I had a full day in London, beginning with a meeting of the Railway Engineers Forum at the Institution of Electrical Engineers, where several papers were read on low-cost railways. Then tea at the Royal Festival Hall was followed by a showing of railway archive film at the Queen Elizabeth Hall, organised by Ian Allan Ltd. The thought occurred to me that I would miss all this if I retired to the sticks. Finally I went across to Euston to join the 00.50 to Manchester, in a sleeper. This was the beginning of 'All Our Yesterdays – a wallow in nostalgia'.

Next morning I rose at 06.30 after a good night's sleep and caught the bus to Manchester Victoria for the 07.15 to Leeds

Bingley signalbox, where I spent many hours in 1945 in my off-duty hours, learning the rudiments of signalling under the watchful eye of the signalman Cliff Nichols. The date is 6 October 1982. *Author*

Bingley station, looking very spick and span on, probably, 6 October 1982. I spent six months there in 1945 as a Booking and Parcels clerk, before joining HM Forces. *Author*

(Trans-Pennine trains used Victoria in those days). I had breakfast at Leeds and then met my escorts for the day – three of my railway colleagues, namely Ken Appleby, Area Manager at York, Les Binns, Divisional Operating Manager, and Paul Watkinson of the Nottingham era, now Divisional Manager at Leeds. We visited my old haunts at Shipley, where I was a clerk following demob in 1948, and then it was on to Bingley, my old home town and the scene of years of schoolboy train-watching. I was a clerk there before I was called up for RAF service in 1945. We also visited the signalbox where I spent many off-duty hours with Cliff Nicholls learning about signalling. Finally, it was on to Keighley so that I could once more enter the booking office where my railway career began in 1943. A lot of memories there!

We went off to the Queen's Hotel in Leeds for lunch before travelling by car to Battyeford, where I was SM in 1951-53 before it closed, then to Ravensthorpe, my next assignment, and finally Huddersfield. Then Les wound it all up by taking me to Wakefield for the 18.01 to King's Cross, and I was home at 21.20. It had been a *tour de force*. However, I had not been pensioned off yet, as a couple of days later I went to the Staff Training College to deliver my usual lecture on Signalling and Safety of Operations to a group of Area Managers. It was my final visit.

PART 5: A FINAL FLING

Across the sea to Ireland

The BRB Signalling Committee had recently played host to a representative from the Irish Railways (CIE), which was somewhat unusual. He wanted our advice on a signalling issue that was causing CIE some problems, and we had been happy to help a fellow railwayman. In response, he invited us to have one of our forthcoming meetings in Ireland, with all expenses paid. It sounded too good to miss, and I was anxious to fit it in before I retired. The visit was scheduled for 12-14 October, after which Val and I would spend a further few days on holiday in Killarney, which neither of us had ever been to before. We travelled by train, of course.

To digress for a moment, back in 1949/50 I went across to Ireland on several occasions, using my LMS free passes, to obtain supplies of food (butter, steak, etc) that were available only on ration in Britain. However, far more precious were nylons, which were freely available in the Republic and quite cheap, whereas in Britain they were like gold and eagerly sought after. Expensive duty had to be paid on them at the first British port, and the customs people expected British travellers to be bringing nylons back. It was therefore politic to declare a few whilst secreting others in various holes and corners where it was hoped the customs officers would not find them. You had to be very cunning and inventive, but the fact that you had declared some seemed to work like a charm and you were waved through. I must have had an innocent face.

But to return to my story. The London-based members of the committee assembled at Euston on 12 October for the 10.00 to Holyhead. (The Crewe and Scottish Region people and their wives met us later.) Three of us brought our wives, who did not want to be left at home whilst their men went off junketing. We sailed at 15.00 on the *St David,* a big ship of about 9,000 tons, which rode very well despite the rough sea. The sky cleared as we approached Dun Laoghaire, where we arrived at 6.30pm, to be welcomed by Tom Quinn of CIE whom we had met before and who took us to the modern and imposing Tara Towers Hotel in Dublin. I recall dining on Tournedos Chasseur.

231

The BRB Signalling Committee held its normal monthly meeting in Dublin at the invitation of CIE, the Irish State Railway, that year. We were treated with great hospitality. The date is 13 October 1982. *Author*

On 16 August 1984, CIE General Motors 2,500hp Co-Co No.086 departs from Dublin Heuston station with the 12.55 service to Cork. *Michael H. C. Baker*

Wednesday 13 October

It was down to business, at least for the men. (The ladies went shopping, of course.) Cars collected us from the hotel and took us to the railway offices, where we met Owen Gahan, a big, genial fellow who was the Rail Manager. He described the impressive new Dublin suburban electrification, assisted by a presentation of slides, and after lunch, whilst the ladies went off for a city tour, we visited the new Signalling Control Centre, which was also very impressive. In the evening a coach took us all to the Abbey Tavern at Howth for a very nice meal, after which we were entertained by an Irish singing group.

Thursday 14 October

The morning was taken up with a normal Signalling Committee meeting before we joined the ladies for lunch. They had clearly been raiding the shops that morning, judging by the bulging shopping bags! Work over, we had an afternoon coach trip to the Wicklow Mountains, with high tea being laid on for us, and some of the party then set off to Dun Laoghaire for the boat back to England after what had been a very enjoyable couple of days. But our little holiday was just beginning, care of CIE.

Friday 15 October

Val and I took a taxi to Heuston station, a journey which took 45 minutes in the morning rush hour. Val said that she had never seen such traffic jams, but the taxi driver kept us entertained with a continuous supply of Irish humour. On our arrival in Killarney, a town full of Waterford glass shops, we were met by a couple of CIE representatives who had obviously been asked to show us around for a couple of hours, during which we visited the scenic Ladies' View and Muckross House.

Saturday 16 October

It was a terrible day of southwesterly gales and rain, so we bravely donned our waterproofs and ventured to the shops. Later, the proprietor of the Ross Hotel, where we had been staying, ran us to the station and we were met by the Stationmaster, Frank Howe. It must be said that throughout our visit to Ireland we received the full treatment and were very well looked after. We set off for the port of Rosslare on the 14.40 train, changing at Limerick Junction, where we had a frugal tea of sandwiches washed down by milk. This being October, it was pitch-dark when we arrived at the grandly named Rosslare Harbour Mainline station and somehow made our way to the also grandly named Great Southern Hotel, perched on the cliffs overlooking the harbour. We were surprised to find a very big and modern edifice rather than a mere hotel with a few run-down bedrooms.

Sunday 17 October

We woke at 7am to huge, crashing waves and a gale blowing. From our bedroom we had a lovely sea view and could see our boat approaching, tossing up and down and disappearing from time to time. Now, I quite enjoyed a rough sea, but Val most definitely did not, and she hadn't forgiven me yet for the very rough sea we experienced (on our honeymoon of all things) on the crossing from Weymouth to St Helier, Jersey. I had learnt fast that a new husband does not enjoy a big cooked breakfast whilst his bride toys with a piece of cold toast, and now history was repeating itself.

We went on board the *Stena Normandia* at 8.45am. It was a big ship, which cheered us up a bit, and we did not set sail until 10.15am, after loading all the cars and lorries and allowing time for the staff to sweep up all the broken glass. But now the fun started. The ship nosed very gingerly into the storm, but it was

On 25 August 1980 Class 47 No.47298 awaits departure from Whitby. The ex-North Eastern Railway signalbox was demolished following the rationalisation of the track at this Yorkshire terminus. *Peter Harris*

not long before a big wave hit us sideways, causing an avalanche of bottles, glasses and crockery to be swept from the shelves in the bar on to the deck. I escorted Val to our cabin before I went for breakfast, to find the staff still grimly providing meals for the diminishing number of diners and trying to avoid being hit by flying plates. Every so often another gigantic wave would hit us, causing yet more mayhem, until the shelves, bars and tables were absolutely bare. However, the few brave souls in the dining room were still clinging gamely to their breakfasts, determined to demonstrate that we British were a nation of seafarers and were not to be put off by a few tiny waves.

The captain had decided to reduce speed to save his ship, so the torment lasted for an extra hour, but fortunately the sea moderated after the halfway mark. It was the roughest crossing I had ever experienced, and I had crossed to Ireland quite a few times over the years. We were looking forward to the comfort of a first-class carriage, but had to be content with a special coach from Fishguard to Swansea – well, it was Sunday – and then it was the glorious comfort of an HST all the way to Reading. We had been on our way for exactly 12 hours, and Val was happy to be home, smiling as ever.

Goodbye to the North-East

On 19 October I went to spend a day with George Wood, my opposite number on the Eastern Region. (I think George was retiring as well, as part of the great clear-out.) In order to make an early start I travelled to Newcastle on the sleeper from King's Cross and had my breakfast in the refreshment room before catching the 08.02 DMU along the coast to Middlesbrough. George was waiting for me there and we had a trip to Whitby. Unfortunately, it was raining when we got there, so we came straight back to Middlesbrough for lunch, with plenty of time to mull over several issues, followed by a trip to Saltburn instead. I came back to King's Cross on the 16.14 HST from Darlington along the now very familiar route that can still be experienced forty years later in true HST comfort.

Back to the major issue of the day

A couple of days later I went to yet another meeting of the Railway Staff Joint Council with the NUR. And the matter in hand? Yes, working trains without guards. We did manage to make a little progress –a chink of light appeared – which was a major breakthrough compared with previous meetings on the issue. A few days later we had a similar RSJC meeting with ASLEF (locomen) and the NUR (who still had quite a following among locomen). We made reasonable progress with the locomen, who had nothing to lose, of course.

Welcome retirement beckoned – only another three weeks to go.

Yet another meeting

This time the meeting was with Ray Buckton and Major Freddie Rose and was about level crossings and the changes that were being introduced. It was a very constructive session. One thing you learnt was that the smaller the meeting, the greater the progress. I liked, and got on with, both Ray and Freddie, but if Ray didn't accept something, he would dig his heels in.

A trip with the RSA to Southampton docks

On the Saturday, Val and I went with the Railway Study Association on a visit to Southampton docks and were fortunate to see the *Canberra* in port. Then we all met in the QE2 Terminal for a buffet lunch, followed by a couple of discussion papers in the afternoon. The ladies had visited Winchester Cathedral and had a guided tour of the city in the morning, and after joining us for lunch they had a trip round Southampton's shops.

The final week

The following Monday, my boss Malcolm Southgate took me to the Great Western Royal Hotel at Paddington for lunch, and then a couple of days later there was a special senior mess lunch for those retiring. And there were a lot of us.

My final day was Thursday 2 December. I had a drinks party in my office for all my staff, and I suspect that the whole building was awash with drinks parties for all those taking early retirement. But what a waste of talent and experience.

PART 6: HELP US OUT ON THIS ONE!

Thursday 2 December – I retire; Friday 3 December – back at my old desk!

On the penultimate day of my railway service, Malcolm Southgate asked me to join him in his office for a discussion about a problem that had just arisen. A parliamentary committee was being set up to review the safety of pedestrians at level crossings. 'What was new?' you might well ask, considering that the ink was barely dry on the 1981 DoT publication 'Railway Construction and Operation Requirements – Level Crossings', which some of us had toiled over for many months.

Sally Oppenheim, the Conservative MP for Gloucester from 1970 to 1987, and Minister of State for Consumer Affairs from 1979 to 1982, was to chair the committee tasked with reviewing the safety of pedestrians at level crossings. Clearly, she needed help from the BRB, and the Board equally needed help from those with a deep knowledge of the subject who were just about to retire. Hence I was one of a small group who were asked to stay on for a short while to help to produce the report for the committee. I was quite happy to do so, and that was how I came to be back at my old desk on the day after my official retirement. I still have copies of all the files relating to the Oppenheim Report.

We then discovered why there are so many clerks in Whitehall. We were bombarded with questions asking for all manner of information in scrupulous detail. On querying the relevance of some of these, the answer was always the same: 'The Minister might ask.' So the expensive machinery of Whitehall was a result of the fear of being unable to answer a Minister's question.

How important was the question in the first place? It was obviously aimed at automatic half-barrier crossings, and the findings surprised even us. In the ten years from 1972 to 1981, five pedestrians were killed at AHBs – ie one every two years. By contrast, the figures for manned crossings with gates were fourteen in the ten years under review. How many tens of thousands of pedestrians were killed on the roads in the same ten-year period was not given. The answer would have been that it was not relevant. It is almost unnecessary to state that when the final report was delivered to the DoT, silence ensued and we all went home. What an absolute farce! In total, I worked for six days before Christmas and 12 days afterwards, compiling the report and answering questions. Ah well, it paid for next year's holiday in Switzerland for Val and me, with a bit left over.

Now I could really settle down and enjoy my retirement.

Not so quick!

It was such a nice feeling to be still wanted and to be irreplaceable – at least for two more days. Sally Oppenheim and her committee wanted to discuss our level crossing report, and Maurice Holmes, the Director of Operations, asked me if I would come out of retirement for a couple of days to help out. Maurice was a nice chap and I was glad to help out, so off we trotted to the DoT, where I had spent so much time with the Inspectorate during the past few years. To be frank, I was flattered that there was no

An SNCF TGV stands in Lyon Perrache station prior to the departure of the IRSE party to Paris in May 1983. *Author*

one else who could help out – they had all been paid off, like me – but if I was hoping for a good lunch, I was to be disappointed. They didn't do things like that at the DoT. I never heard what the outcome was, but I imagine that even the Department had not realised just how safe railway level crossings were compared with the mayhem on the roads.

However, they were not quite 100% safe. A few weeks later there was a collision between a bus and a tram on the Tyne & Wear Metro at Brunton Lane AOCL level crossing (monitored by the tram driver on approach) in Newcastle. Bus drivers were still getting used to these new crossings. Major Peter Olver took the public inquiry, and was not too keen on the friendly relationships that had developed between railways officers and his fellow inspectors, and their respect for each other's technical knowledge and experience. Those relationships continued for several years afterwards in my retirement, culminating in Alan Cooksey, a civilian Railway Inspecting Officer, asking me if I would write the history of the Railway Inspectorate to commemorate its 150th anniversary in 1990, which I was delighted to do.

Another visit to France

I continued to be a member of the IRSE and the RSA after retirement, and I still occasionally attend their meetings. For a good few years, my wife and I attended the annual conventions of both and thoroughly enjoyed their fellowship. The first was the IRSE convention in May 1983 in Paris, always a popular choice, as not only was it close at hand but it also provided plenty of opportunity for the wives to indulge in a bit of fashion shopping whilst their husbands were slaving away (well, some of them were). What was more, the French knew how to entertain, especially the signalling equipment contractors, who were always on the lookout for new business opportunities, and would push

the boat out. The French loved to show off their new trains and signalling equipment, especially the TGVs.

Val and I had a few days together touring around before the convention began, practising our French. On Friday 20 May, we left for France on the time-honoured route via Folkestone and Calais, arriving at the Gare du Nord at 18.35. We then set off for the Hôtel Ibis on the Métro, but only got as far as the first station to find that trains were *se tromper'd* – ie had 'taken the wrong road' (derailed) – so we started walking to the hotel through Montmartre, which was indescribably sleazy and scruffy.

Next morning we went to the Gare de Lyon and caught a train to Dijon. Dijon is a very smart town, and we explored the old part before having a very pleasant dinner at the Hôtel de Paris. After a good night's sleep we decided to go to Lausanne for the day, catching the 10.08 train for a very picturesque journey, with a compartment to ourselves. Arrival was at 12.49, just in time for lunch. Lausanne is an attractive town, elegant and prosperous, and it was a pity that the weather was so poor. It would have been lovely to have sat by Lake Geneva (Lake Léman). We went back to Dijon on a splendid TEE train (Trans Europ Express), the 'Cisalpin', at 18.42.

The next day the sun even shone for half an hour, enabling me to take some photos. It was a Bank Holiday, but all the restaurants and patisseries were open. Beaune was the next stop on our programme – a real wine town, with wine museums and bottles and glasses everywhere. You could drink yourself silly there just sampling the wine at the many outlets. It is the real heart of the Burgundy wine country, and I wished that I could carry some bottles home. Then it was back to Dijon, and asparagus spears and mullet for me, and soup and Niçoise salad for Val.

The next day we rose to leaden skies and rain again, which was a big disappointment. We set off back to Paris on the 11.06

train, clutching our little jar of local mustard, and had a very comfortable journey alone in a first-class compartment.

The IRSE convention in Paris

After arriving at the Gare de Lyon at 13.35, we had lunch and then took the Métro to our hotel. There were student demonstrations going on, but that was nothing new for Paris so it did not bother us. We soon met up with friends and colleagues who were arriving for the convention, and had dinner with them that evening. I seem to recall that the wine flowed freely, but that was par for the course.

The convention began in style the following day, 25 May, with a trip on a special TGV from the Gare de Lyon to, appropriately, Lyon. Despite this being the height of spring, the weather was still diabolical – wet and cold, with leaden skies – but the trip was good, lasting two and a half hours, and we all had a turn in the driving cab, albeit not in the driving seat. It was all very impressive. We visited the Lyon Métro system and then it was back to Paris on our special TGV, arriving just in time for dinner, which we had in a nearby restaurant with our friends Jack and Peggy Reeks and Tony and Brenda Townsend-Rose. The ladies had not joined us for the TGV trip, but had seen various sights of Paris by coach as it was just too wet and cold to be walking around.

Next day the weather relented a little. The men had a business day, visiting the TGV maintenance depot and the Centralised Traffic Control Centre, whilst the ladies had their own enjoyments with a visit to Fontainebleau. The evening seemed to disappear in a fog of champagne – but, after all, it was Paris and it was all free.

The last day of the convention began at the Gare de Lyon and we spent the morning visiting the new underground stations on the RER system at Gare de Lyon, Châtelet-Les Halles and Gare du Nord. It was a sort of high-speed system with a limited number of stops – a bit like our Crossrail project 30 years later. The ladies had also had another interesting day, with a visit to the Eiffel Tower followed by a boat trip on the Seine on a 'bateau mouche'. Our reward for trudging round underground stations came in the evening with the formal dinner at the very impressive Hôtel Trianon at Versailles, beginning with champagne cocktails on the terrace. The dinner lasted for four hours, including the speeches, and was hugely enjoyable thanks to the endless supply of champagne and the good company.

An early start was required next morning for the 08.10 train to Calais, followed by a quiet channel crossing on the *Horsa*. It had been a very good convention, and there must have been about 300 members and guests in attendance. You got an appetite for them.

Back to reality, and to my roots

The most important item on the agenda now was to sell our house at Tilehurst and move back north to our roots. But that was easier said than done. There was a shortage of mortgage funds, which did not bother us much but was a problem for people lower down the scale. It was now the end of May, and the occupiers of the house we were planning to move to, Mr and Mrs Bates, were ready to move out. Unfortunately, we had trouble finding a reliable buyer, but after several wasted months we finally moved north on 16 December 1983, just over a year after I had retired. Now we could start a new life at Coniston Cold on the edge of the Yorkshire Dales. Mr Bates had been clerk to the parish council and asked me if I would take over the reins. It seemed a good idea, so I did. I didn't think the duties would be very onerous – hmm! I wondered what else fate might have in store for us. All I can say is, 'Watch this space!'

After my retirement we moved back north to our roots and settled in the village of Coniston Cold, a couple of miles north of Gargrave. I now had a view of the main line from Skipton to Carlisle and Morecambe, just across the fields. I was soon out with my camera, as these few shots will testify. This is Blea Moor signalbox during the bad winter of 1983/84. *Author*

INDEX